Debunking C++ Myths

Embark on an insightful journey to uncover the truths behind popular C++ myths and misconceptions

Alexandru Bolboacă

Ferenc-Lajos Deák

Debunking C++ Myths

Copyright © 2024 Packt Publishing

Group Product Manager: Kunal Sawant
Publishing Product Manager: Samriddhi Murarka
Book Project Manager: Farheen Fathima
Lead Editor: Kinnari Chohan
Technical Editor: Kavyashree K S
Copy Editor: Safis Editing
Proofreader: Kinnari Chohan
Indexer: Tejal Soni
Production Designer: Shankar Kalbhor
DevRel Marketing Coordinator: Sonia Chauhan

First published: December 2024

Production reference: 2200325

Published by Packt Publishing Ltd.
Grosvenor House
11 St Paul's Square
Birmingham
B3 1RB, UK

ISBN 978-1-83588-478-2

www.packtpub.com

To Maria, my wife and partner. Thank you for your continuous support and advice.

– Alexandru Bolboacă

To my family, my heartfelt thanks; without their unwavering support and encouragement, I wouldn't be where I am today.

– Ferenc-Lajos Deák

Contributors

About the authors

Alexandru Bolboacă is a CTO, passionate polyglot programmer, senior trainer, and advisor at Mozaic Works. With over 20 years in software development, he has worked for various industries, and in various European countries, as well as the UK and the USA. He has been involved in large projects in industries such as banking and financial services, energy, telecommunications, pharma, and eHealth. From practical experience, he advises and teaches architecture and usable software design, evolutionary design, crafting code, clean code, secure coding, and refactoring legacy code. Alex enjoys helping teams and organizations to understand and build strategies for successful and robust products, built-in quality, and motivation.

I want to thank a few people: the editors at Packt Publishing for reaching out to me for this project; the whole production team for supporting a smooth development; my colleagues at Mozaic Works for facilitating my writing schedule; Marius Bancilă for introducing me to Ferenc; and Ferenc for a great collaboration and for inspiring the witty and playful voice of this book. Finally, thank you to my formative mentor in C++, Luc Rogge.

Ferenc-Lajos Deák is a seasoned software developer with a strong foundation in mathematics and theoretical computer science, who is currently based in Trondheim, Norway. His career spans roles in diverse domains, including autonomous vehicles, real-time traffic systems, multimedia, and telecommunications. He is an avid open source fan, having several projects live and running, and has written more than a dozen articles for multiple technical publications concerning one of his passions: programming.

Kudos to my colleagues and managers at Maritime Robotics – their continuous stimulation and positive attitude truly paved the way for this book's completion; to Marius Bancilă for introducing me to Alex; to Alex for a great collaboration and for being the sound voice of prose throughout the book; and to the people at Packt for making sure that what I write will also turn out to be publishable.

About the reviewer

Yuri Khrustalev is a software engineer with a rich background in building things from scratch. During his career, he helped to rewrite many legacy systems through reverse engineering. He enjoys using modern languages such as Zig, cpp, and Rust with a mix of Python and thinks that humanity will continue to demand engineers rather than managers.

Shivanjan Chakravorthy is a Senior Software Engineer at NVIDIA, based in Taiwan. A passionate tinkerer, Shivanjan enjoys coding as a means of innovation and exploration. He's driven by a love for tackling challenging, unconventional projects that push creative boundaries. With expertise in AI, Python, Golang, and Kubernetes, Shivanjan actively seeks to give back to the tech community through his work.

Table of Contents

3

There's a Single C++, and It Is Object-Oriented   35

4

The Main() Function is the Entry Point to Your Application   53

5

In a C++ Class, Order Must There Be   85

6

C++ Is Not Memory-Safe   109

Preface

Imagine C++ as a mythical, ancient language, descended from the ones, forged in the fires of low-level magic, tempered with the precision of high-level incantations. Born out of the need to both control the machine and present an abstraction, it is a tool wielded by those who seek to bridge the chasm between raw machine and high-level constructs, while still accessing the luxury of modern tools.

Imagine this book as unlike any other you have encountered. The authors have embarked on a daring quest, navigating the labyrinthine depths of C++ to shed light on its true nature. With courage and precision, they aim to strip away the layers of myth and mystery that have long surrounded this fabled language, tackling both its triumphs and its perceived flaws.

Approach this book with an open mind, for it promises a journey unlike any other, a journey not suited to the faint of heart. The authors dive headfirst into the complex reputation of C++, confronting its infamous pointers and intricate memory management, and even descending into the depths of low-level C++, where assembly reigns and pointers are simply numbers. We look at the different C++s that exist out there, at the ecosystem around C++, at how to learn it today, and at the things you'd do better to forget about. Through each chapter, we peel back the layers, uncovering the underlying logic and elegance within these powerful constructs. With stories of C++ legends and a touch of humor (albeit sometimes questionable), we aim to keep you engaged while guiding you through both the sublime and the absurd. Expect to encounter some of the worst code you've ever seen, presented intentionally to teach you what not to do, all while illuminating the true potential of C++. This is a book designed not just to teach but also to reveal the soul of C++ through both its virtues and its pitfalls.

Who this book is for

This book, with its myth-busting, semi-humorous approach, is perfect for programmers who already have a working knowledge of C++ but want to go deeper into its nuances and mysteries. It could also appeal to curious learners and computer science students who are intrigued by the language's reputation for both power and complexity.

This audience includes those who appreciate the artistic and philosophical sides of programming – developers who don't just want to use C++ but also understand why it works as it does, and the lore behind its most famous (and infamous) features. It's for those who see programming not just as a skill but as a craft, one shaped by history, quirks, and even a bit of legend.

What this book covers

Chapter 1, C++ Is Very Difficult to Learn, looks at why this is the case: is it the language or is it the teaching method? Should we start with low-level features such as pointers and memory management first, or would it perhaps be better to start with working examples or with the OOP features? Also, does every C++ programmer need to know the same C++? The chapter discusses different approaches to learning a language, with a focus on C++, and decides whether C++ is still difficult to learn today ... with the right method. [**Alex**]

Chapter 2, Every C++ Program Is Standard-Compliant, covers the question that the title suggests. In an ideal world, maybe they would be! In reality, every C++ program should be compliant. However, as we discover in this chapter, when they stray a little to the left or right, using an obscure compiler extension, dabbling in undefined behavior, or relying on a particular platform's quirks, you instantly might find yourself in a tangle of errors only decipherable by ancient mystics. So, sure, every C++ program is "compliant" ... until it's not! [**Ferenc**]

Chapter 3, There's a Single C++, and It Is Object-Oriented, examines different paradigms of organizing code, including functional programming, meta programming, and the lesser-known extreme polymorphism. [**Alex**]

Chapter 4, The Main() Function is the Entry Point to Your Application, covers the topic mentioned in the title. In practice, as we will present in the chapter, the main() function is like the front door of your application: it's where everything begins, but if you peek behind it, you'll often find an intricate web of dependencies, libraries, and OS-dependent system calls that make reaching it feel more like navigating a maze than walking a straightforward path. [**Ferenc**]

Chapter 5, In a C++ Class, Order Must There Be, explores the fact that, sure enough, there must be order in a C++ class, since problems arise without it! Methods, data members, constructors, a place each must find! Yes, flexibility is, but ignored structure cannot be. Respect not the ordered members' order request and crumble the class will! Freedom too much, and behavior, undefined, comes, errors, bugs, crashes! Disorder, C++ does not tolerate. With sequence respect, harmony reigns! The most important rules, this chapter presents, where the specified order of C++ concepts matters. Or it might not be specified at all, but still matters. [**Ferenc**]

Chapter 6, C++ Is Not Memory-Safe, explores the challenges of memory management in C++, the promise of modern language constructs, and their failures, in the context of increased awareness of the general public on software reliability. [**Alex**]

Chapter 7, There's No Simple Way to Do Parallelism and Concurrency in C++, looks at the need for parallelism and concurrency, how modern C++ proposes to deal with them, and how the actor model can help design parallelism in your products. [**Alex**]

Chapter 8, The Fastest C++ Code Is Inline Assembly, covers a fact we were taught three decades ago. While assembly does indeed offer low-level control, modern compilers are highly optimized and often generate more efficient code than hand-written assembly, as we will demonstrate in the chapter. Indeed, inline assembly can improve performance in some cases, but it sacrifices readability and portability, so use it sparingly and only when absolutely necessary. [**Ferenc**]

Chapter 9, C++ Is Beautiful, asserts that C++ is indeed beautiful because where else can you find a language so gracefully tangled in angle brackets, semicolons, curly braces, and periods? It's a poetic dance of keywords, templates, ancient macros, and overloaded operators, all elegantly arranged to make even the most seasoned programmers question their life choices. Truly, as the chapter will showcase, C++ syntax is the epitome of beauty, if beauty means a riddle wrapped in an enigma, with just a hint of confusion after preprocessing again the unpreprocessable. [**Ferenc**]

Chapter 10, There Are No Libraries For Modern Programming in C++, evaluates the need and availability of libraries for C++, the challenges of package management, the difficulties in finding libraries for your target version and architecture, and the increasing problem of supply chain attacks. [**Alex**]

Chapter 11, C++ Is Backward Compatible ... Even With C, explores backward compatibility because, as we will present in the chapter, C++ inherits the family heirloom: a messy pile of global variables, pointy pointers, and undefined behavior. C++ dutifully keeps these relics alive, allowing the two languages to coexist in an awkward, yet somehow functional, embrace. Compatibility, indeed, because who doesn't want the thrill of mixing decades-old C code with modern C++? Or with not-so-modern C++? We mean, hey, tradition is important, and we must clamber for a living! [**Ferenc**]

Chapter 12, Rust Will Replace C++, looks at why we have so many programming languages, how Rust fits into the ecosystem and what it does well, C++'s answer, and the conditions under which Rust might replace C++. [**Alex**]

To get the most out of this book

The ideal audience for this book would be intermediate to experienced C++ developers and scholastic learners who already have a solid understanding of programming fundamentals and are eager to dive deeper into the intricacies of C++.

Professionals working with C++ in real-world applications, those interested in optimizing performance through assembly language or advanced compiler techniques, and enthusiasts who appreciate the language's quirks and complexity might find the book enjoyable.

Computer science students seeking a more thorough introduction to C++, academics in the pursuit of a showcase of the latest modern C++ techniques, or programmers who are in the process of learning the language, please consider that this book does not cover the beginnings of C++, nor does it include the topic of how to learn it. There are books that are definitely much better suited for this task, such as *Programming -- Principles and Practice Using C++ (3rd Edition)* by Bjarne Stroustrup, the creator of the language (or, well, any other book that works for you).

Seasoned C++ developers who want to have an overview of the latest C++ standard, language lawyers, or those of you without a sense of humor, or if you are reading this book to get an answer to a burning question ... well, there are chances that you might not find this book enjoyable at all, since it might not have answers to any of your questions. It might not have answers at all. Instead, you might discover that after reading it, you end up having even more questions than before. For you, I recommend reading through the C++ standard, all your questions have an answer there. You have been warned.

Software/hardware covered in the book	Operating system requirements
Various C++ compilers, which are relevant or not in 2025	Windows, macOS, Linux, or no operating system at all

If you are using the digital version of this book, we advise you to type the code yourself or access the code from the book's GitHub repository (a link is available in the next section). Doing so will help you avoid any potential errors related to the copying and pasting of code.

Download the example code files

You can download the example code files for this book from GitHub at `https://github.com/PacktPublishing/Debunking-CPP-Myths`. If there's an update to the code, it will be updated in the GitHub repository.

We also have other code bundles from our rich catalog of books and videos available at `https://github.com/PacktPublishing/`. Check them out!

Conventions used

There are a number of text conventions used throughout this book.

`Code in text`: Indicates code words in text, database table names, folder names, filenames, file extensions, pathnames, dummy URLs, user input, and Twitter handles. Here is an example: "The `execve()` system call, after several iterations where it leaves the confines of userspace, will end up in the Linux kernel and create a `linux_binprm` structure."

A block of code is set as follows:

```
#include <iostream>
typedef struct S {
    int a;
} S, const *CSP;

int main() {
    S s1;
    s1.a = 1;
    CSP ps1 = &s1;
    std::cout << ps1->a;
}
```

Any command-line input or output is written as follows:

```
$ g++ main.cpp a.cpp b.cpp -o test

$ g++ main.cpp b.cpp a.cpp -o test
```

> **Tips or important notes**
> Appear like this.

Get in touch

Feedback from our readers is always welcome.

General feedback: If you have questions about any aspect of this book, email us at customercare@packtpub.com and mention the book title in the subject of your message.

Errata: Although we have taken every care to ensure the accuracy of our content, mistakes do happen. If you have found a mistake in this book, we would be grateful if you would report this to us. Please visit www.packtpub.com/support/errata and fill in the form.

Piracy: If you come across any illegal copies of our works in any form on the internet, we would be grateful if you would provide us with the location address or website name. Please contact us at copyright@packt.com with a link to the material.

If you are interested in becoming an author: If there is a topic that you have expertise in and you are interested in either writing or contributing to a book, please visit authors.packtpub.com.

Share Your Thoughts

Once you've read *Debunking C++ Myths*, we'd love to hear your thoughts! Scan the QR code below to go straight to the Amazon review page for this book and share your feedback.

https://packt.link/r/1835884792

Your review is important to us and the tech community and will help us make sure we're delivering excellent quality content.

Download a free PDF copy of this book

Thanks for purchasing this book!

Do you like to read on the go but are unable to carry your print books everywhere?

Is your eBook purchase not compatible with the device of your choice?

Don't worry, now with every Packt book you get a DRM-free PDF version of that book at no cost.

Read anywhere, any place, on any device. Search, copy, and paste code from your favorite technical books directly into your application.

The perks don't stop there, you can get exclusive access to discounts, newsletters, and great free content in your inbox daily

Follow these simple steps to get the benefits:

1. Scan the QR code or visit the link below

https://packt.link/free-ebook/9781835884782

2. Submit your proof of purchase
3. That's it! We'll send your free PDF and other benefits to your email directly

C++ Is Very Difficult to Learn

If you want to channel all its power

A prevalent belief between both C++ programmers and those who only hear about the language is that it's very difficult to learn it. But what is this based upon? We will see that part of this belief is historical; not only has C++ been around for almost 30 years, but the initial standard was both unforgiving to programmers and required a lot of knowledge of memory management. Modern C++, after consequent improvements brought by the new standards C++11, C++ 14, C++ 17, C++ 20, and C++ 23, allows programmers to write code that is very similar to Java or C#. However, C++ has its specific niche in systems programming, which makes it necessary for programmers to learn more topics than necessary for other modern languages.

In this chapter, we're going to cover the following main topics:

- Why is C++ perceived as difficult to learn?
- The hard parts of C++ and how to grasp them
- The Stroustrup method for learning C++
- The test-driven method for learning C++
- With great power…

Technical requirements

The code examples in this chapter can be found in the GitHub repository `https://github.com/PacktPublishing/Debunking-CPP-Myths` in the `ch1` folder. The code uses `doctest` (`https://github.com/doctest/doctest`) as a testing library, `g++` and `make` for compilation, and targets C++ 20. You will also need `valgrind` (`https://valgrind.org/`) to check for memory leaks.

Why is C++ perceived as difficult to learn?

The beginnings of C++ saw it as an extension to C, only using the new paradigm, **object-oriented programming** (**OOP**), thus promising to solve the many problems of growing code bases. This initial version of C++ is unforgiving; you, the programmer, had to deeply understand how memory allocation and release works and how pointer arithmetic works, as well as guard against a myriad of subtleties that you'd be likely to miss and that usually ended up in an unhelpful error message. It didn't help that the prevalent cultural zeitgeist of programmers back then was that a real programmer had to know all the intricacies of CPUs, RAM, various assembly languages, OS workings, and compilers. It also didn't help that the standardization committee did almost nothing to reduce the possibility of such errors for decades. No wonder the fame of the language is following it almost 40 years later. My experience learning it only helps to understand the struggles to learn the language back then.

I had my first touches with C++ during my polytechnics studies, in the 90s. They had left me both intrigued and puzzled. I understood the power of the language, while it was actively fighting against me – or that's how I perceived it. I had to struggle to write code that worked. I was not yet familiar with STL, which was yet to gain notoriety as part of the standard, so most of my first C++ programs dealt with pointer usage. A common question at C++ exams was about differentiating between an array of pointers and a pointer to an array. I can only imagine how helpful the complexities of the language were for building exam questions!

For the record, see here the difference between pointer to array and array of pointers, a common exam question for C++:

```
int (*pointerToArrayOf10Numbers) [10];
```

```
int *arrayOfTenPointers[10]
```

I continued learning C++ through practice and from books I could find before the internet would make the knowledge available to everyone. But the biggest jump in my understanding of the language was a project I worked on around the 2000s. The project lead, a very technical Belgian man, set for us very clear guidelines and a process we had to follow to get the best C++ code possible. This need for excellence did not come simply from his desires but from the project needs: we were building a NoSQL database engine many years before they would be given this label.

For this project, I had to study and know all the rules from the two seminal books on C++: *Effective C++* and *More Effective C++* by Scott Meyers. The two books document in total 90 guidelines for C++ programmers, ranging from issues of resource initialization and release to minute ways to improve performance, inheritance, exception handling, and so on. This is also when I started using STL extensively, although the standard library was much more limited in scope than it is today.

This newly acquired knowledge made my C++ programs more reliable and made me more productive. An important contributing factor was the process we used in synergy with the wisdom of the two books. We wrote unit tests, we performed design and code reviews, and we carefully crafted our code knowing that it would be dissected by a colleague before getting accepted in the code base. This made our code quasi-bug-free and helped us implement complex features with high performance in a reasonable time.

However, the language was still fighting against us. We knew how to write good C++ code, only it required a level of attention and care that inevitably slowed us down. Mastering C++ was not enough; the language had to give something back.

After this project, I left the C++ world and learned C# and managed C++, Java, PHP, Python, Haskell, JavaScript, and Groovy, to limit myself to those languages I'd used for professional programming. While every programming language offered higher abstractions and fewer headaches compared to C++, I still had nostalgia for my formative years in programming. The fact that I knew C++ and all the intricacies of memory management gave me a deep understanding of the inner workings of these other languages, allowing me to use them to their fullest. Haskell proved to be very familiar to me since it was closely mapping the meta-programming techniques I'd learned from the seminal book by Andrei Alexandrescu, *Modern C++ Design*. C++ was living on in my mind, not only as the first programming language I used professionally but also as a foundation for every other language I've used since.

To my delight, around 2010, the news came that the C++ standardization committee was finally making bold and frequent changes to the language. The last C++ standard had been for many years C++ 98; suddenly we were seeing a new version every three years. This rolling release of new versions of the standard allowed the introduction of the functional programming paradigm, of ranges, of new primitives for parallel and asynchronous programming, of move semantics. But the biggest change for anyone who wants to learn C++ today is the simplification of memory management and the introduction of `auto` types. The big breakthrough offered by these changes is that a Java or C# programmer can understand modern C++ programs, something we weren't sure about back when Java and C# started.

This means the language is much easier to learn today than in the 90s. A good example of this change is the complete irrelevance of the old exam question on the difference between an array to pointers or a pointer to arrays; naked arrays can easily be replaced with a `vector<>` or a `list<>`, while pointers are replaced with the more precise `shared_pointer<>` or `unique_pointer<>`. This in turn reduces concerns related to allocation and release of memory for the pointers, thus both cleaning up the code and reducing the potential for the inscrutable error messages so prevalent in C++ 98.

We can't say, however, that the C++ language is as easy to learn as the other mainstream ones today. Let's see why.

The hard parts of C++ and how to grasp them

Is C++ as easy to learn as Java, C#, PHP, JavaScript, or Python? Despite all the language improvements, the answer is: most likely not. The important question is: Should C++ be as easy to learn as all these other languages?

The demise of C++ has been predicted for a very long time. Java, then C#, and nowadays Rust were in turn touted as complete replacements for our venerable subject of debate. Instead, each of them seems to carve their own niche while C++ is still leading in programs that require careful optimization or work in constrained environments. It helps that millions of lines of C++ exist today, some of them decades old. While some of them can be turned into cloud-native, serverless, or microservices architectures, there will always be problems better fit for the engineering style serviced by C++.

We conclude, therefore, that C++ has its own purpose in the world of development, and any new programming language faces a steep uphill battle to displace it. This observation comes with its consequence: specific parts of C++ will necessarily be more difficult to grasp than other languages. While Java or C# will spare you from thinking of memory allocation and what happens with the memory when you pass arguments to another method, C++ needs to take these issues head-on and give you the option to optimize your code as your context dictates.

Therefore, if you want to understand C++, you can't escape memory management. Fortunately, it's much less of an issue than it used to be.

Let's analyze the differences by looking at how different languages manage memory allocation and release. Java uses a full **object-oriented (OO)** approach, in which every value is an object. C# designers decided to use both value types that include the typical numeric values, chars, structs, and enums, and reference types that correspond to the objects. In Python, every value is an object, and the type can be established later in the program. All these three languages feature a garbage collector that deals with memory release. The Python language uses a reference counting mechanism in addition to the garbage collector, thus allowing it to be optionally disabled.

The C++ 98 standard didn't provide any built-in mechanism for pointer release, instead providing the full power and responsibility for memory management to the programmer. Unfortunately, this led to problems. Suppose that you initialize a pointer and allocate a large area of memory for a value. You then pass this pointer to other methods. Who is responsible for releasing the memory?

See, for example, the following simple code sample:

```
BigDataStructure* pData = new pData();
call1(pData);
call2(pData);
call3(pData);
```

Should the caller release the memory allocated in pData? Should call3 do it? What if call3 calls another function with the same pData instance? Who is responsible for releasing it? What happens if call2 fails?

The responsibility for memory release is ambiguous and, therefore, needs to be specified for every function or for every scope, to be more precise. The complexity of this problem increases with the complexity of programs and data flows. This would make most programmers using the other mainstream languages scratch their heads or completely ignore the responsibility and end up either with memory leaks or with calls to memory areas that have been already released.

Java, C#, and Python solve all these issues without asking the programmer to be careful. Two techniques are helpful: reference counting and garbage collection. Reference counting works as follows: upon every call to copy the value, the reference count is increased. When getting out of scope, the reference count is decreased. When the reference count gets to 0, release the memory. Garbage collectors work similarly, only they run periodically and check also for circular references, ensuring that even convoluted memory structures get released correctly, albeit with a delay.

Even back in the 2000s, nothing was stopping us from implementing reference counting in C++. The design pattern is known as smart pointers and allows us to think less about these issues.

In fact, C++ had from the very beginning yet another, more elegant way, to deal with this problem: pass-by-reference. There's a good reason why pass-by-reference is the default way to pass objects around in Java, C#, and Python: it's very natural and convenient. It allows you to create an object, allocate its memory, pass by reference, and the best part: its memory will automatically get released upon exiting the scope. Let's look at a similar example to the one using pointers:

```
BigDataStructure data{};

call1(data);

call2(data);

call3(data);

...

void call1(BigDataStructure& data){
    ...
}
```

This time, it doesn't really matter what happens in `call1`; the memory will be released correctly after exiting the scope in which data is initialized. The only limitation of reference types is that the memory allocated for the variable cannot be reallocated. Personally, I see this as a big advantage, given that modifying data can get messy very quickly; in fact, I prefer to pass every value with `const &` if possible. There are, however, limited applications for highly optimized polymorphic data structures that are enabled through memory reallocation.

Looking at the preceding program, if we ignore the & sign from `call1` and rename the functions to fit their corresponding conventions, we could also read Java or C#. So, C++ could have been close to these languages from the beginning. Why isn't it still similar enough?

Well, you can't escape memory management in C++. The preceding code would not make a Java or C# programmer think of anything more; we established that C++ is different, though. The standardization committee realized that there are situations when we need to allocate memory in one function and release it in another and that it would be ideal to avoid using pointers to do that. Enter move semantics.

> **Note**
>
> Move semantics is a key feature introduced in C++11 to enhance performance by eliminating unnecessary copying of objects. It allows resources to be transferred from one object to another without creating a copy, which is especially beneficial for objects that manage dynamic memory, file handles, or other resources. To utilize move semantics, you need to implement a move constructor, which initializes a new object by transferring resources from a `rvalue` (temporary object) to the new object, and a move assignment operator, which transfers resources from a rvalue to an existing object for your class. The `std::move` function is a utility that casts an object to a rvalue reference, enabling move semantics. To help, the compiler creates the move constructor in certain conditions.

See in the following example how we might use move semantics to move the scope of a variable to the function process:

```
BigDataStructure data{};

process(data);

...
void process(BigDataStructure&& data){
}
```

Not much seems different, other than using two ampersand signs. The behavior is, however, very different. The scope of the `data` variable moves into the called function, and `process`, and the memory gets released upon exiting it.

Move semantics allows us to avoid copying big data values and to transfer the responsibility for releasing the memory into called functions. This is a unique mechanic between the languages we've discussed until now. To my best knowledge, the only other programming languages to implement these mechanics are the other contenders for systems programming: Rust and Swift.

This proves to us that, as much as C++ resembles Java or C# nowadays, it does require programmers to understand in more detail the way memory allocation and release work. We may have gotten over the exam questions that focused on minor syntax differences with big effects, but we haven't gotten over the need to learn more than for the other languages.

Memory management, while a big part of the conversation, is not the only thing that makes things more difficult when learning C++. A few things are different and can be a bit annoying for newcomers:

- The need for `#ifndef` preprocessor directives or the non-standard but often supported `#pragma once` to ensure that files are only included once

- Separate `.h` files along with arbitrary rules of what goes in `.h` and what goes in `.cpp`

- The very weird way to define interfaces with `virtual methodName()=0`

While we can ensure we use all these contraptions with rules and guidelines automatically applied by modern IDEs, their presence begs the question: Why are they still needed?

Barring the aforementioned, it is much more difficult to get over the fact that there's no easy way to build a program and add external references. Java, with all its faults, has a single compiler, and Maven/Gradle as standard tools for dependency management that allow the download and integration of a new library with a simple command. C#, although fraught with the same issue for a long time, has pretty much standardized the community-created NuGet command for getting external libraries. Python features the standard `pip` command for managing packages.

With C++, you need to work more. Unlike Java and C#, which count on a virtual machine, your C++ programs need to be compiled for every supported target, and each target matched with the right libraries. Of course, there are tools for that. The two package managers I've heard mentioned the most are Conan and `vcpkg`. For build systems, CMake seems quite popular. The trouble is that none of these tools are standard. While it's true that neither Java's Maven/Gradle nor C#'s NuGet have started as a standard, their integration in tools and fast adoption means that they are the de facto standard today. C++ has a little bit more to go until this part of the language matures. We'll talk more about these issues in a separate chapter, but it's obvious that part of the C++ confusion is also generated by this complexity in trying out simple programs.

We looked at various complications in C++ compared to other languages, and we saw that while the language has gotten easier, it's still not as easy as Java or C#. But the core question is: Is C++ very difficult to learn? To examine this, let's look at three methods beginners can use to learn C++.

The Stroustrup method for learning C++

While the C++ standard has evolved toward simplicity, many of the learning materials have stayed the same. I can imagine it's difficult to keep up with the C++ standard, given its newfound speed of change after 2010, and a question always remains: How much code is using the latest standard? Won't students need to learn anyway the old ways of C++ so that they can deal with decades-old code bases?

Despite this possibility, we must progress at some point, and Bjarne Stroustrup thought the same. The third edition of his book, *Programming: Principles and Practice using C++* (`https://www.amazon.com/Programming-Principles-Practice-Using-C-ebook/dp/B0CW1HXMH3/`), published in 2024, is addressed to beginners in programming and takes them through the C++ language. The book is a very good introduction to C++, and it's accompanied by examples and a slide deck useful for anyone who wants to teach or learn the language.

It's interesting to note that Stroustrup does not shy away from the topic of pointers and memory management, instead discussing the minimum necessary and immediately showing the ways modern C++ avoids them.

Let's take as an example the slides associated with *Chapter 16* that focus on arrays. They start with an explanation of naked arrays, their connection with pointers, and how you can get in trouble when using pointers. Then, alternatives are introduced: `vector`, `set`, `map`, `unordered_map`, `array`, `string`, `unique_ptr`, `shared_ptr`, `span`, and `not_null`. The deck ends with an example of a palindrome implementation in multiple ways, comparing the differences in safety and brevity of the code. Therefore, the whole purpose of this chapter is to show the various issues with arrays and pointers and how STL structures help avoid these issues.

The resulting code closely resembles the Java or C# variants. However, Stroustrup points out that pointer arithmetic is still useful to implement data structures. In other words, use it sparingly and only when you really need heavy optimizations.

We conclude, therefore, that the language creator doesn't shy away from pointers and memory management but is focused on removing a lot of the potential issues that come with it. This enables C++ programmers to care less about memory management than in the C++ 98 era, but still a little bit more than in Java or C#.

The question still stands: Could beginners learn C++ without thinking much about pointers? Another teaching method seems to prove this is possible – if we want to train library users instead of library creators.

The Kate Gregory method – don't teach C

In a talk at *CppCon 2015* (`https://www.youtube.com/watch?v=YnWhqhNdYyk`), Kate Gregory makes the point that C is not a prerequisite for learning C++ and that it's actively harming the learning process to start by teaching `printf`, naked arrays, and char pointers on the first day of a beginner C++ course.

Instead, her proposal is to start with the objects available in STL. The string and vector classes are quite clear to beginners, and operator overloading is also a very natural way to use these objects. Beginners expect that `"abcd" + "efg"` will result in `"abcdefg"`; there's no need to explain the intricacies of operator overloading so that they can write simple programs. Moreover, this approach completely avoids discussing destructors and memory cleanup.

She continues by arguing that teaching lambdas to beginners is also quite easy if you start with an example. Consider trying to find a value in a vector. A first approach would be using a `for` loop that you can skim over. The second method is using `std::find`. But what if we want to find an even value in a `vector<int>` instance? This introduces lambdas very naturally in the conversation, without a whole discussion on all the possible ways to write them.

With this method, she argues that beginners will be able to use existing libraries. They will have some gaps in their knowledge, and in the case of a course for programmers working on a specific code base, you might need to have a section that introduces them to reading specific idioms useful for their work. And if you want these programmers to become library creators, then you need a more advanced course that dives into the depths of memory management and optimizations possible with pointers.

My 15 years of experience training people in complex skills tell me that this teaching method is very good. A key thing in training is to understand your target audience and do your best to avoid the curse of knowledge – the fact that you don't remember how it was not to know something you know very well today. This method caters to the beginner mind by providing fast wins and good progression and giving the learners the courage to write code. So, it's definitely an improvement in the methods of learning C++.

However, this is not the only way to learn a language. It's a structured way, yes, but exploration is an important part of learning. There's a way to learn C++ through exploration that uses a method typically associated with Twitter clashes: **Test Driven Development (TDD)**.

The test-driven method for learning C++

Learning from books or structured courses is only one method; the other one is through personal exploration. Imagine learning C++, but instead of having to look through a bunch of code examples first, write the code as you think it should work and learn incrementally the differences between your intuition and the actual language. In fact, people naturally combine these two methods even when going through a structured learning course.

One downside of learning through exploration is that it's hard to understand your progress, and you might often end up in difficult spots. A method comes to the rescue: TDD.

TDD is a counter-intuitive, effective method for incremental design. Its simplest description is the following:

- **Step 1, also known as red**: Write one test that fails and shows the next case that needs to be implemented
- **Step 2, also known as green**: Write the simplest code to make the test pass (and keep all the other tests passing)
- **Step 3, also known as refactor**: Refactor the production code and the test code to simplify.

This red-green-refactor cycle repeats in very small cycles (often 5-10 minutes) until all the behaviors associated with the current feature or user story have been implemented.

Addressing TDD misconceptions

Personally, I am a fan of TDD, and I've used it for more than 10 years with a lot of success. In fact, I used TDD to write the sample code for this book. However, I know that TDD has been received with mixed feelings by the industry. Part of it is a failure in imagination, a common question being: How can I write a test for a method that doesn't exist? Well, pretty much the same way in which you write code that hasn't existed before: you imagine it's there and focus on the desired inputs and outputs. Other criticism comes from failing to understand what TDD really is and how it works. Examples of faux TDD failures often involve starting with edge cases and showing that things get complicated very quickly when you should start with happy-path cases. Claims of TDD slowing down development are credible, but the truth is that this method helps us be more thorough and calculated, thus avoiding issues that are usually caught much later in the process and fixed with much sweat and stress. Finally, TDD is not a method for designing high-performing algorithms, but it can help you find a first solution that you later optimize with the help of a test suite.

To understand how to learn a programming language with a modified TDD cycle, we need to clarify two things about TDD. First, TDD is counter-intuitive because it requires a prolonged focus on the problem domain, while most programming courses teach us how to deal with the solution domain. Second, TDD is a method for incremental design; that is, finding a code structure that solves a specific problem in a step-by-step manner instead of all at once. These two characteristics make TDD the best fit for learning a new programming language, with some support.

Imagine that instead of learning the whole thing about C++ before being able to run a program, you just learn how to write a test. That is easy enough because tests tend to use a small subset of the language. Moreover, running the tests gives you instant feedback: failure or red when something is not right and success or green when everything is working fine. Finally, this allows you to explore a problem once you have one or more tests and figure out how to write the code such that the compiler understands it – which is what you want when you learn a language. It might be a bit problematic to figure out the error messages, particularly in C++, but if you have a person (or maybe an AI in the future) to ask for help, you'll learn a lot on your way and see the green bar whenever you've learned something new.

This method has been tested on a small scale, and it worked remarkably well. Here's how a learning session might work for C++.

Setup

At least two actors are involved in the learning process; we'll call them the coach and the student. I prefer using a coach instead of the instructor because the goal is to guide the students on their own learning path rather than teach them things directly.

I will discuss the rest of the session as if only a student is involved. A similar setup can work with multiple students as well.

The first thing the actors need to do is to set a goal. Typically, the goal is to learn a minimum of C++, but it can also be learning more about a specific topic – for example, std::vector or STL algorithms.

In terms of the technical setup, this process works best with the two people watching the code on the same monitor and working side by side. While this is best done in person, remote is possible as well through various tools.

To start, the coach needs to set up a simple project composed of a test library, a production code file, and a test file. A simple way to run the tests needs to be provided, either as a button click, a keyboard shortcut, or a simple command. The setup I recommend for C++ is to use doctest (https://github.com/doctest/doctest), a header file-only test library that is very fast and supports a lot of the features needed for production.

Here's the simplest structure for this project:

- A test file, test.cpp
- A production header file, prod.h
- A doctest.h file
- A Makefile allowing us to run the tests

A production cpp file may also be needed depending on the learning objectives.

The coach also needs to provide an example of a first test that fails and show how to run the tests. The student takes over the keyboard and runs the test as well. This test can be very simple, as in the following example:

```
#define DOCTEST_CONFIG_IMPLEMENT_WITH_MAIN
#include "doctest.h"
#include "prod.h"

TEST_CASE("Test Example"){
    auto anAnswer = answer();

    CHECK(anAnswer);
}
```

The production header shows the following:

```
bool answer(){
    return true;
}
```

The first order of business is then to make the test pass. The question the coach will keep asking the student is: "How do you think this will work? Write whatever you find intuitive." If the student finds the correct answer, great! If not, show the correct answer and explain the reasons.

This example is very useful because it introduces a few elements of the language and shows them working: a function declaration, a variable, a test, and a return value. At the same time, the process is very nice because it gives the student a measure of progress: tests passing is good, and tests not passing means there's something to learn.

With all these done, it's time to enter the exploration phase.

Exploring the language

There are two ways to explore a programming language in this manner: through simple problems that introduce concepts one by one, also known as koans, or through solving a more complex problem.

Either way, the method stays the same: first, the coach writes a simple test or helps the student write a simple test that fails. Then, the student is asked to write the solution that seems most intuitive to them. Tests are run, and if they don't pass, the coach needs to explain what is not working. Either the coach or the student makes the change, and when the tests pass, the step ends with clear progress.

During this process, it's important to focus on the next natural step for the student. If the student has specific questions or curiosities, the next test can treat these instead of going through a scripted process. This adaptive way of learning helps students feel in charge, and the process gives them an illusion of autonomy that eventually turns into reality.

What about memory issues?

We spent some time in this chapter discussing the fact that C++ programmers need to learn more about memory management than their colleagues using other mainstream programming languages. How can they learn memory management with this method? Tests will not catch memory issues, will they?

Indeed, we want students to learn that they need to care about memory from the very beginning. Therefore, memory checks need to be integrated into our test suite. We have two options to do this: either use a specialized tool or select a test library that can detect memory issues.

A specialized tool such as `valgrind` is easy to integrate into our process. See the following example of a Makefile:

```
check-leaks: test
    valgrind -q --leak-check=full ./out/tests

test: test.cpp
    ./out/tests

test.cpp: .FORCE
    mkdir -p out/
    g++ -std=c++20 -I"src/" "test.cpp"  -o out/tests

.FORCE:
```

The `test.cpp` target is compiling the tests. The test target depends on `test.cpp` and runs the tests. And the first target, `check-leaks`, runs `valgrind` automatically with options to show errors only when they come up so that students don't get overwhelmed. When running `make` without any parameters, the first target is picked, so the memory analysis is done by default.

Assume we are running the tests with a memory leak, as in the following example:

```
bool answer(){
int* a = new int(4);
return true;
}
```

We are immediately greeted by this output:

```
============================================================ [doctest]
test cases: 1 | 1 passed | 0 failed | 0 skipped
[doctest] assertions: 1 | 1 passed | 0 failed |
[doctest] Status: SUCCESS!
valgrind -q --leak-check=full ./out/tests
[doctest] doctest version is "2.4.11"
[doctest] run with "--help" for options
============================================================ [doctest]
test cases: 1 | 1 passed | 0 failed | 0 skipped
[doctest] assertions: 1 | 1 passed | 0 failed |
[doctest] Status: SUCCESS!
==48400== 4 bytes in 1 blocks are definitely lost in loss record 1 of
1
==48400==    at 0x4849013: operator new(unsigned long) ==48400==    by
0x124DC9: answer()
```

This output provides enough information for a conversation with the student.

The second option is to use a test library that already has memory leak detection implemented. CppUTest (`http://cpputest.github.io/`) is such a library, and it also has the advantage of supporting C and working for embedded code.

With these tools at our disposal, it's now clear that this method works for teaching C++ to anyone who wants to try it or to dive deeper into specific parts, using exploration as a method.

Now that we learned two methods for learning C++ today, let's go back to understanding what C++'s niche is and why it necessarily needs to be more complex than other languages.

With great power...

If there's one thing I'd like you to take away from this chapter, it's that C++ is a very powerful language, and with this power comes the programmer's responsibility to use the appropriate level of abstraction.

I'm certain that a team of C++ programmers starting a new project today that solves specific business problems, using only the latest standard and specific libraries, can write code safely and with good performance without worrying about memory issues more than their Java or C# colleagues. In fact, it's likely their code will resemble quite closely that written in other languages, with the expectation of better performance.

However, even such a team will occasionally face a choice: Do we implement a slightly less performant solution using the existing tools offered to us by STL, or do we optimize it to the stars by recursing to pointer arithmetic, move semantics, or custom memory management? This is when the power of C++ requires an equally high level of responsibility, care, and deep understanding.

> **Note**
>
> As I'm writing these words, the world is still in turmoil after the CrowdStrike incident of July 2024. The causes for the incident are still not 100% clear, despite the official disclosure (`https://www.scmagazine.com/news/crowdstrike-discloses-new-technical-details-behind-outage`). Either way, it looks as if a memory access error in a C++ program has led to a kernel panic in Windows systems around the world, grounding planes, stopping money transfers, and – most dreadfully – shutting down emergency services. Of course, this change should have never reached production, but it's nonetheless a reminder of how much the world depends on software and of the consequences of the misuse of the power of C++.

Summary

In this chapter, we examined a statement: *C++ is very difficult to learn*. So, is it?

We looked at the history of C++ and how initially it was indeed a challenge to write even the simplest of programs. We saw how Java, C#, and Python deal with some of the problems programmers face with C++ and how the C++ standard has evolved unexpectedly fast in the past 15 years to remove its impediments.

While you can write C++ code that resembles Java or C# today, you will likely still need to understand memory management, a fact we exemplified using move semantics. We also saw that the methods for learning C++ have evolved with the language and with the times, with Stroustrup introducing pointers only in passing and quickly switching to higher-level structures available in STL. We saw that a modified TDD cycle can help people learn C++ in an exploratory manner and without getting overwhelmed by the complexity of error messages and the language.

We also pointed out that C++ has a disadvantage when it comes to tooling and portability. Installing a new dependency is a whole thing in C++, unlike Java, Python, or C#, which provide one de facto standard command to manage packages. This can turn off wannabe C++ programmers who make a deeper analysis.

Finally, despite the progress in the standard, we cannot forget the sheer size of C++ code that is in the world and not up to the latest standard. Chances are, even if you learn modern C++, your work will involve dealing with older code sooner or later.

We conclude, therefore, that C++ is still more difficult to learn than Java, C#, or Python, but that it's closer than it's ever been and that the power of the language continues to be attractive for a subset of programmers.

In the next chapter, Ferenc will examine the question: Is every C++ program standard? Or, maybe programmers are driven by solving problems and picking the solutions that work best in their environment, ignoring the standard or even creating idioms that end up in the standard after a while.

2

Every C++ Program Is Standard-Compliant

Except when they are not

In the world of C++ programming, the concept of standard compliance is often held in high regard, with the latest iteration of the C++ standard perceived as the definitive guide for writing correct and efficient code. The C++ standard, meticulously crafted and periodically updated by the C++ committee and the **International Organization for Standardization (ISO)**, serves as the ultimate guide for developers, providing a comprehensive set of rules and best practices to ensure code quality and interoperability. However, the reality of software development is more nuanced and complex than this ideal suggests.

In this chapter, we will delve into the myriad challenges faced by developers who, due to various constraints, cannot always adhere to these standards and carefully balance on the sharp, thin edge between ideal standards and the practical demands of their work. These constraints can include limitations in their development environment, such as outdated compilers, legacy systems, or specific project requirements that mandate the use of non-standard features.

Complex situations can arise when we are forced to use a framework that uses C++ as a base and provides a set of extensions to satisfy a certain use case. As we will present at a later stage, these frameworks build on existing standard C++ and bring in features that are highly specific for a certain scope, but have nothing in common with the C++ standard. So, we might ask ourselves: should we use these frameworks or not? The answer to this question, as we will see, is not as straightforward as one might assume.

In this chapter, we will cover the following major topics:

- Adherence to standards in various compilers, frameworks, and environments
- Why can't everyone learn, use, or write standard C++?
- Compiler extensions drifting away from the standard

Technical requirements

We have to admit that reading this chapter will not be a straightforward process, but we will try to make it as easy as possible. Our minds will wander between platforms, compilers, and different dialects of the C++ language. However, at some point, we must draw the line and conclude that we should be able to transform all this theoretical transfer of information into the practicalities of life and produce some C++ code out of it. So, we kindly ask that at this stage of the book, you have access to the almighty internet, and the go-to place for experimental C++: Matt Godbolt's site:

```
https://gcc.godbolt.org/
```

That place should keep you covered since almost all the compilers we will discuss in this chapter are to be found there.

There is nothing else required for now. That's because at this stage, we have not produced enough valuable code to be able to put anything meaningful into the GitHub repository of the book, and the code that we have produced should not go anywhere.

Somewhere in Ghana, far, far away

When Richard Appiah Akoto posted a few images of himself drawing the user interface of Microsoft Word on a blackboard at his school in Ghana, he instantly became a social media phenomenon overnight[1]. His school was poor and they had no working computers, just a standard blackboard from the turn of the century, but this did not stop him from performing his duties as a teacher. In a very creative manner, he did his best to convey life-altering knowledge to his pupils, hoping that one day, it would be useful for them in their quest for a better life. The rest is history, but the real question is: was this the standard way of teaching Microsoft Word?

Let's not diverge too much from our initial objective. We want to find out about the standard compliance of C++ programs. For zealot C++ programmers, the latest iteration of the standard is perceived as holy scripture, the word, the collection of rules that they should obey, and any deviation from it should be punishable with an erasure and rewrite of the non-standard compliant code. Or one week in the detention center labeled *the maintainer of legacy code*.

Facing the harsh reality, things couldn't be further from an idealistic environment. Some developers do not have the possibility to use the latest version of the C++ standard. This could be because their livelihood is bound to real-life projects that require a specific compiler, or because the environment they program for does not allow the use of specific features of the language.

---

1   https://news.microsoft.com/apac/2018/03/17/teacher-who-used-a-chalkboard-in-computer-class-because-he-had-no-computer-stars-at-microsofts-education-exchange/

Or maybe they are paid to work on a platform that simply has not received updates for the last 20 years because the provider declared bankruptcy a decade ago, and there was no one to take up their business. However, since everything works and it still generates revenue, it is kept and maintained using tools that were available 20 years ago.

This definitely does not include compilers with support for the latest C++ standard. So, does this mean the C++ code the developers working on these platforms write is not standard-compliant?

At the turn of the century, the author of this chapter found himself in a classroom at his university, attending a course called *Introduction to C++ Programming*. It was the only C++ course offered at that place, and there was one book the teacher used to pass on knowledge to more than 30 students.

The small copy shop owner at the end of the road was very happy when, one day, the teacher decided to loan the book to one of the students. The book was a translated and heavily reduced version of Kris Jamsa's *C/C++ programmers' Bible*, the "book with the spotted dog," as we called it.

The local edition of the book contained only the C++ part, but it carried a very important inset: a Turbo C++ Lite IDE and accompanying compiler on a standard 1.44 MB floppy disk. For those who are unfamiliar with the name, Turbo C++ Lite was a dumbed-down version of the popular (and very user-friendly) IDE and compiler Turbo C++ by Borland. The compiler was the same, however, a lot of features and tools were removed in order to fit the entire environment on a single 1.44 MB (megabytes, that is) floppy disk.

This was our first introduction to the complex world of compilers, linkers, and syntax. Some of us found it so fascinating that even now, some 20 years later, we still use it in our daily work. So, as you can imagine, our first C++ program looked like the one in the screenshot that follows.

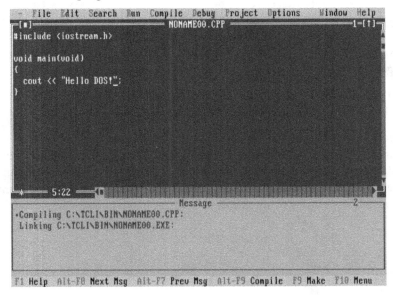

Figure 2.1 – The infamous screen of code, as seen in Life of a Programmer (1997)

Oh, the horror on your face! I can clearly imagine it, dear C++ acolyte. The sheer sight of:

- `iostream.h`: Well, hello, it's 1999, and the C++98 standard came out last year. Why don't you use it, you heretic? Its number is ISO/IEC 14882:1998, go fetch it for a mere 200 Swiss Francs. ... Oh, that is your salary as a part-time dishwasher for three months while studying here?

- `void main(void)`: Oh dear, that was never even in any standard, whether C or C++. What sort of dark concoction did you just dig out? ... Or is this the new thing they call... Java?

- `cout`: Without ever encountering a using directive, how is this even possible?

Here, you can easily afford to give up on trying to understand the reasons for this, sighing with relief, but please bear with me.

Very much akin to the conditions faced by Richard Appiah Akoto, at that stage of our education, we also had access to a classroom with a blackboard, accompanied by one dedicated teacher and the book, as well as several copies of it, as mentioned earlier. Even so, we learned C++. Maybe, from the point of view of the standard, these were ideal circumstances, because the C++ standard is very relaxed, considering the environment, it requires nothing that you can find in a modern computer – no keyboard, no screen, and not even an operating system. Indeed, the only very strict environmental requirement is that `char` must be at least 8 bits in size. This is to ensure that a `char` can hold any member of the basic execution character set (which includes standard ASCII characters). And the fact that `sizeof(char) == 1` is also guaranteed by the C++ standard, together with the signed and unsigned versions of it. Everything else builds on these foundations.

So, we might say that until we were granted access to the computer lab, we had ideal circumstances for learning standard C++. No annoying system dependencies, no computer crashes, and no hardware to kick in case of frustration when your code does not compile. Since we had no compiler running on the blackboard, our teacher soon realized that compiling more complex C++ code on a blackboard is not quite feasible, so we were allocated an early Friday morning time slot at the computer lab. All the troubles began afterward.

The explanation is quite simple: you see, the computer lab that was allocated for teaching C++ at our university back in the day consisted of a bunch of 80286 IBM AT clones.

You read that correctly. 30 students were allocated eight computers (each with a glorious 80286 processors, possibly high-tech at the time of their conception, albeit quite outdated more than one and a half decades later), hand-me-downs from some aid organization that likely did an upgrade, and decided to donate their old equipment to the university for the tax benefit of the ~~company~~ students. Four and a half people were sitting at one machine, with one book (and several copies) for the class, trying to learn C++.

Although the situation was not as bleak as in Richard Appiah Akoto's school two decades later, there were simply no better conditions. Those machines could never run anything else than pure DOS, and there was no better compiler available for them than Turbo C++ Lite, which came out 10 years earlier. Does this mean we intentionally learned to write non-standard C++ code? No, obviously not. We wrote code that we had the possibility to.

However, let's not jump that far back in time. As of 2024, the date of writing of this book, there are 46 questions on Stack Overflow (`https://stackoverflow.com/`), containing the dreaded `void main(void)` phrase. The latest one is surprisingly from 2023. A bit more with the `iostream.h` content but mostly with educational context, and we did not dare count the ones containing `cout` without encountering the using directive or a namespace qualifier because it would have been futile. Does this mean that even in 2024, there are programmers still writing code that relies on non-standard C++? Or are there students learning C++ in a non-standard way?

Digging a bit further on Stack Overflow, another interesting piece of an old dialect of C++ pops up: `conio.h`. This header was shipped with Turbo C (and C++) several years before the official standardization of the language, but considering that there are young padawans still asking questions about it in 2024, we might say that the answer to the previous question is highly likely *yes*.

Depending on their circumstances and possibilities, whether they have to learn using a blackboard, drawing with chalk, or by sharing a keyboard, tapping each other's hands gently in the process, there are still programmers out there today who involuntarily have the process of learning and writing non-standard C++ imposed on them.

Microsoft's tiny, squishy C++

That's enough staring backward for now. Let's look, for a moment, in a different direction and consider a compiler that once was the king of C++, but with time, its shine faded. OpenWatcom is an open source integrated development environment and suite of compilers for C and C++ (and Fortran too, but that language is not in focus in this book), originally developed by Watcom International Corporation and released as open source by Sybase in 2003.

It supports multiple operating systems, including DOS, Windows, OS/2, and also Linux, and is the de-facto compiler for programmers who have an interest in creating fun, free-time projects for retro platforms.

Not necessarily for the money, but instead for that joyful feeling of sweet nostalgia shivering through one's spine when they are in front of an 80x25 screen. Maybe that's the reason most senior programmers today use a grid of VI editors running in a terminal tiled to 6x4 windows, on huge WQUXGA (or larger) screens.

But let's get back to the OpenWatcom compiler. While browsing the release notes of the project[2], we encountered the following, may I say so, quite intriguing phrase (in the *Major differences from version 10.0* section, at item 29):

We have duplicated a Microsoft Visual C++ extension that was required to parse the Windows 95 SDK header files.

Example:

typedef struct S {

*} S, const *CSP;*

^^^^^- not allowed in ISO C or ISO C++

Ehm … what? Did I just read correctly that there is an extension for Visual C++ that allows non-standard code to be compiled?

Yes, we actually read that correctly. The following short sequence of demonstrative code should not compile with any major C++ compiler today, except for Visual C++ (and OpenWatcom's C++ compiler, as per their comments):

```
#include <iostream>
typedef struct S {
    int a;
} S, const *CSP;
int main() {
    S s1; s1.a = 1;
    CSP ps1 = &s1;
    std::cout << ps1->a;
}
```

...and due to some mystery, the author was not able to decipher, the code sequence is also accepted by several versions of ICC (Intel's powerful, but sadly discontinued, C++ compiler). So, we can ask the following question again: since one major, and two relatively esoteric compilers accept this kind of code, does this mean that we should use it? Is it standard?

The answer to the second question is a definitive *no*. However, for the first one, it is a bit more nuanced. This is because before answering, we must take the background, requirements, and other relevant factors that might influence the decisions concerning the development into consideration again.

Do we want to stick to the standard C++ as much as we can? Is it possible to deliver the required solution without extending ourselves to using vendor-specific extensions? Are we bound to a compiler or an operating system, and are we not worried about ever needing to visit foreign lands?

---

2   https://open-watcom.github.io/open-watcom-v2-wikidocs/c_readme.html

Would it save us a lot of trouble to use the managed extensions for C++, offered by adopting the Microsoft platform, or would we rather stick to the good old syntax (and types) that we know and are familiar with?

Microsoft is famous for providing platform-specific extensions for the C and C++ languages, to the extent that there is an entire section dedicated to Microsoft-specific C++ keywords[3]. This tells us that there is a market for non-standard C++, and with just cause, because some of these extensions are very handy, at the expense of binding ourselves to a platform, compiler, and toolchain.

One of the Microsoft extensions manifests itself within the __declspec keyword. The __declspec keyword in C and C++ is part of Microsoft's extended C++ syntax, which allows developers to specify Microsoft-specific storage-class attributes for certain C++ constructs.

This keyword provides additional control over behaviors such as DLL exporting and memory alignment, which are not covered by the standard ANSI keywords such as static and extern. By using __declspec, developers can easily and non-standard compliantly apply these features specific to Microsoft's own compiler (behold: a surprise follows!) to their code, enhancing the capabilities and performance of their code, such as in the following code sequence:

```
struct person {
    void set_age(int page) { m_age = page; }
    int get_age() const { return m_age; }
    __declspec (property(get = get_age, put = set_age)) int age;
    person() = default;
private:
    int m_age;
};
int main() {
    person joe;
    joe.age = 12;
    std::cout << "Hello " << joe.age;
}
```

Using Microsoft's __declspec(property(...)) syntax, the preceding code sequence creates an age property that allows indirect interaction with m_age through the methods provided, properly encapsulating the age data while providing a simplified interface for accessing and modifying it.

The list of attributes that one can harness with the __declspec extension is quite long and pragmatic, and __declspec also seems to be catchy in the compiler development world. In fact, it's so catchy that **Clang** provides an argument dedicated to understanding this Microsoft-specific extension. This flag, -fdeclspec, makes it possible to use the __declspec keyword in code compiled by Clang too. So, the question naturally arises: is this a Microsoft-specific extension anymore, or are we witnessing the emergence of a cross-platform feature?

---

3   https://learn.microsoft.com/en-us/cpp/cpp/keywords-cp-p?view=msvc-170

A truth that is still considered to be taboo in hardcore C++ programmer circles is that in real life, rare are the situations, when one needs to write true cross-platform code. Most programmers work for a specific company, developing or supporting a particular product. They'll mostly use one operating system, with one compiler toolchain, complying with the restrictions imposed by their employer and happily compiling their code using all the extensions their compiler supports.

This does not mean they don't explicitly want to write standard compliant C++ code. No, on the contrary, I believe they write the highest quality code they can come up with. This just means that they merely use the possibilities provided by a specific compiler: the one they have to work with. At their next company, there is a high chance that they will be using a different compiler that runs on a different OS, thus forgetting all about the advantages provided by their ex-compiler at their ex-place. This is because compiler-specific syntax and extensions are not bound to one compiler exclusively.

Let's consider the following code sample, for example:

```
char arr[6] = {'a', 'b', "cde"};
```

Other than hurting our eyes, this sequence is obviously as standard and non-conformant as possible. Who in their right mind would ever attempt to initialize an array of 6 chars like this? However, the Microsoft Visual C++ compiler happily digests it. Let's start with a few normal characters, and when we get bored of typing in all the apostrophes and commas, we'll just throw everything else in a constant string literal, because why not? And it is quite clever about it, detecting the size that was requested for the array and matching it to the accumulated length of the parts, signaling an error if there are any mismatches.

Microsoft's C++ compiler is a very innovative one when it comes to adding features not found in the standard, or allowing code that would break a language lawyer's tongue. Let's look at the following piece of code, for example:

```
class person {
public:
    int age;
    class {
    public:
        std::string name;
    };
};
```

This code sequence is anything but standard C++. Its sheer existence even allows us to write code that looks like the following:

```
int main() {
    person joe;
    joe.name = "Joe";
    std::cout << "Hello " << joe.name;
}
```

The preceding example compiles and runs without any issues when compiled using Microsoft's own C++ compiler. Please carefully observe the anonymous class, which contains the name member, is an object that has a constructor.. This is an object that has a constructor, a destructor, and lots of other interesting features. This is another (very handy, if I may say so) Microsoft deviation from the standard because anonymous unions are a well-known beast of C++. However, anonymous structs only dwell in the C language (starting from C11) and no other compiler accepts the preceding code.

As a side note, if you're not familiar with the notion of anonymous structs in the C language, they are a useful feature for simplifying nested structure declarations. They do not require the naming of inner structs when they are not needed elsewhere, and they make the code more concise and readable. While the members are enclosed in a structure, it is still possible to have direct access to them. By encapsulating related fields within anonymous structs, and introducing logical blocks within these members, the cluttering of the code with unnecessary type definitions becomes less overwhelming.

The realm of free compilers

Two of the three major compilers today are developed and maintained in an open-source manner. This means that, in theory, anyone can contribute and provide useful new features to their compiler of choice. However, in practice, it means that there is a tiny core of professional programmers who have the necessary knowledge and dedication, and also the backing of a large corporation benefiting from the development of the aforementioned compiler working on it.

In no particular order, GCC and Clang (and MSVC, which we discussed in the previous section) are the most standard-compliant compilers as of 2024. This standard compliance, however, does not mean that these compilers don't come with their own perks that a developer once thought would be a great idea to incorporate.

Let's take, for example, the **computed goto** feature of GCC (and Clang too, of course; those two tend to go hand in hand). We all have learned in school that goto is just plain evil, and should not be ever used. If you did not learn this in school, please do not learn it from this book. That's because it is, again, not true. Instead, let's focus on what we can think of the computed goto. If goto is evil, then is computed goto calculated evil? So is the following code sequence pure evil, or calculated evil? Let's have a look:

```
int main() {
    std::vector<void*> labels = { &&start, &&state1, &&state2, &&end };
    int state = 0;
    goto *labels[state];
    start:
        std::cout << "In start state" << std::endl;
        state = 1;
        goto *labels[state];
    state1:
        std::cout << "In state 1" << std::endl;
```

```
        state = 2;
        goto *labels[state];
    state2:
        std::cout << "In state 2" << std::endl;
        state = 3;
        goto *labels[state];
    end:
        std::cout << "In end state" << std::endl;
        return 0;
}
```

There is nothing wrong with the first line. The problems start after that. This very handy feature can be used for implementing interpreters or state machines efficiently and in a non-standard manner by allowing jumps to labels based on the value of a pointer, initialized from the address of the label itself. Since we are dealing with pointers, it is entirely possible to use the dreaded pointer arithmetic and do some calculations on the addresses.

Also, this can be a dangerous feature if not used properly. Unlike in the case of the standard goto, the calculated one does not take into calculation the objects whose lifetime ends upon leaving a specific scope. So, no destructors are called. Consider yourself warned!

Another pretty useful deviation from the standard C++ syntax comes from GCC (and again, it's implemented by Clang too, what a surprise), which makes the following code sequence compilable with these two compilers:

```
int y = ({ int x = 10; x + 5; });
```

Neat, ain't it? This feature is called *Statements and Declarations in Expressions* and has all the benefits that you can think of: nice encapsulation of the objects declared inside, and somewhat safer macros if used properly. It's too bad it is not standard C++.

Clang, the new kid on the block (well, if we can call a 15-year-old compiler the "new" kid, although compared to GCC, with a birth date dating back to 1987, Clang is still a very young, albeit skilled, player in the field) takes the feature fight a bit further. The following piece of code only compiles with Clang, with the benefit of a very special library and a new command line switch to the compiler:

```
#include <iostream>
int main() {
    int (^square)(int) = ^(int num) { return num * num; };
    int y = square(12);
    std::cout << y << std::endl;
}
```

This feature is called **Blocks** in Clang. In order to get it right, you will need to install the `BlocksRuntime`[4] library, then specify a special `-fblocks` flag to Clang, and, after all this blocking has been done, we can finally compile the preceding code.

This pretty much resembles the behavior of a standard C++11 lambda, but considering that this feature was created and introduced in Clang in 2008, we might call this the father of the standard C++ lambda. In case you're curious, the standard C++ lambda providing the same functionality is as follows:

```
auto square = [](int num) ->int { return num * num; };
```

That's not black magic, unlike the following piece of code:

```
auto generate(int n) -> std::vector<int>{
    int array[n] = {0};
    for(int i=0; i<n; i++) array[i] = i;
    return std::vector<int>{array, array + n};
}
```

So, in case you are wondering what is happening there, here's just a small refresher of your C++ freshman memories: under no circumstances is `int array[n] = {0};` standard C++. The **variable length array** is a feature present in C, but the C++ standard does not include it due to various safety considerations. Regardless, the preceding code is accepted by the GCC compiler, but Clang complains about it:

```
error: variable-sized object may not be initialized
    5 |     int array[n] = {0};
```

According to the error message, the fix is easy:

```
auto generate(int n) -> std::vector<int>{
    int array[n];
    for(int i=0; i<n; i++) array[i] = i;
    return std::vector<int>{array, array + n};
}
```

Now, even Clang (and several other compilers, such as ICC) accept it, regardless of the state of standardness of the code... or rather, the lack of it.

A tribute to attributes

Both GCC and Clang (and also Microsoft Visual C++) can, however, agree on the usefulness of one very specific extension to the C++ language: we need a way to attach metadata to some of the language constructs (such as types, functions, variables, etc.). This metadata can then be used by the compiler and other tools to generate optimized code, perform checks, or provide other features.

---

4   https://github.com/mackyle/blocksruntime

Before modern C++ (i.e., C++11) introduced the standardized way to specify attributes using the double square bracket syntax `[[attribute]]`, each compiler had their own way of specifying these so required attributes:

- GCC and Clang used `__attribute__((attribute-name))`
- Microsoft Visual C++ used `__declspec(attribute-name)`

With the release of C++11, however, the standardization committee realized the usefulness of these, and lifted the most applicable attributes into the language (such as `[[noreturn]]`) while later improvements to the standard added even more attributes (such as `[[fallthrough]]`, `[[nodiscard]]`, etc.). However, a lot of these attributes remained confined to the compilers that have introduced them. The following code snippet showcases some of these:

```
void old_function() __attribute__((deprecated));
void fatal_error() __attribute__((noreturn));
int pure_function(int x) __attribute__((pure));
int x __attribute__((aligned(16)));
void old_function() {
   std::cout << "This function is deprecated.";
}
void fatal_error() {
   std::cerr << "This function does not return.";
   exit(1);
}
int pure_function(int x) {
   return x * x;
}
```

The code sequence above contains a few attributes shared by GCC and Clang, such as the following:

- `__attribute__((deprecated))` marks `old_function` as deprecated
- `__attribute__((noreturn))` is used to indicate that `fatal_error` does not return
- `__attribute__((pure))` is used to indicate that `pure_function` has no side effects except for its return value
- `__attribute__((aligned(16)))` is used to align the x variable to a 16-byte boundary

The list of attributes these compilers[5] provide is huge [6], and we can highly recommend that if you are in a situation where you are working with one of these compilers on a very specific platform, and your main concern is not code portability, platform independence, and standard compliance, then

---

5   https://gcc.gnu.org/onlinedocs/gcc/Function-Attributes.html

6   https://clang.llvm.org/docs/AttributeReference.html

you should go and check them out. That's because a lot of power can be harnessed by properly using the tools your compiler provides you with.

When the header is not even C++

The long list of standard-non-compliant-but-still-working-and-useful features does not end with the preceding examples. However, if we had only focused our attention on those, we could still have filled several books with them. Sadly, for the moment, we have only dedicated one chapter to this topic, so let's move our attention to somewhat more exotic features.

Qt has been the de-facto cross-platform programming framework for GUI applications (but not only) for quite some time. Throughout its fateful history, while exchanging owners several times since its inception in 1994, the Qt framework has evolved significantly, with each release giving a new set of features to the C++ (but not only) programming community. However, one feature has remained more or less the same: the signal/slot implementation and the **Meta Object Compiler** (**MOC**). The pillar of the framework, the MOC makes it possible to connect events from components (i.e., signals) to receivers (i.e., slots) for proper handling.

However, this very handy feature comes at the expense of having to support several non-C++ constructs, which makes the connection between seemingly unrelated elements of the application possible. For example, the class declaration of objects that must respond to an event is extended by several non-standard "access modifiers", such as signals:, private slots:, and so on. Also, there is a new **keyword** called emit, which makes it possible to, well, emit signals.

Long story short, the following is an excerpt from a header file, making the compilation of the following code possible:

```
#ifndef MYCONTROL_H
#define MYCONTROL_H
#include <QObject>
#include <QPushButton>
#include <QWidget>
class MyControl : public QWidget {
    Q_OBJECT
public:
    MyControl(QWidget *parent = nullptr);
private slots:
    void onButtonClicked();
signals:
    void nameChanged(const QString &name);
private:
    QPushButton *myButton;
};
#endif
```

Should we adopt the luxury provided to us by Qt and use the very convenient signal/slot mechanism with the drawback that we have to write non-standard C++ code? Or would we rather stick to tradition and create every little button and connection by writing pure C++ code, as we would do in GTK?

This chapter cannot answer this question because, in the end, it is up to every project's specific requirements. Those include what is imposed by the environment, what the project stakeholders expect from it, and how the development team decides the path forward. However, despair not: even if this does not feel like standard C++, it solves a very real-life problem. Behind the scenes, there hides a cutting-edge implementation, which has been tested, approved, improved, and used in several small- and large-scale projects. It has stood the test of time.

Microsoft's own large-scale extension to the C++ language comes from a different approach. While not being a specific tool such as Qt's MOC, C++/CLI extends C++ with .NET-specific syntax. The Visual Studio compiler for C++/**CLI** (as in, **Common Language Infrastructure**, not Command Line Interface) can parse this extended syntax and generate valid Common Intermediate Language (which is a low-level, platform-independent instruction set used by the .NET framework) and native code. The following code sequence is an example of this managed C++. It does nothing special; it just concatenates the elements of an array of strings and prints the result:

```
#include <iostream>
#include <atlstr.h>
#include <stdio.h>
using namespace System;
int main() {
    array<String^>^ args = { "managed", "world" };
    String^ s = "Hello";
    for each (String ^ a in args) s += " " + a ;
    CString cs(s);
    wprintf(cs);
}
```

I totally agree; it is anything but standard C++. It does not look like standard C++, it does not feel like standard C++, and it doesn't even quack like standard C++. So, it must not be that. The standard-compliant C++ code having the same functionality would look like the following:

```
#include <array>
#include <iostream>
#include <string>
int main() {
    std::array<std::string, 2> args = { "unmanaged", "world" };
    std::string s = "Hello";
    for(const auto& a : args) {
        s += " " + a ;
    }
```

```
    std::cout << s;
}
```

Isn't it nicer, shorter, and more concise than the previous one? Not to mention the fact that it is also standard-conformant.

It will be interesting to observe the evolution of the managed extensions of C++ in the future.

Right now, it serves as a bridge between native and managed code, which is a very niche field for the moment. However, in the long term, its survival is heavily dependent on how the developer communities will embrace it (or not), whether the ecosystem it has created will be of enough use to keep it alive, or whether other technologies, such as P/Invoke or COM Interop, will take over the specific uses cases that C++/CLI handles right now.

There are interesting times ahead, indeed.

The curious case of C++ locked in a box

Up until now, we have observed cases where the standard compliance was at the developers' own discretion. They had the option to choose their platform, use the extensions provided by their favorite compiler, or go for pure standard C++. However, out there in the wild wide world, there are certain circumstances wherein we cannot fully comply with the standard due to some restrictions imposed upon us by the environment that disallows the usage of certain features found in the C++ standard.

Not considering obscene scenarios, when we must maintain decades-old legacy code written in the golden age of C++ (i.e., before the standardization committee took over and ruined all the fun by demanding standard compliance, in order to avert the uncontrollable spread of C++ dialects as happened with **BASIC**), there are situations outside of our control that make the usage of the full C++ standard features impossible. For example, there might be certain requirements that disallow the usage of exceptions. Other environments may lack the proper support for memory allocation, while others still simply force us to write to direct hardware addresses in order for something to happen. However, this last one can happen in a standard-compliant way too.

Some embedded systems, for example, actively encourage the usage of their platform-specific assembly instructions. As we know, there is no such thing as a platform-independent assembly language because that is the lowest level one can go to in today's C++. Below that is pure hexadecimal machine code, but long gone are the times when we had to use that in C++ code.

There might also be scenarios wherein the requirements formulated for our code by the hardware require deterministic behavior. This, by definition, excludes exceptions (because who would like to be unable to follow the code flow at every nanosecond during its execution?) and memory allocations (because of allocation latency, memory fragmentation, and a myriad of other issues your code is again not behaving in a deterministic manner). Thus, a large chunk of the C++ standard falls out of our grace.

There are certain solutions tackling the problem of memory allocation in embedded systems, such as the usage of memory pools, object pools, compile time memory allocation, and various other resources, which may be even platform-specific in turn. Then there are the exceptions. In his excellent paper[7], Bjarne Stroustrup discusses the challenges, costs, and risks involved in replacing C++ exceptions with alternatives such as deterministic exceptions. However, as the paper concludes, at this moment, there are no clear advantages to replacing the current exception-handling mechanisms with something else. That would include another fragmentation in the C++ developer community, as if there aren't enough of those already. Instead, the paper argues for the importance of focusing on enhancing the current exception-handling system rather than complicating the language with additional mechanisms, emphasizing that exceptions, despite their imperfections, have effectively served a vast number of developers for decades.

Past days of future C++

The last scenario that we will explore concerning the standard compliance of the code you write relates to the most fundamental item in the C++ ecosystem: the compiler itself.

You see, compilers are also programs, consisting of millions and millions of lines of code. There are several contributors spread out on the globe working on them, adding new features, fixing bugs, making them more standard compliant, releasing the latest versions, and generally making sure that your compiler just works.

These compilers also have a development timeline. The implementation of features does not happen overnight, and there simply might be situations wherein, at a certain point in time, some compiler does not support some feature of the standard because there was not enough manpower to implement it.

There is a very handy document available at the source of all C++ knowledge[8], which details the support of various C++ standard features and which compilers have support for a specific feature.

At the turn of standards (or when forced to use outdated compilers that have not implemented some of the features yet), there have been several tricks employed by the C++ developer community to compensate for the lack of features in upcoming versions of various compilers.

When the `mutable` keyword was introduced in C++98, its implementation in certain compilers took a bit longer than in others. For programmers using these compilers, it was challenging to modify member variables in `const` member functions (a feature introduced in the same standard).

---

7   https://www.open-std.org/jtc1/sc22/wg21/docs/papers/2019/p1947r0.pdf

8   https://en.cppreference.com/w/cpp/compiler_support

In situations like this, the following (quite ugly) hack had to be used to counteract the missing keyword:

```cpp
class Counter {
    int viewCount = 0;
public:
    void view() const {
        const_cast<Counter*>(this)->viewCount++;
    }
    void print() const {
        std::cout << "Count: " << viewCount << std::endl;
    }
};
```

Assuming that your computer supports `const_cast`, there is nothing wrong with the preceding code. However, if `const_cast` is not in the list of supported keywords, then you are pretty much back to a standard C style cast, such as `((Counter*)(this))->viewCount++;`. This should fix all your problems.

The `mutable` keyword was not the first one whose lack of support in compilers caused trouble for developers. Before C++11 introduced `constexpr` (and a few years after that too, for Microsoft Visual C++ programmers), compile-time constant expressions had to be evaluated using various template tricks (or just macros, but as we all know, they are evil, so let's avoid them for as long as we can).

> **Note**
>
> As a side note, the code demonstrating how to bypass a missing 'mutable' keyword using const_cast can lead to undefined behavior - specifically, if this actually points to a const object, then removing const and dereferencing it results in UB. This risk is even greater on operating systems with proper memory protection mechanisms in place, and for almost sure it will result in a crash if the object was created in the global namespace. And no, DOS, this doesn't apply to you.

For example, the following piece of code calculated the famous factorial of some number, before `constexpr` (but still at compile time):

```cpp
template <unsigned int N>
struct Factorial {
    static const unsigned long long value = N * Factorial<N -
1>::value;
};
template <>
struct Factorial<0> {
    static const unsigned long long value = 1;
};
const unsigned long long fac5 =  Factorial<5>::value;
```

The current standard implementation using a compiler that supports `constexpr` of the same function is certainly shorter and much easier to understand:

```
constexpr unsigned long long factorial(unsigned int n) {
    return n <= 1 ? 1 : n * factorial(n - 1);
}
const unsigned long long fac5too =  factorial(5);
```

Certainly, a huge jump in the readability of the code, if I may say so.

Summary

As this chapter has demonstrated, writing standard C++ ensures code portability, compatibility, and maintainability across different platforms and compilers. We learned that by adhering to the ISO/IEC C++ standard, we can create code that behaves predictably and is less prone to bugs and platform-specific issues. Standard-compliant C++ code also benefits from generic compiler optimizations and future language enhancements, while ensuring long-term relevance and performance, as we learned in this chapter.

On the other hand, using C++ compiler-specific extensions can provide performance optimizations specific to a platform and compiler, access to advanced features that are not yet standardized, and integration with vendor-specific tools. However, the extension may introduce portability issues, dependencies on specific compiler versions, as well as divergence from standard C++ practices, which can impact code maintenance and interoperability across different platforms and compilers. We also covered this in this chapter.

Therefore, we learned that adoption should be carefully considered based on project needs, balancing the benefits of enhanced functionality with potential drawbacks related to compatibility and long-term support. At this stage, we trust that you can make the right decision that has the best impact on your project and code base while allowing you to deliver the required product. Even if it's your pet project that you coded in your free time on a 30-year-old machine. Compiled with a 30-year-old compiler.

Our next chapter, courtesy of Alex, will go on a deep exploration and try to uncover the basic truth of whether C++ is indeed just another object-oriented language, or whether there is something more lurking below the surface...

3

There's a Single C++, and It Is Object-Oriented

Only if you ignore all the others

C++ was born as C with objects, which makes many developers still consider it an OOP language. We will see in this chapter that C++ allows multiple paradigms, and you could safely describe it as multiple programming languages in one. We will look at a few paradigms supported in C++, including structured programming, OOP, functional programming, and metaprogramming, in combination with the choice of strong versus quasi-optional types.

In this chapter, we're going to cover the following main topics:

- The multiple facets of C++
- Functional programming in C++
- Metaprogramming
- Strong types to the limit
- What about ignoring types?

Technical requirements

The code for this chapter is available from the GitHub repository `https://github.com/PacktPublishing/Debunking-CPP-Myths`, in the ch3 folder. It uses Makefile, g++, and the doctest library (`https://github.com/doctest/doctest`) for unit testing. The code is compiled for C++20.

The multiple facets of C++

If you, like me, frequently move between different organizations, teams, and technical conferences, you will quickly notice two things: C++ programmers have distinct interests compared to other developers, and the C++ community is more aptly described as small, specialized pockets of C++ developers. That's different from other communities; if you discuss Java, you'll likely end up talking about Spring Framework and REST APIs or the Android toolkit. C# is mostly fairly standardized around the Microsoft libraries, and JavaScript is mostly about React. But get 100 C++ programmers in a room from different organizations and you'll soon notice the differences. Embedded C++ is all about keeping all the resources in check because adding an extra 1 MB of memory to a device sold in millions of units quickly pumps up the cost. Game developers are on the other side of the spectrum, looking at how to squeeze extra frame rate out of next-generation GPUs and CPUs. The high-frequency trading people know all about avoiding CPU cache misses and how to brush off a picosecond of the automated transaction algorithm because the smallest time fraction can mean millions of euros. Engineering software developers are more relaxed, but still worried about the validity of the changes in a complex rendering model. And then you find the programmers dealing with automated systems for rails, cars, or factories, whose main concern is resilience and robustness.

This picture, while far from complete, is enough to show us the immense variability of C++ programmers, unlike their peers using any other language. We could almost say that from a certain point of view, C++ is the last remaining de facto general-purpose language, since the other mainstream ones are used in practice mostly for specific types of programs: Java for enterprise backend services and Android development, C# for web and Windows applications and services, JavaScript for rich web frontends and serverless backends, and Python for scripts, data science, and DevOps. But C++ is in embedded software, factory systems, trading, simulations, engineering tools, operating systems, and so on.

The old saying "form follows function" is about design applying to everything built by people, including programming languages, and applies equally well to C++. The large variability in projects and types of programmers fed into the language, along with Stroustrup's desire to make it as capable as possible. C++ is not a single language; every programmer uses a subset of C++ that is often different from their colleagues working in the same organization.

Yes, C++ started as C with objects, at a time when OOP was on the rise. But, at the same time, C++ is backward compatible with C, which means you can still write structured programming in C++. Then, templates were needed. Then, lambdas were useful. While C++ has always been a collection of different languages, today it's even more so. To prove this point, let's look at a few paradigms you can use in C++, starting with functional programming.

Functional programming in C++

I remember being in university, fascinated about programming, and already quite adept at writing BASIC, Pascal, Logo, and simple C++. I think it was in my second year when I took a course on functional programming. The teacher was very passionate and eager to show us the wonders of this paradigm, explaining a lot of concepts that I couldn't quite grasp. The course turned into a complete miss for me, since the only thing I learned was how to write imperative code in Lisp and how to translate the idioms I knew into something that would work in this weird language that wears its parentheses on the outside of expressions.

I tried to go back to functional programming after starting my career as a software engineer. There were plenty of resources online, only the way they explained the paradigm didn't help. "It's basically category theory," they said. Everything is a function, even numbers (check out Church encoding). You can easily understand monads since they are a monoid in the category of endofunctors. This style of explanation uses a more complicated concept to explain a practical one and doesn't facilitate understanding.

This is why it took me years to understand what functional programming is and how it helps with software development. I became a fan, but not a fanatic, of this paradigm. Like any engineer, I like to solve problems, and in my case, most often I solve them with code. Having code that is simpler is always great, although often simpler does not mean more familiar.

If I were to explain functional programming today, I would focus on three important things: *immutability*, *pure functions*, and *operations with functions*. Perhaps unexpectedly, C++ is a good fit for all these traits. Immutability is where C++ shines compared to the other mainstream programming languages (although less than Rust, but we'll talk about that in the final chapter).

However, there's one catch: functional programming is a different paradigm, with its own trade-offs. I've noticed that C++ programmers find it difficult to think about lambdas since they see lambdas not as a fundamental concept but as something built on top of the existing language. That's fair enough since lambdas are objects and not first-class design elements in C++. However, thinking in a functional paradigm requires the programmers to temporarily forget this knowledge and embrace the functional design elements. You can go back to this knowledge when you have implemented something that works and are looking for improvements.

Let's explain the three characteristics in more detail and then discuss the impact of using functional programming on our software architecture.

Immutability

Immutability fundamentally means that each variable is initialized with a value, but a new value cannot be assigned to the variable. In C++, this can be done with `const` or `constexpr`, depending on whether we want the value to be immutable at runtime or at compile time.

While immutability is easy to understand for simple types, collections and objects introduce challenges. An immutable collection is one that returns a new collection upon every change. So, for example, the following code shows a mutable collection:

```
vector<int> numbers {1, 2, 3};
numbers.push_back(4);
assert(numbers == vector<int> {1, 2, 3, 4});
```

Contrast this example with a hypothetic immutable collection, shown in the next code sample, that returns a new collection upon adding to it:

```
immutable_vector<int> numbers {1, 2, 3};
immutable_vector<int> moreNumbers = numbers.push_back(4);
assert(numbers == immutable_vector<int> {1, 2, 3});
assert(moreNumbers == immutable_vector<int> {1, 2, 3, 4});
```

This trait guarantees that you're using the correct version of the data structure that you need. But the memory optimization bells might ring in your C++ brain. There seems to be a lot of memory allocation happening for immutable collections! Isn't that a waste?

It is indeed possible to be temporarily using more memory than you'd expect upon performing a change in an immutable collection. However, functional languages have found smart ways to avoid this, and C++ is perfectly capable of using the same mechanisms. It depends on the implementation.

The way to optimize memory for immutable collections is to use *smart pointers*. Remember that values are immutable once assigned to a variable. Therefore, when the collection is first initialized, memory is allocated for each element of the collection and each memory area is assigned to a specific value. When a new element is added, the pointers to each element are copied and a new memory area is allocated for the new value. If an element is removed from the collection, all the pointers to existing elements are copied except the one pointing to the removed element. Once a memory area is no longer referenced by any pointer, it gets deleted.

While immutable collections are not implemented as such in STL, libraries such as immer (`https://github.com/arximboldi/immer`) allow you to use this pattern without worrying too much about the internal details.

OK, but what about immutable objects? Isn't the whole purpose of OOP to mix behavior with data?

To this, I have three things to say.

First, good question!

Second, OOP was misunderstood to be about encapsulation, inheritance, and polymorphism when in fact it's about message passing. C++ was unfortunately the trendsetter for what I like to call "class-oriented programming": a style of programming focused on classes and their relationships instead of objects and their relationships.

And third, functional programming has in fact no qualms with objects. Implementing immutable objects is very simple: either we implement an immutable data structure using `const`, or every method that changes data returns instead a new object with the modified data.

It's worth mentioning at this point that you don't have to use immutability to its fullest in your programs to benefit from functional programming. I write enough code that maximizes constness but still uses the standard STL collections and objects that change their internal data. However, you need to be aware that the level of immutability described previously allows you to introduce parallelism much more easily into your programs. If values cannot change, you have no problems with critical sections. Each thread works with its own value, and changing the value will change it only for the specific thread. Indeed, this is one of the side benefits of immutability. I say side benefits because immutability combined with pure functions and good naming gives you programs that are easier to understand once you get used to the building blocks. So, let's look at pure functions next.

Pure functions

A pure function is a function that returns the same output for the same input and doesn't change any value in the context. By definition, a pure function cannot do **Input/Output (I/O)** operations. However, any non-trivial program can be written as a combination of pure functions and I/O functions.

Pure functions are the simplest types of functions you can think of. They are easy to understand, very predictable, and cacheable because they lack side effects. This leads to easy testing with data-driven unit tests and potential optimizations such as caching the result of the function upon first call with specific inputs and reusing it later.

Pure functions are at the core of functional programming. In C++, they are very easy to implement using the support for immutability.

The original way of writing functions in pure functional languages is lambdas. Lambdas have made their way into the standard since C++11. However, C++ lambdas can be mutable because they can change the variables they capture in their context. So, writing pure functions in C++, even with lambdas, requires you to ensure the constness of all variables involved.

In a functional paradigm, everything is either a function or a data structure, and in pure functional languages, the two are interchangeable. So, how do we create complex behaviors from simple functions? We compose functions using various operations, of course.

Operations on functions

Since functions are the main design element of functional programming, it's par to the course to think about how functions can change through operations. The most common functional operations are partial application and composition.

Partial application refers to creating a new function by binding the value of one parameter of a function to a specific value. For example, if we have a function, `add(const int first, const int second)`, we can obtain the `increment(const int)` function by binding the `second` parameter to the value `1`. Let's take a moment to consider the consequence: every function, no matter how many arguments it receives, can be reduced through subsequent partial applications to functions that take no parameters. This gives us a universal language for expressing anything in code.

To implement a partial application in C++, we can use the `std::bind` function from the `<functional>` header. Let's see how we can obtain the `increment` function from the `add` function by binding the second parameter of `add` to the value 1:

```
#include <functional>
auto add = [](const int first, const int second){ return first +
second; };
auto increment = std::bind(add, std::placeholders::_1, 1);
TEST_CASE("add"){
      CHECK_EQ(10, add(4, 6));
}
TEST_CASE("increment"){
      CHECK_EQ(10, increment(9));
}
```

This is a neat solution from a functional programming perspective. However, the return value is complicated and approximates a function instead of being a function. This is one of the mental hurdles for C++ programmers when trying functional programming. I've been away from the language long enough to allow myself to think in higher-level concepts instead of always analyzing the implementation. So, when I use `std::bind` to do the partial application, I treat the result as a function and hope the implementors have done their job of optimizing and providing the necessary behaviors.

The other fundamental operation with functions is functional composition. You've probably encountered this construct in mathematics. Functional composition refers to creating a function, f, from two functions, g and h, such that $f(x) = g(h(x))$ for any value x. This is commonly denoted in math as $f = g \circ h$.

Unfortunately, there's no function or operation in the C++ standard that implements functional composition, but it's easy to implement this operation with templates. Once again, the result of this operation in C++ is complicated, but I encourage you to think about it as a function rather than the actual data structure.

Let's see a possible implementation for functional composition in C++. The `compose` function takes two type parameters, F and G, that each denote the type of functions f and g to compose. The compose function returns a lambda that takes one parameter, `value`, and returns `f(g(value))`:

```
template <class F, class G>
auto compose(F f, G g){
   return [=](auto value){return f(g(value));};
}
```

> **Note**
>
> The preceding example is borrowed from Alex's other book on the topic with Packt Publishing, *Hands-On Functional Programming in C++*.

Let's see how we could use this function with a simple example. Let's implement a price calculator that takes as parameters the price, a discount, a service fee, and tax and returns the final price. Let's look first at an imperative implementation, using a single function that computes everything inline. The `computePriceImperative` function takes the price, subtracts the discount, adds the service fee, and then adds the tax percentage on top:

```
double computePriceImperative(const int taxPercentage, const int
serviceFee, const double price, const int discount){
return (price - discount + serviceFee) * (1 + (static_
cast<double>(taxPercentage) / 100));
}
TEST_CASE("compute price imperative"){
        int taxPercentage = 18;
        int serviceFee = 10;
        double price = 100;
        int discount = 10;
                                double result =
computePriceImperative(taxPercentage, serviceFee, price, discount);

        CHECK_EQ(118, result);
}
```

This is a simple implementation, and good enough to give a result. Challenges usually appear for this type of code when we need to add more types of discounts, modify taxes depending on items, or change the order of discounts. Of course, we can apply an imperative or object-oriented style when the time comes, and extract multiple functions, one for each operation, that we then combine however we need.

But let's look at the functional style now. The first thing we can do is to use lambdas for every operation, and another lambda for the final computation. We implement a few lambdas: one that subtracts the discount from the price, a second that applies the service fee, a third that applies the tax, and a final one that computes the price by chaining calls to all the previously defined lambdas. We end up with the following code:

```
auto discountPrice = [](const double price, const int discount){return
price - discount;};
auto addServiceFee = [](const double price, const int serviceFee){
return price + serviceFee; };
auto applyTax = [](const double price, const int taxPercentage){
return price * (1 + static_cast<double>(taxPercentage)/100); };
auto computePriceLambda = [](const int taxPercentage, const int
serviceFee, const double price, const int discount){
```

```
return applyTax(addServiceFee(discountPrice(price, discount),
serviceFee), taxPercentage);
};
TEST_CASE("compute price with lambda"){
int taxPercentage = 18;
int serviceFee = 10;
double price = 100;
int discount = 10;

double result = computePriceLambda(taxPercentage, serviceFee, price,
discount);

CHECK_EQ(118, result);
}
```

Is this code better? Well, it depends. One factor is familiarity with this paradigm, but don't let that stop you; as I said before, familiarity is often confused with simplicity, but the two are not the same. Another factor is to see the lambdas as functions and not as data structures. Once you pass these two challenges, we notice a few things: the lambdas are very small, they are easy to understand, and they are pure functions, which are objectively the simplest types of functions out there. We can chain the calls in multiple ways, for example, applying the discount at the price with tax, so we have more options with this implementation. Still, there's nothing we couldn't do with imperative programming until now.

Let's then take the next step and make this fully functional. We will use the lambdas we created, but instead of returning a value, our implementation will use partial application and functional composition to return a function that gives us the answer we are looking for. Since the preceding lambdas have two parameters, we need to bind one of the arguments to the corresponding input before applying the functional composition. So, for the discountPrice lambda, we bind the discount argument to the value passed to the computePriceFunctional function and we obtain a lambda that takes a single parameter, the initial price, and returns the price with a discount. For the addServiceFee lambda, we bind the serviceFee argument to the value passed to the computePriceFunctional function and obtain a function that takes a single parameter, the price before service, and returns the price with the service fee. For the applyTax lambda, we bind the taxPercentage argument to the value passed to the computePriceFunctional function and we obtain a function that takes a single parameter, the price without tax, and returns the price with tax. Once we obtain these functions that take a single parameter, we compose them using the compose function shown previously, and we obtain a function that takes a single argument price and, when called, computes the correct final price. Here is the result:

```
auto computePriceFunctional(const int taxPercentage, const int
serviceFee, const double price, const int discount){
using std::bind;
using std::placeholders::_1;
```

```
auto discountLambda = bind(discountPrice, _1, discount);
auto serviceFeeLambda = bind(addServiceFee, _1, serviceFee);
auto applyTaxLambda = bind(applyTax, _1, taxPercentage);
return compose( applyTaxLambda, compose(serviceFeeLambda,
discountLambda));
}
TEST_CASE("compute price functional"){
int taxPercentage = 18;
int serviceFee = 10;
double price = 100;
int discount = 10;

auto computePriceLambda = computePriceFunctional(taxPercentage,
serviceFee, price, discount);
double result = computePriceLambda(price);

CHECK_EQ(118, result);
}
```

This style of programming is at first glance very different from what OOP or structured programming does. But if you think for a little bit, you will realize that an object is just a set of cohesive, partially applied functions. If you extract the functions from objects, you need to pass in the data members used in the object, a style familiar to those who have ever programmed in C. Including a method in an object is therefore equivalent to binding a few of the arguments to the object data members that are initialized by the constructor. Therefore, OOP and functional programming are not really enemies, just different and equivalent ways of expressing the same behavior, with different trade-offs.

As a prelude to the *Metaprogramming* section coming later, let's look at making all these functions available at compile time. We need to do a little bit of magic with templates and pass in the value parameters as template arguments, and we need to add a lot of constexpr, but the following code works equally well:

```
template <class F, class G>
  constexpr auto compose(F f, G g){
    return [=](auto value){return f(g(value));};
  }
constexpr auto discountPriceCompile = [](const double price,   const
int discount){return price - discount;};
  constexpr auto addServiceFeeCompile = [](const double price,   const
int serviceFee){ return price + serviceFee; };
  constexpr auto applyTaxCompile = [](const double price,
cons t int taxPercentage){ return price * (1 + static_
cast<double  >(taxPercentage)/100); };
  template<int taxPercentage, int serviceFee, double price, in t
discount>
```

```
constexpr auto computePriceFunctionalCompile() {
        using std::bind;
        using std::placeholders::_1;
        constexpr auto discountLambda = bind(discountPrice,    _1,
discount);
        constexpr auto serviceFeeLambda = bind(addServiceFee   , _1,
serviceFee);
        constexpr auto applyTaxLambda = bind(applyTax, _1,
t  axPercentage);
        return compose( applyTaxLambda, compose(serviceFeeLa   mbda,
discountLambda));
    }
TEST_CASE("compute price functional compile"){
        constexpr int taxPercentage = 18;
        constexpr int serviceFee = 10;
        constexpr double price = 100;
        constexpr int discount = 10;

        constexpr auto computePriceLambda =
computePriceFunctionalCompile<taxPercentage, serviceFee, price,
discount>();
        double result = computePriceLambda(price);

        CHECK_EQ(118, result);
}
```

With this, we have seen the fundamental blocks of functional programming in C++. Let's now look at where and why they are useful.

Architectural patterns in functional style

Let's first look at how we would implement an application going all the way to the functional style. We can't discuss all the possible design patterns of such an application, but we can show a few examples.

We notice first that functional programming places a few constraints upon our design. We favor immutability and pure functions. We use data structures, but they are immutable, meaning that every change to the data structure gives us a new version. Finally, the I/O part needs to be separate and as thin as possible since it needs mutations.

A simple design pattern using these constraints is the pipe pattern. Let's imagine we receive a file in XML format, and we call web services with data from it. We have an input layer that reads the XML file, an output layer that writes to web services, and a layer in the center that uses a functional style. We can now consider the input and output data and implement consequent transformations on the input that lead to the desired output. Each of these transformations is a pure function working on immutable data structures.

Such a process is highly parallelizable because of the lack of mutation. In fact, C++17 introduced the `<execution>` header, which allows running the common STL algorithms in parallel. Similar patterns are used in data transformation architectures such as **Extract, Transform, Load** (ETL) and in the MapReduce architecture made popular by Hadoop.

The pattern can be extended beyond data transformation, to the more loosely defined **functional core, imperative shell** architecture, aptly named by Gary Bernhardt. If you want more specific details, look into the hexagonal architecture with a functional core.

This shows not only that we can design programs using a functional paradigm in C++ but also that there are situations when this architecture fits. It also shows that we can take some parts of this style of programming and use it on pieces of our implementation.

Metaprogramming

One thing seems to unite programmers, no matter how different they are otherwise: the enjoyment of jokes on recursion. There's something in the programmer's mind that appreciates a certain type of symmetry. When it comes to programming languages and programming paradigms, you'd be hard-pressed to find a more symmetrical type of language than one that can understand itself.

The corresponding programming paradigm is called metaprogramming, and programming languages that take this idea to the limit are known as homoiconic, meaning that a program can manipulate another program's representation or its own as data. Programming languages that have this property include Lisp and its derived dialects, the latest being Clojure.

Metaprogramming is very powerful, but also very difficult to master, and can introduce a lot of issues in large projects. Some features connected to metaprogramming are available in modern languages, such as instrumentation, reflection, or dynamic execution of instructions. But other than using annotations, very little of all this is used in practice.

C++ is different, however. One feature of metaprogramming is the ability to move computations from runtime to compile time, and C++ has fully embraced it with template metaprogramming. In more recent versions of the language, the implementation of compile-time computations has been simplified with the introduction of generalized constant expressions with `constexpr` and `consteval`.

A typical example of this technique is the factorial implementation. A recursive factorial implementation computed at runtime looks like this:

```
int factorial(const int number){
    if(number == 0) return 1;
    return number * factorial(number - 1);
}
```

The same implementation can be done using template metaprogramming. It is perhaps a lesser-known characteristic of C++ templates that they can take a value as a parameter, not just a type. Moreover, both a generic template, for example, one that takes any integer value as a parameter, and a specialization, which takes only a specific value, can be provided. In our case, we can implement a factorial template that takes an integer and a specialization for the value 0, resulting in the following code:

```
template<int number>
struct Factorial {
enum { value = number * Factorial<number - 1>::value};
};
template<>
struct Factorial<0>{
enum {value = 1};
};
```

This implementation achieves the same goal as the previous one, with the exception that a call to `Factorial<25>`, for example, will be computed at compile time rather than runtime. Starting with C++11 and generalized constant expressions, we can avoid templates altogether and instead use `constexpr` and `consteval` to tell the compiler which values are to be computed at compile time. Here's a simplified implementation of the same code with a constant expression:

```
constexpr int factorial(const int number) {
return (number == 0) ? 1 : (number * factorial(number - 1));
}
```

These metaprogramming techniques available to C++ programmers allow more flexibility in decisions related to what happens at compile time versus runtime. They offer a trade-off of CPU cycles versus the executable size. If you have a lot of memory available but the computations need to happen extremely fast, caching results in the executable can be the way to go, and `constexpr` and `consteval` become your friends.

But the possibilities don't stop here. We can create in C++ programs that are demonstrably valid from compilation. We just need to take strong types to their limit.

Strong types to the limit

One of the biggest challenges in software development is avoiding bugs. This is such a pervasive problem that we have taken to naming it something that suggests something bad has happened to our code. In fact, however, we should be calling bugs *mistakes*, because that is what they are.

Since we have compilers, why can't we place enough restrictions on the code so that they tell us when there's a bug? We might be able to do just that, only not for free. We discussed template metaprogramming in the previous section, but we have left out one important characteristic: template metaprogramming is Turing complete. This means that for any program that we can write in the normal way, we can also write it using template metaprogramming.

This idea is very powerful, and it has been discussed in various contexts over time. If you want to try a programming language built entirely around this notion, try Idris (`https://www.idris-lang.org/`). Many programmers might be familiar with the support available in Haskell for validation at compilation time. But my first encounter with this idea was Andrei Alexandrescu's seminal book *Modern C++ Design: Generic Programming and Design Patterns Applied*, published in 2001.

Let's consider a simple problem. One of the common sources for bugs and code smell is the so-called **primitive obsession**, that is, the obsession to use primitive types to represent complex data. A typical example of primitive obsession is to represent length, money, temperature, or weight as a number, by completely ignoring their units of measure. Rather than doing this, a specific type for money would use a value that allows for a specific precision depending on the context, such as seven decimals for accounting and banks, and the currency. This is often useful in software development even when the program deals with a single currency because one thing you can bet on when it comes to features is that eventually, one thing will become more – there will be a time when your client will ask you to add a second currency.

A typical challenge relating to primitive obsession is with constraining primitive types. For example, consider a type that can store the hour of the day. Not only is this value an unsigned int, but it can only be from 0 to 23, assuming a 24-hour format for simplicity. It would be great to be able to tell the compiler that no value outside of the 0-23 range is ever accepted as an hour and to give a relevant error when passing, for example, a value of 27.

In this case, an enum can be a solution, since the number of values is small. But we'll ignore this option and consider first how we would implement this at runtime. We can imagine a class called `Hour` that throws an exception if the value passed in the constructor is not between 0 and 23:

```
class Hour{
private:
int theValue = 0;


void setValue(int candidateValue) {
if(candidateValue >= 0 && candidateValue <= 23){
theValue = candidateValue;

}
else{
throw std::out_of_range("Value out of range");
}
}

public:

Hour(int theValue){
```

```
setValue(theValue);
}
int value() const {
return theValue;
}
};
TEST_CASE("Valid hour"){
Hour hour(10);

CHECK_EQ(10, hour.value());
}

TEST_CASE("Invalid hour"){
CHECK_THROWS(Hour(30));
}
```

What if we want to move the check at compile time? Well, time to use the power of constexpr to tell the compiler what values are defined at compile time, and static_assert to verify the range:

```
template <int Min, int Max>
class RangedInteger{
private:
int theValue;

constexpr RangedInteger(int theValue) : theValue(theValue) {}

public:
template <int CandidateValue>
static constexpr RangedInteger make() {
static_assert(CandidateValue >= Min && CandidateValue <= Max, "Value
out of range.");
return CandidateValue;
}

constexpr int value() const {
return theValue;
}
};

using Hour = RangedInteger<0, 23>;
```

With the preceding implementation, the following code works perfectly:

```
TEST_CASE("Valid hour"){
constexpr Hour h = Hour::make<10>();

CHECK_EQ(10, h.value());
}
```

But if we try to pass a value outside the range, we get a compilation error:

```
TEST_CASE("Invalid hour"){
constexpr Hour h2 = Hour::make<30>();
}
Hour.h: In instantiation of 'static constexpr RangedInteger<Min, Max>
RangedInteger<Min, Max>::make() [with int CandidateValue = 30; int Min
= 0; int Max = 23]':
Hour.h:11:87: error: static assertion failed: Value out of range.
   11 |                                static_assert(CandidateValue
>= Min && CandidateValue <= Max, "Value out of range.");
      |                     ~~~~~~~~~~~~~~~^~~~~~
Hour.h:11:87: note: '(30 <= 23)' evaluates to false
```

This error tells us that we can't have an hour with the value 30, which is precisely what we needed!

This is just one technique in the toolbox of C++ programmers who want to create programs that are provably valid at compile time. As we mentioned, template metaprogramming is Turing complete, which means we can theoretically implement any program at compile time that we can implement at runtime. As always, there are trade-offs. Notice how the Hour value must be constexpr, which means the value will be stored in the executable. This is by design, since the only way to constrain the types to the maximum is to compile them into the unit.

In practice, I noticed that this technique can easily lead to code that is extremely difficult to understand and modify. Making changes to this code requires a strong discipline, since modifying existing code can still introduce bugs that we otherwise have weeded out through our strong types. The fundamental technique is always to add, never to modify, unless to fix issues. We have kept this code clean until now, but types can get very abstract very quickly, which makes reconstructing the reasoning that led to them very difficult after, say, six months. On the upside, this technique works best when creating libraries focused on a very specific domain.

While I find this technique intriguing, I tend to prefer more freedom when I program. I use my own disciplines – test-driven development, merciless refactoring, extreme attention to names, and simple design – when I code. I'd rather have a way to write the code that I want and let the compiler figure out the details, which is why the last paradigm I'm going to discuss ignores types as much as possible.

What about ignoring types?

A few years ago, I led a team that built a few web applications in a language called Groovy with a framework named Grails. Groovy is an optionally typed and dynamic language, meaning that it assigns types at runtime, but you can provide type hints for the compiler. It can also be compiled statically, and since it's built on JVM, the code ends up in a Java unit.

I had noticed in previous web projects that types were useful at the edges of the system, for checking request parameters, interacting with databases, and other I/O operations. But types in the core of a web application tended to make things more difficult. We often had to change code or write extra code to accommodate new ways of using the already-implemented behaviors, since users of web apps often notice a scenario that is useful and want it to work in other contexts or for other types of data. So, I decided from the very beginning that we would use types for request validation, to ensure security and correctness, and for the interaction with external systems, to ensure simplicity. But we did not use types in the core.

The plan was always to use a sound strategy for automated testing so that all the code was proven valid through tests. I expected that the lack of types would make us write more tests, but I was in for a big surprise: the number of tests was relatively the same as before, but we had less code. Also, the code we wrote, because there were no types involved, pushed us to name things very carefully since names were the only hints we had as programmers as to what a function or a variable was doing.

This is, to this day, my favorite style of programming. I want to write the code as I want, and as expressive as I can, and let the compiler work out the types. You can think about this approach as extreme polymorphism: if you pass a variable of a type that has the required methods, the code should work irrespective of the type you pass in. It is not a style I would recommend for everyone, because it's not obvious if it works solely in combination with a specific design experience, but it is a style that you can experiment with. However, the first hurdle is to let go of controlling what the compiler does, a feat more difficult to achieve for C++ programmers who are very detailed-oriented.

How would this work in C++? Well, fortunately for me, the `auto` keyword was introduced in C++ since C++11, and its features were improved little by little in consequent standards. On the downside, C++ is not as permissive as Groovy on dynamic typing, so occasionally I need templates.

First, let me amaze you with the most polymorphic function you can write:

```
auto identity(auto value){ return value;}
TEST_CASE("Identity"){
CHECK_EQ(1, identity(1));
CHECK_EQ("asdfasdf", identity("asdfasdf"));
CHECK_EQ(vector{1, 2, 3}, identity(vector{1, 2, 3}));
}
```

This function works no matter what we pass into it. Isn't that neat? Imagine that you have a bunch of functions like this that you can use in the core of your system, without needing to change them. That sounds like an ideal programming environment to me. Alas, life is more complicated than this, and programs need more than identity functions.

Let's look at a slightly more complicated example. We'll start by checking whether a string is a palindrome, that is, whether it reads the same both forward and reversed. A simple implementation in C++ is to take the string, reverse it by using `std::reverse_copy`, and then compare the initial string with its reverse:

```
bool isStringPalindrome(std::string value){
std::vector<char> characters(value.begin(), value.end());
std::vector<char> reversedCharacters;
std::reverse_copy(characters.begin(), characters.end(), std::back_
insert_iterator(reversedCharacters));
return characters == reversedCharacters;
}
TEST_CASE("Palindrome"){
CHECK(isStringPalindrome("asddsa"));
CHECK(isStringPalindrome("12321"));
CHECK_FALSE(isStringPalindrome("123123"));
CHECK_FALSE(isStringPalindrome("asd"));
}
```

What if we were to make this code less interested in types? First, we would change the parameter type to `auto`. Then, we need a way to reverse it without constraining ourselves to a string input. Fortunately, the `ranges` library has a `reverse_view` that we can use. Finally, we need to compare the initial value with the reversed one, again without restraining the type too much. C++ provides us with `std::equal`. So, we end up with the following code, which we can use not only for strings but also for a `vector<string>` that represents a phrase, or with tokens defined in an enum. Let's see the extreme polymorphism in action:

```
bool isPalindrome(auto value){
auto tokens = value | std::views::all;
auto reversedTokens = value | std::views::reverse;
return std::equal(tokens.begin(), tokens.end(), reversedTokens.
begin());
};
enum Token{
X, Y
};

TEST_CASE("Extreme polymorphic palindrome"){
CHECK(isPalindrome(string("asddsa")));
CHECK(isPalindrome(vector<string>{"asd", "dsa", "dsa", "asd"}));
CHECK(isPalindrome(vector<Token>{Token::X, Token::Y, Token::Y,
Token::X}));
}
```

Perhaps I have now shown you why I find this style of programming very appealing. If we ignore the types, or make our functions extremely polymorphic, we can write code that applies to future situations without needing to change. The trade-off is that the code has its constraints in the deducted types and that the names of the parameters and functions matter a lot. For example, if I pass in an integer value to `isPalindrome`, I will get a complicated error instead of the simple one telling me that the parameter is of the incorrect type. This is the beginning of the g++ compiler output on my computer when trying to pass in an integer:

```
In file included from testPalindrome.cpp:3:
Palindrome.h: In instantiation of 'bool isPalindrome(auto:21)
[with auto:21 = int]':
testPalindrome.cpp:30:2:    required from here
Palindrome.h:14:29: error: no match for 'operator|' (operand t
ypes are 'int' and 'const std::ranges::views::_All')
   14 |         auto tokens = value | std::views::all;
      |                                 ^
      |                             ~~~~~~^~~~~~~~~~~~~~~~~~~
```

It's now up to you: do you prefer strong types or extreme polymorphic behavior? Both have their trade-offs and their own application domains.

Summary

We have seen in this chapter that we can use multiple paradigms to program in C++. We looked briefly at a few: functional programming, metaprogramming, types that ensure compile-time validation, and extreme polymorphism. Each of these approaches, as well as the standard object-oriented and structured programming, are useful for various contexts when building libraries or specific programs. Each of them has something to offer to the curious programmer who wants to learn as much as possible about their craft. Each of them has its trade-offs and its own implementations in the world of software development.

We have shown that C++ programmers perhaps only use a subset of the language, and it doesn't have to be an object-oriented one. Instead, it's best to experiment with all of them, making the most of the fact that C++ is powerful enough to offer so many options, and to pick and choose depending on the task at hand.

In the next chapter, we will see that the `main()` function might not actually be the entry point of our applications.

4

The Main() Function is the Entry Point to Your Application

What happens before main stays in main

For programmers working with C++ on various operating systems, the entry point of an application is a concept that requires a deep understanding of the underlying architecture. In this chapter, we'll analyze how an application starts, focusing on the initialization code that's executed before we reach the user-defined `main()` function.

While exploring this process under Linux, we'll analyze the **Executable and Linkable Format (ELF)**, detailing how the `execve()` system call loads and executes a `_start()` function, which prepares the runtime environment before calling `main()`. We'll also explore some compiler-specific extensions that we can use to manipulate this process. Then, we'll shift our focus to Windows by offering a detailed examination of the **Portable Executable (PE)** file sections on Windows.

We'll also use a tool called **Ghidra** to dissect and analyze the executables under both platforms since this is one of the tools that provides practical insights into the low-level operations that underpin application startup.

After completing this chapter, you'll have a deeper understanding of the following aspects:

- The format of executable files and starting processes under Linux and Windows
- How to tinker with the startup process of applications

What is Ghidra?

Ghidra is an open source software reverse engineering suite developed by the NSA for analyzing compiled code across various formats and platforms. It offers tools for decompiling, disassembling, and debugging binary files, making it easier for users to understand and analyze machine code.

The main() function

When we took up C++ in school, or maybe at university, on our first C++ course, we were told by our teacher: "Dear fellows, here's the main function: `void main(void)`. That's where your program will start." That's it.

Chapter done – turn the pages and see you in the next one.

However, this statement isn't true. I wrote `void main(void)` just to wake your curiosity and put you in a state of alertness. At this point in their career, all C++ programmers should know that `void main(void)` is as far as standard C++ as Point Nemo is from the closest piece of dry land.

Oh – you're still here! This means that you must have read the fine print. Excellent – we programmers should always pay attention to the finer details, such as how our application is loaded and executed in memory by the underlying operating system.

Since we live in a free world, we have the option to choose from several operating systems at our discretion, so we've opted to present how this application loading happens under Linux and Windows.

There's a significant difference between these two operating systems concerning the way they load and execute the compiled binaries, and while in one of them (it's not that hard to guess which one) we can track all the code paths of this peculiar process down the deepest layers of the underlying kernel, for the other one, we must rely on existing documentation, books, and various sources of information that are to be gathered by the enthusiast low-level scholar.

Since the way Linux deals with this operation is very similar to how the operating systems from the BSD family (FreeBSD, NetBSD, and so on) approach the same problem, we'll refrain from actively mentioning these while we debate the problem in the upcoming paragraphs. Since we want to keep you entertained while in the pursuit of knowledge, we still want to offer information that's up to date, so we've decided not to offer this information for peculiar operating systems, such as MS-DOS, that are no longer used in active production environments as of 2024 (except if you happen to work at Deutsche Bahn[1]).

But before we dig deeper, we'll present the test application that we'll be using in this chapter to exemplify the aforementioned functionality:

```cpp
#include <cstring>
#include <cstdio>
struct A {
    A(const char* p_a):m_a(new char[32]) { strcpy(m_a, p_a);
        printf("A::A : %s\n", p_a);
    }
    ~A() {
```

---

[1]   https://www.theregister.com/2024/01/30/windows_311_trundles_on/

```
        printf("A::~A : %s\n", m_a);
        delete[] m_a;
    }
    volatile const char* get() const {return m_a;}
private:
    char* m_a;
};
const char* my_string= "Hello string";
A my_a(my_string);
const char* my_other_string = "Go away string";
A my_other_a(my_other_string);
int main() {
    printf("Hello, World, %s, %s\n", my_a.get(), my_other_a.get()); }
```

When compiled and run on a standard compliant system, the preceding application produces the following output, as expected by a standard compliant programmer:

```
A::A : Hello string
A::A : Go away string
Hello, World, Hello string, Go away string
A::~A : Go away string
A::~A : Hello string
```

Yes, we've intentionally used no cout and other stream operations as we want to keep this simple. We don't want to pollute the generated code since we plan to dig deep into the compiled executables.

Also, please note that this is synthetic code that's been written specifically for this chapter to exemplify the features we want to present. The authors are totally aware of the potential memory overflow error induced by strcpy, so the readers are advised to do what the author tells them to do, not what the author does: *"Don't use strcpy."*

Going back to our initial goal, let's present how operating systems load and execute applications. In case, dear reader, you feel that the discussion below is of a too low level, please bear in mind: C++ programs compile to native code while running at the highest possible speed allocated by the underlying operating system.

With this in mind, we consider that it's in the interest of any C++ programmer to know how the operating system is handling their code, and what happens after the compiler has digested their source files and spat out an executable. We will try to keep out the lowest level details and present only what is really necessary, in order to fully grasp the seriousness of the situation.

The penguin farm

When Linux loads and executes an application (say we want to execute an application, not a shell script or something else), usually a fork()/execve() pair of system calls are initiated to start the execution of the application.

These system calls are responsible for duplicating the current process (`fork()`) and replacing the current process image with a new process image (the application to be executed – that is, `execve()`).

These API calls are presented in great detail in *Advanced Linux Programming*, by Mark Mitchell, Jeffrey Oldham, and Alex Samuel, but there are countless online resources dedicated to this subject. So, if you're interested in this subject, you might find good sources of information there.

But let's continue loading the executable. The `execve()` system call, after several iterations where it leaves the confines of userspace, will end up in the Linux kernel and create a `linux_binprm` structure[2].

According to the documentation, this structure is used upon loading binaries and contains all the major details that are needed upon loading and executing a binary file.

If you have lots of free time, are armed with a large cup of tea, and have deep knowledge of the intricacies of the C language, you can easily read through the lengthy implementation of the `do_execveat_common` function to learn more about the behind-the-scenes of this function in the current Linux kernel source tree[3].

The kernel, in turn, determines the format of the executable file. On Linux systems, the most common executable format is ELF.

All fields are described in the official standard document,[4] but a quick summary of the fields that are relevant to our use case are as follows:

Field Name	Offset	Description
MAGIC	0x00	A magic number indicating that the file is an ELF file ("ELF" in ASCII and 0x7F)
CLASS	0x04	Specifies the class (32-bit or 64-bit) of the ELF file
e_type	0x10	Identifies the object file type (for example, executable, shared object, and so on)
e_machine	0x12	Specifies the architecture for which the file was compiled
e_entry	0x18	The virtual address to which the system transfers control first, starting the process

2   https://github.com/torvalds/linux/blob/master/include/linux/binfmts.h

3   https://github.com/torvalds/linux/blob/master/fs/exec.c

4   https://refspecs.linuxfoundation.org/elf/elf.pdf

Please remember this table as we'll be referring to it shortly. But for now, let's continue loading a program. It's time for the kernel to read the ELF header to understand the structure of the executable. The following operations happen at this stage:

1. **Memory allocation**: The kernel allocates memory for the new process. This includes setting up the process's address space, which consists of different segments such as text (code), data, the heap, and the stack.

2. **Section mapping**: The kernel maps sections of the executable file into the process's address space. For example, the text segment (containing executable code) is mapped as read-only, while the data segment (containing global variables) is mapped as read-write.

3. **Dynamic linking**: If the executable depends on shared libraries, the dynamic linker/loader (`ld.so`) is invoked to load the necessary shared libraries and resolve symbol references. The dynamic linker also maps these libraries into the process's address space.

These operations all happen deep inside the Linux kernel, but if you're interested in this domain, we encourage you to go and read the source – perhaps you can spot something teasing there.

Once all these interesting and very low-level operations have been performed successfully, the kernel sets up the initial environment stack for the process. This stack contains the following:

*   **Argument vectors** (`argv`): An array of command-line arguments

*   **Environment variables** (`envp`): An array of environment variables

*   **Auxiliary vectors** (`auxv`): Additional information needed by the program, such as system page size, entry point of the program, and so on

All this happens in the same kernel source file mentioned previously (`binfmt_elf.c`), in the following function:

```
static int create_elf_tables(struct linux_binprm *bprm,
const struct elfhdr *exec, unsigned long interp_load_addr,
unsigned long e_entry,unsigned long phdr_addr) { ... }
```

After creating the runtime environment, the kernel sets up the **instruction pointer** (**IP**) to point to the entry point of the program (as specified in the ELF header). The CPU registers are also initialized as required. Finally, the kernel switches the CPU back to user mode and transfers control to the entry point of the program.

In Linux, transfer of control i occurs primarily in the `start_thread()` function, which is architecture-specific. At the time of writing, for x86, this function is defined in `arch/x86/include/asm/processor.h` and is implemented in `arch/x86/kernel/process_64.c`. The program starts executing from this point. Now comes the interesting part – at least from a C++ developer's point of view.

First, the program's initialization code (often part of the C runtime library) is executed – typically the `_start()` function, not `main()`. The `e_entry` field of the ELF header lists the offset in the file where the program starts executing. Usually, it's the offset of the `_start()` method, or at least if the executable was compiled with the standard GNU toolchain. This code is responsible for setting up any runtime environment variables and calling the `main()` function of the program. From this point, the program runs as per the instructions written.

So, let's examine what exactly is the initialization code. We'll use our handy tool, **Ghidra**, which allows us to dissect Linux executables and examine their inner workings. This tool provides the following summary of our almost empty application:

```
Project File Name:                          main
Last Modified:                              Mon Jun 24 12:39:55 CEST 2024
Readonly:                                   false
Program Name:                               main
Language ID:                                x86:LE:64:default (3.0)
Compiler ID:                                gcc
Processor:                                  x86
Endian:                                     Little
Address Size:                               64
Minimum Address:                            00100000
Maximum Address:                            _elfSectionHeaders::000007bf
# of Bytes:                                 7658
# of Memory Blocks:                         33
# of Instructions:                          24
# of Defined Data:                          133
# of Functions:                             24
# of Symbols:                               62
# of Data Types:                            39
# of Data Type Categories:                  2
Created With Ghidra Version:                11.0.2
Date Created:                               Mon Jun 24 12:39:55 CEST 2024
ELF File Type:                              shared object
ELF GNU Program Prop[processor opt 0xc0000002]:03 00 00 00
ELF GNU Program Prop[processor opt 0xc0008002]:01 00 00 00
ELF Note[GNU BuildId]:                      d985831ac95d0c4f0ce4bd4b557bc5917152ddba
ELF Note[required kernel ABI]:              Linux 3.2.0
ELF Original Image Base:                    0x0
ELF Prelinked:                              false
ELF Source File [   0]:                     Scrt1.o
ELF Source File [   1]:                     main.cpp
ELF Source File [   2]:                     crtstuff.c
ELF Source File [   3]:                     crtstuff.c
ELF Source File [   4]:
Elf Comment[0]:                             GCC: (Ubuntu 11.4.0-1ubuntu1-22.04) 11.4.0
Executable Format:                          Executable and Linking Format (ELF)
Executable Location:                        /home/fld/tmp/loadtest/main
Executable MD5:                             8b0b3489ea812140b3b8a3f98c909ae8
Executable SHA256:                          22977e98d5bd4b26b0341b38a71ae3ed0e82d1a4e936d915858c9541f
FSRL:                                       file:///home/fld/tmp/loadtest/main?MD5=8b0b3489ea812140b3
Preferred Root Namespace Category:
Relocatable:                                true
Required Library [   0]:                     libstdc++.so.6
Required Library [   1]:                     libc.so.6
```

Figure 4.1 – The structure of our synthetic application

When looking at the **ELF Source File** section, we can see our initial `main.cpp` file; however, there are a few other items that we're not familiar with yet – for example, `crtstuff.c`. This file is part of `libgcc` and can be found in the `libgcc` repository[5], with the following comment written at the top:

```
/* Specialized bits of code needed to support construction and
   destruction of file-scope objects in C++ code.
```

---

5   https://github.com/gcc-mirror/gcc/blob/master/libgcc/crt-stuff.c

With that, one of the mysteries has been resolved and the comment is self-explanatory. However, another remains: **Scrt1.o**. To understand this, we need to know about the difference between **fixed-address executables** and **position-independent executables (PIEs)**.

Fixed-address executables are compiled to be loaded at specific, predetermined memory addresses, making them simpler but less secure and flexible since their addresses are predictable and vulnerable to attacks. This is the preferred manner of loading executables on embedded devices and some older platforms (such as MS-DOS, which also had this "feature" of requiring .com applications to be loaded at a specific offset).

On the other hand, **Position Independent Executable (PIE)** executables are compiled and linked to be position-independent, allowing them to be loaded at any address in memory.

When you compile a program, you can use various flags to control how the compiler generates the code. The -fPIE, -pie, and -fPIC flags are related to how the code is positioned and handled in memory. Here's a quick breakdown of what each flag does:

- -fPIE (**position-independent executable**): The -fPIE flag tells the compiler to generate position-independent code for executables. This is useful for creating executables that support **Address Space Layout Randomization (ASLR)**, a security feature that randomizes the memory address where the executable is loaded to make it harder for attackers to predict the location of specific code.

- -pie (**position-independent executable linker flag**): The -pie flag is used during the linking stage. It instructs the linker to produce a position-independent executable. This means that the final output file (the executable) will be able to be loaded at any address in memory supporting ASLR. It complements the -fPIE flag, which is used during compilation, ensuring that all the code in the executable is position-independent.

- -fPIC (**position-independent code**): The -fPIC flag tells the compiler to generate position-independent code for shared libraries. Position-independent code for shared libraries means that the library can be loaded at any address in memory. This is essential for shared libraries because they may be loaded into different memory locations in different programs.

Now that we know about these important notions, let's get back to where we left off and cover the one remaining mystery in our binary: **Scrt1.o**. Do you remember the _start() function? Since you didn't write it yourself, it must come from somewhere. For us, it comes from this magic **Scrt1.o**. There are several variations of **crtX.o**, some with a leading S, some without, but for us, the presence of **Scrt1.o** tells us that our application is a PIE executable. Several other files can be linked to our application:

- **crt0.o**, **crt1.o**, and so on: These files contain the _start symbol, which is crucial for bootstrapping program execution. Their specific naming conventions may vary between **libc** implementations.

- **crti.o**: This defines function prologues for .init and .fini sections, triggering linker-generated dynamic tags (DT_INIT and DT_FINI), to support We'll discuss these notions here, so don't worry about the unknown terminology yet.

- **crtn.o**: This provides function epilogues for `.init` and `.fini` sections, complementing `crti.o`.

- **Scrt1.o**, **gcrt1.o**, and **Mcrt1.o**: These are variants of `crt1.o` that are used under different circumstances, such as generating PIEs or including profiling information.

- **crtbegin.o**, **crtbeginS.o**, and **crtbeginT.o**: These are used by GCC to locate constructors and their variations (`crtbeginS.o` for shared objects/PIEs and `crtbeginT.o` for static executables).

- **crtend.o** and **crtendS.o**: Similar to `crtbegin.o`, these are used by GCC to locate destructors (`crtendS.o` for shared objects/PIEs).

Now that we've demystified the content of our executable, we need to understand something else: the `.init_array` section in an ELF file is used to store an array of function pointers that are automatically executed by the operating system's runtime loader during program startup.

These functions are typically referred to as "init functions" or "initialization functions." They're called before `main()` and are responsible for initializing global data. For our synthetic application, this is how this section looks once it's been analyzed by **Ghidra**:

```
                    //
                    // .init_array
                    // SHT_INIT_ARRAY  [0x3d80 - 0x3d8f]
                    // ram:00103d80-ram:00103d8f
                    //
                    __DT_INIT_ARRAY                        XREF[4]:    00100168(*), 001002f0(*),
                    __frame_dummy_init_array_entry                     00103de0(*),
                                                                       _elfSectionHeaders::00000590(*)
00103d80 60 12 10    addr        frame_dummy
         00 00 00
         00 00
00103d88 10 11 10    addr        _GLOBAL__sub_I_my_string
         00 00 00
         00 00
```

Figure 4.2 – The .init_array section for global variables

As we can see, there are two functions here – a dummy one and something called `_GLOBAL__sub_I_my_string`. Interesting choice of name, so let's use the assembly to C-like code feature of the tool and see what it does:

```
void _GLOBAL__sub_I_my_string(void)

{
  A::A((A *)&my_a,my_string);
  __cxa_atexit(A::~A,&my_a,&__dso_handle);
  A::A((A *)&my_other_a,my_other_string);
  __cxa_atexit(A::~A,&my_other_a,&__dso_handle);
  return;
}
```

Figure 4.3 – How global objects are created according to Ghidra

Intriguing, isn't it? This is just what you would expect to happen in the global namespace.

Here, the my_a and my_other_a objects are being created, their constructor is called, and the destructor of class A is being invoked for __cxa_atexit. It is quite an intriguing observation though, how the constructor calls behind the scenes work.

From this queasy disassembly, you may feel that the constructor gets an invisible parameter for the object it's constructing. This is true: this is the this variable, and it's implicitly added to all the methods of a class without being explicitly required. This is how we gain access to the object itself.

As its name suggests, the __cxa_atexit function is just like atexit. However, you don't have to worry about it because it isn't a function that should be dealt with outside of the library it resides in.

Now that we understand what happens here, it's time to pick up another thread we mentioned previously: the infamous _start() function.

As mentioned previously, this function should do some housekeeping and start our main function. According to Ghidra, it can be indeed found in the ELF header. According to the ELF specification, it occupies the e_entry field in the long list of ELF entries: :

```
00100000 7f 45 4c          Elf64_Ehdr
         46 02 01
         01 00 00 ...
00100000 7f                db      7Fh                        e_ident_magi...
00100001 45 4c 46          ds      "ELF"                      e_ident_magi...
00100004 02                db      2h                         e_ident_class
00100005 01                db      1h                         e_ident_data
00100006 01                db      1h                         e_ident_vers...
00100007 00                db      0h                         e_ident_osabi
00100008 00                db      0h                         e_ident_abiv...
00100009 00 00 00 00 00    db[7]                              e_ident_pad
         00 00
00100010 03 00             dw      3h                         e_type
00100012 3e 00             dw      3Eh                        e_machine
00100014 01 00 00 00       ddw     1h                         e_version
00100018 80 11 00 00 00    dq      _start                     e_entry
         00 00 00
00100020 40 00 00 00 00    dq      Elf64_Phdr_ARRAY_00100... e_phoff
         00 00 00
00100028 28 39 00 00 00    dq      Elf64_Shdr_ARRAY__elfS... e_shoff
         00 00 00
00100030 00 00 00 00       ddw     0h                         e_flags
00100034 40 00             dw      40h                        e_ehsize
00100036 38 00             dw      38h                        e_phentsize
00100038 0d 00             dw      Dh                         e_phnum
0010003a 40 00             dw      40h                        e_shentsize
0010003c 20 00             dw      20h                        e_shnum
0010003e 1f 00             dw      1Fh                        e_shstrndx
```

Figure 4.4 – The ELF header according to Ghidra

Now, after applying some disassembly magic, courtesy of **Ghidra**, it looks like this:

```
void processEntry _start(undefined8 param_1,undefined8 param_2)

{
  undefined auStack_8 [8];

  __libc_start_main(main,param_2,&stack0x00000008,0,0,param_1,auStack_8);
  do {
                    /* WARNING: Do nothing block with infinite loop */
  } while( true );
}
```

Figure 4.5 – The _start routine function, disassembled and converted into C pseudocode

The scary-looking `__libc_start_main` function isn't as scary as it seems and is responsible for loading our `main()` function alongside the parameters provided by the operating system. This function is part of **glibc** and can be obtained free of charge[6], just like every other free piece of software with good behavior, so that we can study its internals.

At this stage, with the outcome of `__libc_start_main`, we've reached the actual main function. This is where we would expect our program to reside.

These details offer deeper insights into program execution, optimization opportunities, and debugging capabilities. Mastery of the ELF file format enables you to optimize performance by leveraging specific linker options and understanding dynamic linking intricacies. Moreover, it facilitates effective debugging by tracing initialization sequences and identifying startup-related issues.

Oh no, there's more!

Now that we're here, typing on our favorite Linux machine, let's not waste any more time and dive a bit deeper into the internals of some of the compilers that come with this great operating system. For example, let's dig into the **.init_array** section of the ELF file. As mentioned previously, it's responsible for starting different functions before the main one.

But before we continue our journey through these swampy fields, a warning must be mentioned: what we're going to discuss isn't for faint-hearted C++ programmers, to the extent that it isn't even standard C++. Please read *Chapter 2* concerning C++ standardness. If you can live with the unholy scripture of compiler extensions, then please read on.

---

6   `git clone git://sourceware.org/git/glibc.git`

GCC (as well as Clang) has a very handy extension for executing functions before main(). These functions are called constructor functions and they need to be spawned with a specific attribute:

```
__attribute__((constructor)) void welcome() {
    printf("constructor fun\n");
}
```

If we add this specific piece of code to our synthetic application, we can expect the following output:

```
constructor fun
A::A : Hello string
A::A : Go away string
Hello, World, Hello string, Go away string
A::~A : Go away string
A::~A : Hello string
```

As you can see, the constructor function is being executed before the global initialization code. If we dig into the executable with our favorite nine-headed spades, we'll see the following content in the **.init_array** section:

```
                      //
                      // .init_array
                      // SHT_INIT_ARRAY  [0x3d78 - 0x3d8f]
                      // ram:00103d78-ram:00103d8f
                      //
                      __DT_INIT_ARRAY                       XREF[4]:    00100168(*), 001002f0(*),
                      __frame_dummy_init_array_entry                    00103de0(*),
                                                                        _elfSectionHeaders::00000590(*)
00103d78 80 12 10     addr        frame_dummy
         00 00 00
         00 00
00103d80 e0 10 10     addr        welcome
         00 00 00
         00 00
00103d88 30 11 10     addr        _GLOBAL__sub_I_my_string
         00 00 00
         00 00
```

Figure 4.6 – The .init_array section with a constructor function

With this knowledge, we now possess two methods of writing code that will be executed before the main() function in a C++ application: constructor functions and global variables.

At this point, we're in a place where we've started scratching the surface of something dangerous: the **static initialization order fiasco**. This is a subject that's been debated several times, in various places. These debates summarize that this issue arises from the undefined order of initialization of static or global variables across different translation units. There are various techniques for resolving these issues, but our recommendation is to just **avoid them**.

The following example illustrates why this can conjure up dangerous situations. Here, we've created several short files, again with synthetic content, trying to emulate a real-life situation:

a.h

```
#ifndef A_H
#define A_H
class C;
extern C a_c;
#endif
```

b.h

```
#ifndef B_H
#define B_H
class C;
extern C b_c;
#endif
```

C.h

```
#ifndef C_H
#define C_H
#include <cstring>
#include <cstdio>
struct C {
    C(const char* p_c) : m_c(nullptr) {
        m_c = new char[32];
        strcpy(m_c, p_c);
        printf("C::C : %s\n", p_c);
    }
    ~C() {
        printf("C::~C : %s\n", m_c);
        delete[] m_c;
    }
private:
    char* m_c;
};
#endif
```

a.cpp

```
#include "C.h"
C a_c("A");
```

b.cpp

```
#include "C.h"
C b_c("B");
```

main.cpp

```
int main()
{
}
```

This isn't extraordinarily complicated code – it's just a diagnostic C class that's used to print out some debugging information and some separate C++ files creating objects of the aforementioned diagnostic class.

Normally, these files are compiled with gcc, so let's compile them and execute the resulting file:

```
> $ g++ main.cpp a.cpp b.cpp -o test
> $ ./test
C::C : A
C::C : B
C::~C : B
C::~C : A
```

There's nothing special here – we compiled and created an executable that performed what it's supposed to: print out when a specific object was created and destroyed.

But what happens if we specify the files in a different order?

```
> $ g++ main.cpp b.cpp a.cpp -o test
> $ ./test
C::C : B
C::C : A
C::~C : A
C::~C : B
```

What a surprise. Now, the b_c object from b.cpp is created before the a_c object from a.cpp. Now, imagine the disastrous situation where our program is made up of global objects that depend on the pre-existence of some other global objects to be initialized correctly.

Thankfully, the compiler ecosystem under Linux provides us with the necessary tools to achieve a sane state of our applications concerning this matter, with the help of a very handy extension. This extension is used to specify the initialization order for global members and it manifests itself using the __attribute__((init_priority(XXX))) syntax.

Both gcc and clang provide this way to control the initialization order of namespacescope objects across translation units using the init_priority attribute. This attribute allows users to assign a relative priority to the initialization, with priority values ranging from 101 to 65535 inclusive. Lower numbers correspond to higher priority, meaning objects with lower init_priority values will be initialized earlier.

Armed with this knowledge, let's modify our synthetic example files so that they use this extension:

a.cpp

```
#include "C.h"
__attribute__((init_priority(1000))) C a_c("A");
```

b.cpp

```
#include "C.h"
__attribute__((init_priority(1001))) C b_c("B");
```

Now, regardless of the order in which a.cpp and b.cpp are introduced to the compiler, the result will be the same:

```
> $ g++ main.cpp a.cpp b.cpp -o test
> $ ./test
C::C : A
C::C : B
C::~C : B
C::~C : A
> $ g++ main.cpp b.cpp a.cpp -o test
> $ ./test
C::C : A
C::C : B
C::~C : B
C::~C : A
```

Now, let's return to our first synthetic application – the one that tried to create global objects but in the same translation unit. And also introduced the notion of "constructor" functions. Let's see what happens if we specify initialization priority for one of the global objects, and what the order will be in that case:

```
__attribute__((init_priority(1000)))
                          A my_other_a(my_other_string);
```

Surprisingly, the output will be as follows:

```
A::A : Go away string
constructor fun
A::A : Hello string
Hello, World, Hello string, Go away string
A::~A : Hello string
A::~A : Go away string
```

In order to grasp a deeper understanding of the mechanics behind the scenes, and to understand why this scenario happened we run our beloved tool on the compiled binary. The result confirms our finding as per the following screenshot:

```
               //
               // .init_array
               // SHT_INIT_ARRAY  [0x3d70 - 0x3d8f]
               // ram:00103d70-ram:00103d8f
               //

               __DT_INIT_ARRAY                          XREF[4]:     00100168(*), 001002f0(*),
                                                                     00103de0(*),
                                                                     _elfSectionHeaders::00800590(*)
00103d70 30 11 10    addr      _GLOBAL__sub_I.01000_my_string
         00 00 00
         00 00

               __frame_dummy_init_array_entry
00103d78 90 12 10    addr      frame_dummy
         00 00 00
         00 00
00103d80 e0 10 10    addr      welcome
         00 00 00
         00 00
00103d88 70 11 10    addr      _GLOBAL__sub_I_my_string
         00 00 00
         00 00
```

Figure 4.7 – The .init_array section according to gcc with the specified init priority

The output happens to be as it is because the **.init_array** section has gained a new member that's to be executed before the constructor and the standard global initialization code.

It isn't hard to guess that the name of the new function contains the initialization priority. What however still baffles the author is why gcc decided to continuously use my_string as a postfix for the variable names. This must be a gcc specificity because the same executable compiled with clang produces the following **.init_array** section:

```
                //
                // .init_array
                // SHT_INIT_ARRAY  [0x3da0 - 0x3dbf]
                // ram:00103da0-ram:00103dbf
                //

                __DT_INIT_ARRAY                              XREF[4]:   00100168(*), 001002f0(*),
                                                                        00103e30(*),
                                                                        _elfSectionHeaders::00000550(*)

00103da0 30 11 10      addr        _GLOBAL__I_001000
         00 00 00
         00 00


                __frame_dummy_init_array_entry
00103da8 30 12 10      addr        frame_dummy
         00 00 00
         00 00
00103db0 40 12 10      addr        welcome
         00 00 00
         00 00
00103db8 40 11 10      addr        _GLOBAL__sub_I_main.cpp
         00 00 00
         00 00
```

Figure 4.8 – Clang's different .init_array section for the same init priority

The author has found it interesting why there's such a difference between how gcc and clang handle this critical section of the object file. However, without analyzing the source files of these compilers further, this will remain a mystery.

A library is the delivery room for the birth of ~~ideas~~ unexpected behavior

So far, we've been the happy parents of a single application. Now, the time has come for our lovechild to mature and marry a … meaning, in order to adhere to some common sense and more advanced programming practices, we want to factor out some very useful functionality of our synthetic code into a synthetic library and call it **synth**. Pardon – I mean **libsinth**.

And since the main focus of this chapter is still the dissection of code execution before main() (*1*), and since we are happily advocating for gcc (and clang) extensions (2), let's see what happens if we hitch all these together in an unholy matrimony of code and data.

As a side note, we'll use our second synthetic example, where a.cpp and b.cpp remained unchanged from their last stage, which includes the required initialization order. We'll create a new main.cpp file to utilize the library itself, and we'll also introduce the library's source code.

Our library will be constructed from the following code:

synth.cpp

```
#include "C.h"
#include <cstdio>
__attribute__((init_priority(2000))) C synth_c("synth");
__attribute__((constructor)) void welcome_library() {
    printf("welcome to the library\n");
}
void print_synth() {
    printf("print_synth: %s\n", synth_c.get());
}
```

synth.h

```
#ifndef SYNTH_H
#define SYNTH_H
void print_synth();
#endif
```

Besides defining the global object synth_c of type C (as defined in the C.h header) and has an initialization priority of 2000, we also define a function called welcome_library marked with __attribute__((constructor)), ensuring it runs before main() and prints "welcome to the library."

Additionally, the print_synth function prints a message that states the value that was obtained from synth_c.get(). The C.h header is the one from a few pages prior – it defines the class C, along with all the required methods and constructors to create objects properly.

To use this library, we'll need to create the corresponding underlying infrastructure for it. This consists of the two aforementioned files and an application that uses the features exposed by it.

To keep on track, we'll need to modify our main file so that it uses the library's features. However, we also want to keep the test source files we created for this scenario.

So, our application will contain the aforementioned `a.cpp` and `b.cpp` files, as well as our new `main.cpp` file:

main.cpp

```cpp
#include "synth.h"
#include "C.h"
__attribute__((constructor)) void welcome_main() {
    printf("welcome to the main\n");
}
C main_c("main") ;
int main() {
    print_synth();
    return 0;
}
```

To make everything work properly, we need to link these items and turn them into a working application:

```
> $ g++ -c -o synth.o synth.cpp
> $ ar rcs libsynth.a synth.o
> $ g++ -o main main.cpp a.cpp b.cpp -L. -lsynth
```

As you can see, at this stage, we've created a **static** library, **libsynth.a**, and linked our main application to it to incorporate all the code in the library properly.

Please note that there is no *c.cpp* file because, to be as compact as possible, we've provided all the implementation of the class in the header file. For bigger projects, this isn't best practice because a small change in the implementation of any functions of the class will require all the files that include the header to be recompiled. However, for this very peculiar situation, we can live with it.

Since we're interested in the order of execution of the various constructs we've created, after running the resulting application, we get the following output:

```
> $ ./main
C::C : A
C::C : B
C::C : synth
welcome to the main
C::C : main
welcome to the library
print_synth: synth
C::~C : main
C::~C : synth
C::~C : B
C::~C : A
```

To dig a bit deeper into the innards of the freshly compiled executable file, we'll open it with our beloved tool, **Ghidra**, and locate the section we're most interested in: the **.init_array** section.

After a quick inspection, we can see that the order of the printouts corresponds to the order of the functions in the **.init_array** section:

```
                //
                // .init_array
                // SHT_INIT_ARRAY  [0x3d50 - 0x3d87]
                // ram:00103d50-ram:00103d87
                //

                __DT_INIT_ARRAY                              XREF[4]:    00100168(*), 001002f0(*),
                                                                         00103dd8(*),
                                                                         _elfSectionHeaders::00000590(*)
00103d50 a4 13 10     addr        _GLOBAL__sub_I.01080_a_c
         00 00 00
         00 00
00103d58 1d 14 10     addr        _GLOBAL__sub_I.01001_b_c
         00 00 00
         00 00
00103d60 e1 14 10     addr        _GLOBAL__sub_I.02000_synth_c
         00 00 00
         00 00


                __frame_dummy_init_array_entry
00103d68 e0 11 10     addr        frame_dummy
         00 00 00
         00 00
00103d70 e9 11 10     addr        welcome_main
         00 00 00
         00 00
00103d78 77 12 10     addr        _GLOBAL__sub_I_welcome_main
         00 00 00
         00 00
00103d80 36 14 10     addr        welcome_library
         00 00 00
         00 00
```

Figure 4.9 – The .init_array section for different init priorities in different files

Here, _GLOBAL__sub_I_welcome_main is the function creating the global object in main.cpp – that is, C main_c ("main") ;. Interesting! At this point, we're convinced that the order of initialization for global objects works even after libraries – at least static ones.

But we're still not done. Let's see what happens if we create a shared library. That isn't that complicated. After removing the generated files – that is, synth.o, libsynth.a, and main – so that we have a clean plate, we need to run the following command to create a shared library:

```
> $ g++ -fPIC -c -o  synth.o synth.cpp
> $ g++ -shared -o libsynth.so synth.o
> $ g++ -pie -o main main.cpp a.cpp b.cpp -L. -lsynth
```

Now, we can see how easily those magic switches fall into place from the beginning of this chapter, where we created a shared library and application that uses it.

With all these pieces in place, we can see an interesting change in how Ghidra presents the application overview:

```
Relocatable:                                    true
Required Library [     0]:                       libsynth.so
Required Library [     1]:                       libstdc++.so.6
Required Library [     2]:                       libc.so.6
```

Figure 4.10 – The synth library as a dependency, as shown in Ghidra

Here, we can see a dependency on the **libsynth.so** library we just created. Now, we can examine the part that interests us most regarding the executable – **.init_array**:

```
             //
             // .init_array
             // SHT_INIT_ARRAY  [0x3d48 - 0x3d6f]
             // ram:00103d48-ram:00103d6f
             //
                        __DT_INIT_ARRAY                        XREF[4]:    00100168(*), 001002f0(*),
                                                                           00103dd0(*),
                                                                           _elfSectionHeaders::00000590(*)
00103d48 c4 13 10       addr      _GLOBAL__sub_I.01000_a_c
         00 00 00
         00 00
00103d50 3d 14 10       addr      _GLOBAL__sub_I.01001_b_c
         00 00 00
         00 00

                        __frame_dummy_init_array_entry
00103d58 00 12 10       addr      frame_dummy
         00 00 00
         00 00
00103d60 09 12 10       addr      welcome_main
         00 00 00
         00 00
00103d68 97 12 10       addr      _GLOBAL__sub_I_welcome_main
         00 00 00
         00 00
```

Figure 4.11 – No reference to libsynth in the .init_array section

There's no reference at all to the objects and functions in our synth library… No wonder – it's a library. But at least we can still see that our application links to the library properly:

```
> $ LD_LIBRARY_PATH=. ldd ./main
    linux-vdso.so.1 (0x00007fff17387000)
    libsynth.so => ./libsynth.so (0x00007ea84ee45000)
    libstdc++.so.6 => /lib/x86_64-linux-gnu/libstdc++.so.6
```

Please observe that we have to specify LD_LIBRARY_PATH=. explicitly to find the library (note that we've also truncated unnecessary output lines to keep things clear).

At this point, we're curious about what happens when we execute the application:

```
> $ LD_LIBRARY_PATH=. ./main
C::C : synth
welcome to the library
C::C : A
C::C : B
welcome to the main
C::C : main
print_synth: synth
C::~C : main
C::~C : B
C::~C : A
C::~C : synth
```

First, according to the expectations set by the single application test, the object(s) with the specified priority(ies) is(are) created in the library. Then, the constructor function from the library is called. If there were any other non-prioritized global objects in the library, they would have been created after these, before the prioritized objects from the main application were created and the constructor from the main application was called. All these operations were performed before the main() function even had the chance to say *hush*.

Almost as we expected it to happen. There's just one dark corner of these function constructor extensions that I've been unable to find a cure for at the moment – what if a.cpp and b.cpp contain the following lines?

```
__attribute__((constructor)) void welcome_a() {
    printf("welcome to the 'a' file\n"); }
__attribute__((constructor)) void welcome_b() {
    printf("welcome to the 'b' file\n"); }
```

This unholy scribbling of spooky code adds two more constructor functions to our executable. Now, we have three. If you want to have a predictable order of execution for these constructor functions too, you need to specify their priority using __attribute__((constructor(205))) void welcome_b(). This will guarantee that these functions will also be executed in a specific order and that you're not facing the global constructor invoking order fiasco.

The behavior in case the library was dynamically loaded (dlopen/dlclose) is the one that one would expect, i.e. it follows the execution flow of the main application, and at the point where the library is loaded, it will jump and execute the various constructors and object initializations from the library.

Famous last words

This chapter dealt with code that is executed before the main function. However the same attention would require the topic covering the code that is executed after the main function, but that debate will go in a different chapter, in a different book.

But just to spoil you, here's a small hint: the same way as there are constructor functions, there are also destructor functions. They're not like C++ destructors – more like `__attribute__((destructor))`.

Spicing those up with the standard application exit routines, we have twice as much fun as the startup because we have to consider a myriad of other alternatives, such as functions registered for `std::atexit` (or even `std::quick_exit`), or abnormal program termination. For example, let's say an exception is thrown in a destructor or we use `std::terminate` or `std::abort`.

The documentation on `gcc` and `clang` offers a nice escapade from the standard world, and any good book on C++ will offer a great overview of the standard termination routines, so please head over to them for a good lecture. A combination of these two will provide the best overview of how applications start and exit.

For now, we'll shift our attention toward other platforms before we get a good wigging from the folks at Packt – instead of the agreed-upon 16 pages for this chapter, we're already at 22 and covered only half of the promised subject.

Let's open the Windows (unless you're on ISS)

Before we delve deep into the internals of how an application is executed under Windows and the steps we must take to reach our main function, please note that from C++'s point of view, there should be no real difference from Linux or any other operating system. The C++-only standard functionality is (should be) identical to the functionality presented in the previous pages, so we won't repeat the same information here.

We will, however, present how and why the application starts under Windows the way it does and present some techniques that can directly influence this behavior, just like we did under Linux. We'll also be using a Visual Studio compiler since `gcc` and `clang` for Windows behave identically, so there's no sense in presenting them again.

Due to its closed nature, to understand process creation under Windows, we need to resort to the few available resources that deal with this kind of information. One of these resources is the best book I've managed to find in this domain: *Windows Internals, 7th edition (Part 1),*[7] by Pavel Yosifovich, Alex Ionescu, Mark E. Russinovich, and David A. Solomon.

---

7   https://learn.microsoft.com/en-us/sysinternals/resources/
windows-internals

The information gathered from that book is complemented by various scraps gathered from the world wide internet, and filtered in order to offer our readers a light introduction to the Windows side of process creation. We will reference back however some of the notions encountered in the Linux subsection of this chapter, so reading it would be beneficial. Also, a small observation: security, thread handling, and user management are much more fine-tuned in Windows than in Linux, and all this is reflected in the way processes are treated. If you're interested in understanding this domain, there are several resources available, such as the excellent *Windows Security Internals: A Deep Dive into Windows Authentication, Authorization, and Auditing*, by James Forshaw. We recommend reading through it if you're interested in the domain.

Let's get back to the processes. The process creation mechanism in Windows involves several stages that are executed by different components of the operating system: the Windows client-side library, **kernel32.dll**, the Windows executive, and the Windows subsystem process (**csrss.exe**). Due to the simple fact that we don't have access to the sources of these Windows components, our presentation on this matter will be a very high-level one.

Processes in Windows are created by a function of the CreateProcess family, which comes with several relatives and uncles (`create process` as a different user, create process with various security clearances, etc…) but all members of the extended family routines after several iterations end up in the CreateProcessInternalW function in **kernel32.dll**, which first validates and converts some of the parameters and flags to an internal representation (to which sadly we have no access).

The priority class for the new process is determined by the `CreationFlags` parameter. In Windows, there are six priority classes: Idle, Below Normal, Normal, Above Normal, High, and Real-time. If no priority class is specified, the priority class defaults to Normal. If Real-time is requested but the caller lacks the necessary privileges, the priority is downgraded to High.

Next, **kernel32.dll** initiates a connection to the native debugging interface if the process is to be debugged and sets the default hard error mode if specified. The user-specified attribute list is converted into its native format, and any additional internal attributes are added. The security attributes for the process and initial thread are also converted into internal representations.

The next step is to open the executable image to be run. This task is handled within the `NtCreateUserProcess` system call. First, the function validates the arguments again to ensure they haven't been tampered with. Then, it attempts to find and open the appropriate Windows image and create a section object, which will be mapped into the new process's address space at a later date.

If the image isn't a valid Windows executable, the function searches for a support image to run it. For instance, if the executable is an MS-DOS or Win16 application, it uses **ntvdm.exe** (for 32-bit Windows) to run it. This ensures that older DOS or Win16 applications can be executed correctly within the Windows environment. However, this feature has been slowly deprecated on modern Windows systems, so you need to enable it so that it can function.

Once the executable image has been opened, the next stage is to create the Windows executive process object. This involves setting up the process's virtual address space and other critical structures. The executive process object serves as a container for all the resources needed by the process, including memory, handles, and threads.

With the process object in place, the initial thread is created. This step involves setting up the thread's stack, context, and executive thread object. The thread is responsible for executing the program's entry point and managing the process's execution flow.

After the initial thread is created, Windows performs subsystem-specific initialization tasks. These tasks are essential for integrating the new process into the Windows subsystem, which provides the environment and resources necessary for the process to run correctly.

The initial thread is then started, unless the CREATE_SUSPENDED flag is specified, in which case the thread remains suspended until it's explicitly resumed. Starting the thread involves switching to user mode and executing the process's entry point.

Finally, in the context of the new process and thread, the address space is initialized. This includes loading any required DLLs and performing any other necessary setup tasks. Once these steps are complete, the process begins executing its code, and process creation is considered complete.

To PE or not to PE

Like every other file with a specific meaning, the bytes that conjure up Windows-based executables also have a special meaning.

The Windows **Portable Executable** (**PE**) format is a file format for executables, object code, DLLs, and other system files that are used in Windows operating systems. It's the standard file format for executables in DOS (as well as FreeDOS), Windows, and ReactOS and encompasses both the **executable** (**EXE**) and **Dynamic Link Library** (**DLL**) file types.

The PE format is designed to be extensible and capable of supporting modern operating system features. If you're interested in this domain, there are excellent learning opportunities online, so we encourage you to study this subject since this book can't encompass all the required information due to lack of space.

Here's a filtered explanation of its structure and components, mostly the ones relevant to this chapter:

- **DOS header (IMAGE_DOS_HEADER):**

  The file begins with **MZ**, the initials of Mark Zbikowski, the engineer who created this format while working at Microsoft. This is followed by a DOS header, which is a relic from the MS-DOS days. This header includes a small DOS stub program that displays a message ("This program can't be run in DOS mode") if the executable is run in a DOS environment. The last section of the DOS header contains a pointer to the PE header's location.

- **PE header (IMAGE_NT_HEADERS):**

  - **Signature:** This identifies the file as a PE file. The signature is a 4-byte value – that is, `PE\0\0`.

  - **File header** (`IMAGE_FILE_HEADER`): This contains basic information about the file, such as the target machine type, the number of sections, the time and date the file was created, and the size of the optional header.

  - **Optional header** (`IMAGE_OPTIONAL_HEADER`): This provides essential information for loading and running the program. Despite its name, this header is required for executable files and includes the following aspects:

    - **Magic number:** Identifies the format (for example, PE32 for 32-bit and PE32+ for 64-bit)

    - `AddressOfEntryPoint`: The address where execution starts

    - `ImageBase`: The preferred base address for the executable in memory

    - `SectionAlignment`: Alignment of sections in memory.

    - `SizeOfImage`: The total size of the image in memory

    - `Subsystem`: Identifies the required subsystem (Windows GUI or CUI)

- **Section headers (IMAGE_SECTION_HEADER):**

  Following the PE header, there are one or more section headers, each describing a section of the file. These sections contain the actual data and code of the program. The following are some common sections:

  - `.text`: Contains executable code.

  - `.data`: Contains initialized global and static variables.

  - `.bss`: Contains uninitialized data.

  - `.rdata`: Read-only data (such as string literals and constants).

  - `.idata`: Import table, listing the functions and DLLs that the executable depends on.

  - `.edata`: Export table, listing functions and data that the executable exposes to other modules.

- **Data directories**:

    Part of the optional header, these directories provide information about the location and size of various tables and data structures within the executable file, including:

    - **Import table**: Lists the DLLs and functions imported by the executable.

    - **Export table**: Lists the functions and data exported by the executable.

    - **Resource table**: Contains resources that are built into the application, such as icons, menus, and dialogs. These resources are stored in a resource tree, depending on their type. There's also support for variations in multiple languages for the same resource.

    - **Exception table**: Contains information for exception handling.

    - **Relocation table**: Used for address fixups.

- **Sections**:

    The actual sections follow the headers and contain the executable code, initialized data, and other components that the program needs to run.

    Each section is aligned based on the SectionAlignment value specified in the optional header.

For us, the most important and interesting part of this list of sections and subsections is the AddressOfEntryPoint field.

Getting our hands dirty

Our initial approach will be a very clean application to work on, a classical "Hello World!"

```
#include <iostream>
int main() {
    std::cout << "Hello World!\n";
}
```

This will allow us to understand how a very simple application is loaded and executed under Windows. However, before taking things further, a small remark: under Windows, there are different kinds of applications, as indicated by the OptionalHeader/Subsystem field in the PE header.

For our purpose, which is to dissect an application to examine how it starts, we'll create a Console Application. There are other types of applications we could look at, but they're overly complex. For example, if they have a GUI, then we must implement complicated message loops and dependencies, so we'll stick with something simple.

Assuming that we've successfully compiled our synthetic console application, we can fire up Ghidra and see that a large section of the file resembles the standard PE header shown previously:

```
004000e0 50 45 00            IMAGE_NT_HEADERS32
         00 4c 01
         09 00 e2 ...
004000e0 50 45 00 00         char[4]                   "PE"              Signature
   004000e0 [0]              'P', 'E', 00h, 00h
004000e4 4c 01 09 00 e2      IMAGE_FILE_HEADER                           FileHeader
         f4 7b 66 00 00
         00 00 00 00 00...
   004000e4 4c 01            dw                        14Ch              Machine
   004000e6 09 00            dw                        9h                NumberOfSections
   004000e8 e2 f4 7b 66      ddw                       667BF4E2h         TimeDateStamp
   004000ec 00 00 00 00      ddw                       0h                PointerToSymbolTable
   004000f0 00 00 00 00      ddw                       0h                NumberOfSymbols
   004000f4 e0 00            dw                        E0h               SizeOfOptionalHeader
   004000f6 02 01            dw                        102h              Characteristics
004000f8 0b 01 0e 1d 00      IMAGE_OPTIONAL_HEADER32                     OptionalHeader
         74 00 00 00 4c
         00 00 00 00 00...
   004000f8 0b 01            dw                        10Bh              Magic
   004000fa 0e               db                        Eh                MajorLinkerVersion
   004000fb 1d               db                        1Dh               MinorLinkerVersion
   004000fc 00 74 00 00      ddw                       7400h             SizeOfCode
   00400100 00 4c 00 00      ddw                       4C00h             SizeOfInitializedData
   00400104 00 00 00 00      ddw                       0h                SizeOfUninitializedData
   00400108 23 10 01 00      ibo32                     entry             AddressOfEntryPoint
   0040010c 00 10 00 00      ibo32                     __enc$textbss$begin  BaseOfCode
   00400110 00 10 00 00      ibo32                     __enc$textbss$begin  BaseOfData
   00400114 00 00 40 00      addr                      IMAGE_DOS_HEADER_00400... ImageBase
   00400118 00 10 00 00      ddw                       1000h             SectionAlignment
   0040011c 00 02 00 00      ddw                       200h              FileAlignment
   00400120 06 00            dw                        6h                MajorOperatingSystemVersion
   00400122 00 00            dw                        0h                MinorOperatingSystemVersion
   00400124 00 00            dw                        0h                MajorImageVersion
   00400126 00 00            dw                        0h                MinorImageVersion
   00400128 06 00            dw                        6h                MajorSubsystemVersion
```

Figure 4.12 – The contents of the PE header

This is a lot of information to digest, but what's interesting for us is the `AddressOfEntryPoint` field. At the moment, it points to a method called `entry`. This is where our application will start executing, so let's examine this function in a bit more detail. If we dig deeper and see what the entry is, we'll reach the following function:

```
ulong __cdecl entry(void *param_1) {
    ulong uVar1;
    uVar1 = __scrt_common_main();
    return uVar1;
}
```

This in itself is an interesting discovery as it seems to be the entry point of console-based Windows applications. Let's explore this further. The next function that's run is as follows:

```
int __cdecl __scrt_common_main(void) {
  int iVar1;
  __security_init_cookie();
  iVar1 = __scrt_common_main_seh();
  return iVar1;
}
```

Microsoft's page[8] contains a detailed description of the __security_init_cookie() function. However, the other function is a different kind of beast. It does a large amount of initialization, such as setting up the terminal and handling initialization errors. At some point, the following piece of code is executed:

```
                  LAB_00412a82                    XREF[2]:    00412a5f(j)
00412a82 e8 79 01    CALL    invoke_main
         00 00
```

Figure 4.13 – The invocation of main()

As you may have guessed, invoke_main is responsible for invoking main():

```
int __cdecl invoke_main(void) {
  char **_Argv;
  char **_Env;
  undefined4 *puVar1;
  int *piVar2;
  int iVar3;
  _Env = (char **)__get_initial_narrow_environment();
  puVar1 = (undefined4 *)___p___argv();
  _Argv = (char **)*puVar1;
  piVar2 = (int *)___p___argc();
  iVar3 = main(*piVar2,_Argv,_Env);
  return iVar3;
}
```

At this point, we've reached the stage where our main() function is called. Even for a simple "Hello World!" application, there's a large amount of boilerplate code that needs to be executed.

---

8   https://learn.microsoft.com/en-us/cpp/c-runtime-library/
reference/security-init-cookie?view=msvc-170

Now, it's time to go one step further and take our synthetic application on a ride through Ghidra (for brevity's sake, we'll omit that we must create a project, compile it, and link the application; let's just assume the application summons itself by magic).

Since we're mostly interested in determining the order of function calls before main(), and we know that we initialize the my_a and my_other_a variables globally, we need to look through the binary. At some point, we'll spot the following interesting data:

```
                .CRT$XCU
                my_a$initializer$
00419208 d0 18 41 00        void _func___cdecl_...  `dynamic_initializer_for_'my_a''


                my_other_a$initializer$
0041920c 40 19 41 00        void _func___cdecl_...  `dynamic_initializer_for_'my_other_a''
```

Figure 4.14 – The .CRT$XCU section according to Ghidra

Well, this looks interesting, especially that cryptic .CRT$XCU text. This takes us back to a few paragraphs prior, where the sections of a PE file were discussed: sections are distinct areas within the executable file that hold different types of data and code.

Each section serves a specific purpose and has attributes that define its behavior and how it should be handled by the operating system. There's excellent documentation[9] on Microsoft's site that discusses the sections responsible for initializing CRT, a quick summary of it follows.

According to the documentation, by default, the CRT library is included via the linker, which ensures that the CRT is initialized properly, global initializers are called, and, subsequently, the user-defined main() function is executed. When the compiler encounters a global initializer, it creates a dynamic initializer and places it in the .CRT$XCU section.

The CRT uses specific pointers such as __xc_a and __xc_z in the .CRT$XCA and .CRT$XCZ initialization sections to define the start and end of the list of initializers, ensuring they're called in the correct order. The __scrt_common_main_seh() function, which we discussed previously, is responsible for setting these up correctly.

These names are predefined by the CRT, and the linker arranges these sections alphabetically. This ordering ensures that user-defined initializers in .CRT$XCU are executed between the standard sections.

To manipulate the initialization order, developers can place their initializers in unused reserved sections such as .CRT$XCT (before compiler-generated initializers) and .CRT$XCV (after compiler-generated initializers) using specific pragmas, as detailed in the CRT startup documentation mentioned a few paragraphs prior, but before jumping on that technique, please read below because things are a bit more complicated than they seem.

---

9   https://learn.microsoft.com/en-us/cpp/c-runtime-library/crt-initialization?view=msvc-170

According to Microsoft, that subject is so platform and compiler-specific that we don't wish to explore those fields, especially considering the warning that comes from the official site:

> *"The names .CRT$XCT and .CRT$XCV aren't used by either the compiler or the CRT library right now, but there's no guarantee that they'll remain unused in the future. And, your variables could still be optimized away by the compiler. Consider the potential engineering, maintenance, and portability issues before adopting this technique."*

So, once again, we'll just repeat what the official warning said: unless you have to do this kind of hackery, please refrain from using these halfheartedly documented "features" of the language and compiler since (again, as mentioned in the official warning) there's no guarantee that if it works today, it will work tomorrow, or even after the next system update.

Instead, let's turn our attention toward the functions that we "discovered" in the `.CRT$XCU` section and see what kind of sorcery lies behind this very explicit name, which undoubtedly isn't standard C (nor C++):

```
void __cdecl `dynamic_initializer_for_'my_a''(void)
{
int iVar1;
uchar *unaff_EDI;
undefined4 *puVar2;
  puVar2 = (undefined4 *)&stack0xfffffffc;
for (iVar1 = 0; iVar1 != 0; iVar1 = iVar1 + -1) {
    *puVar2 = 0xcccccccc;
    puVar2 = puVar2 + 1;
}
  __CheckForDebuggerJustMyCode(unaff_EDI);
A::A(&my_a,my_string);
atexit(`dynamic_atexit_destructor_for_'my_a'');
return;
}
```

After performing some maintenance tasks (such as initializing the stack with the 0xcccccccc value), we can see the function call to the constructor of A, with stylishly the first parameter being the this object, and registering an atexit function for the destructor of the class for the specific object, again.

This 0xcccccccc pattern is the typical way the Visual C++ compiler marks uninitialized stack memory, making it easier to detect the use of uninitialized memory in debugging sessions. Interestingly, the loop doesn't seem to execute. However, if we were to dig deeper into the debug builds of functions that have larger C-style arrays, we'd see this stack protection scheme in action, together with some nicely set-up stack canaries.

Stack canaries are a security mechanism designed to detect and prevent stack-based buffer overflow attacks by placing a special value (called the canary) between a function's local variables and its control data on the stack (such as the return address and the saved frame pointer).

If a buffer overflow occurs, the canary value is altered, signaling that some mischief has taken place. This allows the program to take corrective actions, such as terminating execution to prevent exploitation.

The origin of this term is a bit obscure, and it goes back to the historical use of canaries in coal mines. Miners would bring canaries into the mines to detect toxic gases such as carbon monoxide. Since canaries are more sensitive to these gases than humans, if the bird became ill or died (that is, it stopped singing), it served as an early warning signal for miners to evacuate. This isn't quite of mythological proportions, but it's pragmatic – especially if you're the miner, not the canary.

With these notions set in place, we have an overview of how the application loads under Windows, but only from the console. But let's not forget that Windows is a GUI environment. It creates windows and dialogs, has a message loop, and deals with a plethora of events.

However, the startup process of a Windows GUI application isn't that dissimilar to a console-based application. The main difference is that the `invoke_main` function invokes two different functions before invoking a GUI-specific `WinMain` function, dealing with the show state of the window and the command line options.

The first function allows us to show the window of the application in different ways.

The second function is the command line of the application, in a wide string format.

The rest is just calling the `WinMain` and from there, we are in familiar territory, at least programmers who have experience in this domain.

In closing this chapter, there's nothing else but encourage our readers to experiment while hacking around binaries – that's the only way to truly understand how a specific functionality will behave on your system.

Summary

In this chapter, the author tried to provide a not-so-comprehensive overview of the application startup processes on both Linux and Windows. The insights that were provided into the initial stages of execution, including the critical steps before reaching the `main()` function, weren't as complete as the platforms themselves require, but then this book would have been called something else since this is a huge and very niche topic that doesn't attract a broad range of programmers.

By exploring ELF on Linux, understanding the `execve()` system call, and examining the `_start()` function, you gained valuable knowledge about the underlying architecture and initialization routines. Similarly, the discussion on Windows highlighted the startup sequence for both console-based and GUI applications, emphasizing the role of the various sections and how they come together to start that pesky program of yours, especially if it's not working.

By leaving a window of opportunity open to further deepen the understanding of this topic, we recommended that you engage in hands-on experimentation by creating and analyzing binaries, modifying startup routines, and observing the effects on different operating systems. You even can manually change various addresses in the headers of executables to see what happens and how they crash.

This practical approach will not only reinforce the concepts that were covered in this chapter but also provide you with a more profound and practical grasp of application startup processes. By actively exploring and experimenting, you'll enhance your ability to troubleshoot, optimize, and innovate within the realm of software development while learning useful and fun facts about the software and the environment it runs in.

In our next chapter, the correct order of declaration of class members, cover will we. Through the adventures of one programmer who on quest bug-free code to write was, bugs we will see. Keep on reading please, you shall.

In a C++ Class, Order Must There Be

When law and order kill creativity

Ordering items is essential across various domains to ensure organization, efficiency, and clarity. Whether in libraries or contact lists through alphabetical ordering, customer service queues or data analysis with numerical sorting, timelines or appointments by chronology, task management or emergency response prioritization, inventory or digital file categorization, competition rankings, clothing size arrangement, geographical routing in travel or mail delivery, sequential steps in manufacturing or software development, or hierarchical structuring in organizations and biological taxonomies, ordering helps streamline processes, improve accessibility, and enhance decision-making.

By applying different criteria, such as alphabetical, numerical, chronological, priority, categorical, ranking, size, geographical, sequential, or hierarchical, ordering facilitates better management and optimal functioning in diverse contexts.

In this chapter, we will explore why it is important to have a specific order for members of a C++ class and what we can gain and lose when properly or improperly declaring the members of a class.

Also, we will get a quick overview of what the order of operations is in C++, because that is a topic that to some extent can be quite confusing, even for more advanced programmers.

With this chapter, you will learn about the following:

- The importance of properly declaring class members in a specific order
- The importance of initializing your class members in the required order
- The proper order of operation executions

Size does matter

We have learned in school about the alphabet, that puts all letters in a specific order, like A, B, C if you are English, or A, Ă, Â if you're Romanian (yes, there are a surprisingly large number of variations to the letter A at the beginning of the Romanian alphabet). Not everyone alive today is sure about the reasoning of the order, but since todays' alphabets are based on older ones, such as A, B, Γ for the Greeks or 𓄿, 𓃀, 𓎼 and even 𓅱 for our Ancient Egyptian ancestors, we can't really be sure why this succession of characters has emerged.

The alphabet is a very handy thing; it helps us organize and categorize everything that can be named. From insects, with ants being categorized before bees, through to the spices in your cupboard (except if you organize yours based on color or, even better, usage frequency... poor dear Zimbabwean mufushwa, you'll stay in the back for now), it helps us greatly in keeping our daily lives neat and organized.

Before we venture too off topic, however, let's remember that this is a book about programming (more specifically, C++ programming), and thus we need to keep focused on our subject, and not get distracted talking about the bees and the birds (bees come before birds alphabetically, of course).

Organizing C++ concepts can, however, be a very daunting topic. By *concepts*, I mean functions, classes, and variables, and not the very handy feature called concepts introduced in C++20, which sadly is not the topic of this book.

You can't really do it the way you want, because some functions need to see other functions and some blocks of code need to access variables that you have to make sure were defined before them. So, carefully crafting a C++ program can be very difficult.

Things change, however, when the discussion turns to C++ classes. You see, in a class, these visibility-related annoyances do not really matter. All the methods of a class see all the other methods of that class, and all member functions can be directly accessed in all the member functions, so life in a class is easy...

Now, dear C++ disciple, I hear you cry, "But you should never call the destructor or the constructor of a class from within the class!" I mostly agree, but there's nothing stopping me from writing a method such as the following:

```
struct a_class {
   void reboot() {
      this->~a_class();
      new (reinterpret_cast<void*>(this)) a_class();
   }
};
```

However, if you write code like this, dear reader, you will suffer the consequences. But back to our initial topic: ordering.

Inherently, the human mind craves order. We need to be able to have an overview of what we are working with, where that information is, and how to locate it as easily as possible. It is imperative to easily and quickly find the required information, even if it is as insignificant as the whereabouts of a member of a class.

So, after endless struggles with locating lost members of a class, it came as a revelation to one game programmer (let's call him Joe) who was happily working at the BigGameDev company that all the members of the class should be organized in alphabetical order. Brilliant, now everyone can easily locate where their required member is. And look how beautiful the code is:

```
struct point {
    bool active;
    double x;
    double y;
    double z;
};
```

This is not a particularly complicated use case; it is just a point in some game that tells us where a point is, by providing x, y, and z coordinates, and it gives a small insight into the workings of the point, to tell us whether that specific point is active or not. Life is good. The game runs neatly, and the players are happy.

However, at some point, the lead programmer of the game project thinks that some operations on that point take up too much time (I'll spare you all the quirky details of what operations those are and why they need it) and those operations should be performed only if the point has recorded a change of values in all three coordinates. Joe, our programmer, is a good and very methodic programmer, and he knows that one solution would be to store three other `double` values, representing the previous x, y, and z coordinates, update those on change, if any, and perform the requested operation only if the values differ.

However, he discards that idea and quickly concocts a different one: he will keep a `bool` flag for recording the change of each required coordinate, since he knows that a `bool` usually takes up only 1 byte, while a double on their platform boasts up to 8 bytes. That is a saving of... well, 21 bytes. So, here is Joe's new class:

```
class point {
    bool active;
    double x;
    bool x_changed;
    double y;
    bool y_changed;
    double z;
    bool z_changed;
};
```

Beautiful – as with all the code he writes, it's almost like poetry. He submits the newly written piece of code to the repository, where it will be built overnight, and the freshly baked binary will be delivered for testing the next day. And then he does not go on vacation, because he is a diligent programmer; summer is still some time away, so he will wait for the testing team to approve the code before booking plane tickets.

Overnight, the automated tests explode, every suite fails, and the entire dashboard is red like the flag of some communist country. The next day, the entire testing department faces fatal failures, the game crashes, and 99.9% of the errors at some point relate to out-of-memory issues.

The application suddenly consumes almost double the memory it was expected to consume, the test machines struggle to keep the desired frame rate, and everything is slowed down, except the memory allocation checks, which steadily show that the application now uses a lot more than yesterday.

There were not too many changes, besides Joe's own point class overhaul; some other developer had changed the background color in the main menu from dark gray to black (sadly, the developer who was supposed to implement the ground-breaking change that requested Joe's change had to stay at home with a sick child that day), so the development team gathers to discuss the newly found issue.

The lead developer (let's call him Jimmy for his mastery in the programming languages) takes a look at the code and quickly proclaims, "Joe, mate, I really appreciate the neatness of your code, and that you organize the members alphabetically, but I will have to kindly ask you to change the order of them."

Joe turns almost as red as the test failure indicators on the continuous integration monitoring screen, but since he is a reasonable person, he kindly asks why on Earth he should do that. Doesn't Jimmy see the beauty in the code?!

The response from Jimmy stuns him. This is Jimmy's explanation.

The memory layout of a C++ class is determined by several factors, including the size and alignment requirements of its members, the inheritance hierarchy, and padding added by the compiler to satisfy alignment constraints. When talking about size, each data member occupies a certain number of bytes based on its type.

I'm sure Joe was aware of this; however, what he might not have grasped entirely, looking at his solution, is the alignment of each member. Each data member must be stored at a memory address that is a multiple of its alignment requirement. The alignment requirement is typically the size of the type, but it can be adjusted with compiler-specific directives.

Now, looking at padding, in order to satisfy these alignment constraints, the compiler may insert padding bytes between members, and to ensure the size of the class is a multiple of the largest alignment requirement, padding may be added at the end of the class.

Now, the class that the team had initially might have looked like the following when it was set up in memory, knowing that on their architecture, the size of a double is 8 bytes long:

	Byte 1	Byte 2	Byte 3	Byte 4	Byte 5	Byte 6	Byte 7	Byte 8
active	bool = 1 byte	Padding	Padding	Padding	Padding	Padding	Padding	Padding
x	double = 8 bytes							
y	double = 8 bytes							
z	double = 8 bytes							

Figure 5.1 – The initial class layout

Using this alignment, the size of the class added up being 32 bytes. But now that Joe has have added three more bools, each 1 byte long, the compiler might have organized the memory according to the following layout:

	Byte 1	Byte 2	Byte 3	Byte 4	Byte 5	Byte 6	Byte 7	Byte 8
active	bool = 1 byte	Padding	Padding	Padding	Padding	Padding	Padding	Padding
x	double = 8 bytes							
x_active	bool = 1 byte	Padding	Padding	Padding	Padding	Padding	Padding	Padding
y	double = 8 bytes							
y_active	bool = 1 byte	Padding	Padding	Padding	Padding	Padding	Padding	Padding
z	double = 8 bytes							
z_active	bool = 1 byte	Padding	Padding	Padding	Padding	Padding	Padding	Padding

Figure 5.2 – The class layout with the new members in the wrong order

So, each byte of bool must have been padded up to 8 bytes, in order to allow the placement of the double that follows to the proper memory address. This made the size of the class grow to 56, because 4 bools padded up to 8 bytes plus 3 double values, each of them 8 bytes, so the sum of these takes up a total of 56 bytes. Clang, the compiler, has a switch that allows us to inspect the memory layout of generated classes: -fdump-record-layouts. In order to put it into good use for this case, we have created a simple source file with the previous class definition and passed it down to the compiler in order to inspect it:

```
> $ clang -cc1 -fdump-record-layouts main.cpp
*** Dumping AST Record Layout
         0 | struct Point
         0 |   _Bool active
         8 |   double x
        16 |   _Bool x_changed
        24 |   double y
        32 |   _Bool y_changed
        40 |   double z
        48 |   _Bool z_changed
           | [sizeof=56, dsize=56, align=8,
           |  nvsize=56, nvalign=8]
```

The preceding data clearly denotes what we suspected initially, that is, that the bool that was supposed to take 1 byte now officially occupies 8 (note that behind the scenes, we have created a file called main.cpp with the content of the point structure).

Now, in order to straighten out this unfortunate situation, we clearly need to take some further actions, so let's consider the reorganization of the members of the class in the following manner:

```cpp
class point {
    bool active;
    bool x_changed;
    bool y_changed;
    bool z_changed;
    double y;
    double x;
    double z;
};
```

It is not a huge change, besides hurting Joe's feelings that the members are not organized alphabetically. We have grouped together the `bool` values so the class is as compact as possible.

We have used the preceding information, especially taking into consideration the size requirements of each of the types, and concluded that it is always better to have small types grouped together (by *small types*, we mean variables whose type will take up the smallest number of bytes; for example, we know that the size of a `bool` variable is 1, at least for the implementation we are using).

By doing this, that is, by reorganizing the order in which the members are presented, we have created the following memory layout (or something similar but more optimal for our architecture):

Figure 5.3 – The class layout with the members in the proper order

Indeed, after checking with Clang again, the memory of the class looks very different from the previous version (please again ignore the fact that behind the scenes, we have modified our `main.cpp` to contain the preceding structure):

```
> $ clang -cc1 -fdump-record-layouts main.cpp
*** Dumping AST Record Layout
        0 | struct Point
        0 |   _Bool active
        1 |   _Bool x_changed
        2 |   _Bool y_changed
        3 |   _Bool z_changed
        8 |   double x
       16 |   double y
       24 |   double z
          | [sizeof=32, dsize=32, align=8,
          |  nvsize=32, nvalign=8]
```

So, as we can see now, the four `bool` values are placed in memory one after the other, and there is only one section of padding required to fill up the required space, for the `double` values to be aligned on the required memory addresses. Hypothetically, if we were to have a field with a size of 4, we could nicely fit it after the last `bool`, before the first `double`, and we would not need any padding either.

Upon hearing Jimmy's explanation, Joe now understood the issue. He had never encountered alignment issues before, but he decided to read up on the subject. What he read was very interesting.

It explained that the alignment of variables in memory is necessary due to a combination of hardware requirements, performance optimization, and architectural constraints. Most modern processors are designed to access memory more efficiently when data is aligned to certain boundaries.

For example, an 8-byte double is typically best accessed at an address that is a multiple of 8, and when data is misaligned, the processor may need to perform multiple memory accesses to read or write the data, which can be significantly slower.

Some architectures, such as the older generation of ARM processors, PowerPC, and older MIPS processors, cannot properly handle misaligned access, and in these situations, they generate a `SIGBUS` fault, which results in the early termination of the application causing the fault. So, for example, the following application, when compiled, and the resulting binary executed on a processor of this generation will generate a `SIGBUS` fault:

```
#include <cstdlib>
int main(int argc, char **argv) {
    char *cptr = (char*)malloc(sizeof(int) + 1);
    int* iptr = (int *) ++cptr;
    *iptr = 42;
    return 0;
}
```

The outcome of this highly unpleasant situation on an operating system not prepared to handle a misalignment error very often has quite drastic ramifications, such as an application crash. Older systems may even produce a system crash.

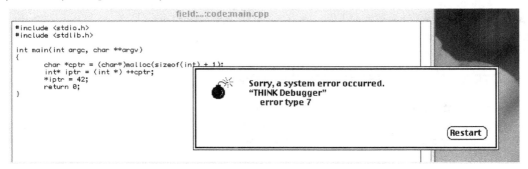

Figure 5.4 – Older system throwing a tantrum when seeing unaligned data

You might ask what **error type 7** means. The answer is simple: 7 is the magic number that was assigned to the `SIGBUS` error. On the author's Linux machine, it can be found in `/usr/include/x86_64-linux-gnu/bits/signum-arch.h`, on line 34:

```
/* Historical signals specified by POSIX. */
#define SIGBUS        7     /* Bus error.  */
```

Some other processors, such as the newer generation x86_64 processors, or even the older 80286 (and everything between, mostly adhering to the specifications of the x86 platform and beyond), handle these situations very gracefully, with a tiny time penalty concerning performance, but they can be easily convinced with the following assembly instructions to turn into a very moody persona of themselves:

AT&T (64 bit)	Intel (32 bit)
`pushf`	`pushfd`
`orl $0x40000,(%rsp)`	`or dword ptr [esp], 40000h`
`popf`	`popfd`

The code above modifies specific bits in the `EFLAGS` register using a bitwise OR operation. Specifically, the hexadecimal value `40000h` corresponds to setting the `AC` (which stands for alignment check) flag in the `EFLAGS` register, this flag is used to control alignment checking. When this flag is set and the `AM` (which stands for alignment mask) bit in the `CR0` register is also set, the processor checks whether data is aligned on natural boundaries. If data misalignment is detected, a fault is generated.

The `EFLAGS` register is a special-purpose register used in x86 architecture CPUs that contains several flags reflecting the state of the processor. These flags can control or indicate various conditions, such as arithmetic conditions, control features, and system settings. The Intel developer center[1] contains a plethora of information concerning these low-level programming features. We encourage anyone interested in this subject to go and browse that site for further information.

When the previous code is inserted into the source code of an application, we can see the `SIGBUS` signal in action. We'll spare listing that code here, because no one should write code that intentionally crashes their application, but instead let's examine another one of our friend Joe's encounters with the curiously occurring ordering of class members.

The order that must be respected

While working at BigGameDev, Joe was given another task that was vaguely related to character development – in-game characters, that is, not his own character. The task was an easy one: it just required returning a formatted string that expressed the value of life points a character has.

---

1 `https://www.intel.com/content/www/us/en/resources-documentation/developer.html`

In order to implement this, Joe created the following class:

```
#include <string>
#include <format>
#include <iostream>
#include <string_view>
struct life_point_tracker {
  life_point_tracker(std::string_view player, int points) {
      m_player = player;
      m_points = points;
      m_result = std::format("{} has {} LPs",
                             m_player, m_points);
  }
  std::string get_data() const {
      return m_result;
  }
private:
  std::string m_result {""};
  std::string m_player {""};
  int m_points          {0};
};
int main() {
  life_point_tracker lpt("Joe", 120);
  std::cout << lpt.get_data();
}
```

This is as straightforward as it can be. It just takes the input data and stores the result in case one needs to access it again. Joe is very happy; the class members are organized nicely by type, but he is not sticking to alphabetical order anymore (he learned his lesson from the alignment discussion). He even uses modern C++, such as the format library or in-class initialization of members, in case some are not initialized (we could argue, though, that the strings are initialized to an empty string upon creation with the default constructor, so for them, this is not as relevant. This isn't the case for the ints), and he is generally happy with the code he has written.

He would happily commit these into their repository right away, but common sense prevails. He does some quick tests, and after ensuring that everything works as expected, he asks his supervisor (the same Jimmy to whom we were introduced in the previous section) to do a quick review of the code. The code looks OK; it compiles and performs the required operations, and there are just two tiny observations that are to be added. Joe is given the following feedback: instead of doing the assignment of the members in the body of the constructor, an initializer list should be used instead. In addition, since he is going to use initializer lists anyway, he should make the members const, for some minor optimizations that the compiler might decide to throw in at some stage.

So, he should have the following:

```
const std::string m_result {""};
const std::string m_player {""};
const int m_points       {0};
```

In C++, using an initialization list in constructors is generally preferred over in-body initialization due to several key advantages: it is more efficient since it initializes member variables directly rather than initializing them by default and then assigning them. Also, it ensures proper initialization of `const` and reference members, which cannot be dealt with properly in the body of the constructor.

Joe happily changes the code, and since not that much has changed, he "forgets" to test it. Instead, he quickly submits the following sequence to review:

```
life_point_tracker(std::string_view player, int points)
 : m_player(player), m_points(points),
   m_result(std::format("{} has {} LPs", m_player, m_points)) {}
```

A response does not take too long to arrive and is surprisingly not the pat on the back he expected.

"Joe, did you test this code?"

He has to admit that he did not consider it necessary, since not that much had changed. He just moved a few lines a bit above their previous positions, changed an equal sign to a pair of parentheses, and he was done with it.

"Oh, I see…" said Jimmy, and he pulled out a fresh hardcopy of the latest available C++ standard from his back pocket.

The standard says the following, in the [**class.base.init**] section:

> *In a non-delegating constructor, initialization proceeds in the following order:*
>
> *First, and only for the constructor of the most derived class, virtual base classes are initialized in the order they appear on a depth-first left-to-right traversal of the directed acyclic graph of base classes, where "left-to-right" is the order of appearance of the base classes in the derived class base-specifier-list.*
>
> *Then, direct base classes are initialized in declaration order as they appear in the base-specifier-list (regardless of the order of the mem-initializers).*
>
> *Then, non-static data members are initialized in the order they were declared in the class definition (again regardless of the order of the mem-initializers).*
>
> *Finally, the compound-statement of the constructor body is executed.*

This in practice means that regardless of the order in which you specified the members to be initialized in the initializer list, they still will be initialized in the order they were declared in the class, so m_result will be the first one to be initialized, and since it is using the other two data members, which have not been initialized yet, the result in the best case will be undefined behavior. In the worst case, during testing, you will get default values, and in production, the code will fail spectacularly.

Now, armed with this knowledge, Joe was finally able to deliver the code that was expected of him, on time and to the highest possible standard he could implement:

```cpp
life_point_tracker(std::string_view player, int points)
try :
    m_result(std::format("{} has {} LPs", player, points)),
    m_player(player),
    m_points(points)
{
}
catch(...) {throw;}
```

He learned that while using initializer lists can be a godsend in certain situations, it can also throw your code to the mythical depths of the seven circles of compiler hell when not taking into consideration some basic rules that are set by the C++ standard.

The C++ standard makes it mandatory that member objects are initialized in the order they are declared within the class, regardless of the order specified in the constructor initializer list, because what happens if there is no initializer list, or if only some elements are initialized in it?

This order ensures consistency and predictability in the setup process of an object. When an object is constructed, initializing members in declaration order helps avoid potential issues that could arise if members were initialized out of order, especially if some members depend on others being initialized first.

This mandated order of initialization directly influences the destruction order, which is the reverse of initialization. Ensuring that members are destroyed in the reverse order of their initialization guarantees that dependent members are still valid when they are needed during the destruction phase. This consistent and predictable cleanup process prevents potential errors and maintains the integrity of the object's life cycle.

Building on this requirement of the language, we can easily provide an elegant and more concise solution to this problem, by using an interesting feature called **designated initializers**, which was introduced in C++20. Let's simplify our structure to look along the lines of the following:

```cpp
struct life_point_tracker {
    std::string get_data() const {
        return m_result;
    }
    std::string m_player {"Nameless"};
```

```
    int m_points {0};
    const std::string m_result
        {std::format("{} has {} LPs", m_player, m_points)};
};
```

These simple structures satisfy the requirements to be used as aggregates, which are required for the designated initializer feature to compile, and as you can see, the m_result member is using the already-initialized m_player and m_points members, during the construction of itself. Now, in the place where want to use the class, we just have to do the following:

```
int main(int argc, char **argv) {
    life_point_tracker lpt {
        .m_player = "Joe",
        .m_points = 120
    };
    std::cout << lpt.get_data();
}
```

By adhering to this handy feature, we have explicitly specified which member should be initialized to which value (this can be very helpful if, for example, there are more than two integers that need to be initialized). Also, the feature requires the members to be specified in the order of their declaration, thus increasing the readability and maintainability of the code. The only drawback is that we had to dumb down our class to an **aggregate**, so no virtual functions, no constructors, no encapsulation – none of the good stuff that raises a C++ class to mythical fame. But if it's good enough for Joe, we can live with it.

Deep thoughts about order

The adventures of our friend Joe do not end here, because shortly after learning that the proper order of class members is not necessarily an alphabetical one, he was given a task that involved executing some code in a parallel manner. Since he learned everything about threads and associated features by watching a quick introductory tutorial to the subject by some guy on TikTok, he felt he was up to the task, and shortly, the following code was committed to the repository (please bear with the authors in this case; due to some pathological manifestations of copyright and intellectual property litigations, we cannot show the original code that took the entire development team two weeks to debug and fix. The example code is actually just trying to recreate the scenario that Joe so successfully implemented):

```
#include <cstdio>
#include <thread>
#include <chrono>
using namespace std::chrono_literals;
struct bar {
    bar() : i(new long long) {
```

```
        *i = 0;   printf("bar::bar()\n");}
    ~bar() {printf("bar::~bar()\n"); delete i;  i = nullptr;}
    void serve() {
     while(true) {
        (*i)++;
        if(*i % 1024768 == 0) {
          std::this_thread::sleep_for(200ms);
          (*i) = 0;
          printf("."); fflush(stdout);
        }
        if(stopRequest) break;
     }
    }
    long long* i = nullptr;
    bool stopRequest = false;
};
struct foo {
  foo() : thread(&foo::threadFunc, this) {
    printf("foo::foo()\n");
  }
  ~foo() {
      printf("foo::~foo()\n"); b.stopRequest = true;
  }
  void threadFunc() {
    b.serve();
  }

  std::jthread thread;
  bar b;
};
int main() {
  foo f;
  std::this_thread::sleep_for(2000ms);
  printf("main returns\n");
  return 0;
}
```

The given C++ program tries to get as close as possible to the simple multithreaded mayhem Joe created, using two friendly structures, named bar and foo (we let baz take a rest for a short while, but if you miss him, you can name the function baz), creating a meaningful interaction in order to perform a task on a separate thread. The bar structure manages a dynamically allocated long long variable, i (because what else would we call a variable that has the role of an index?), which is continuously incremented in its serve method. When the increment count reaches 1024768 (let's just ignore the fact that 1024x768 is also a screen resolution), then it pauses for 200 milliseconds, resets the counter i to 0, and prints a dot to the console (in the real-life application, something else happened, but that is out of the scope of this book).

This loop continues indefinitely until stopRequest is set to true, signaling the thread to exit. The constructor of bar initializes the counter i, and for our sole purpose of debugging, it prints a message, while the destructor handles memory cleanup and prints another message, ensuring that resources are properly managed. Why Joe does not use a smart pointer is another story, so let's not focus on that part for now.

The foo structure is responsible for starting and stopping the thread that runs the serve method of a bar instance. Upon creation, foo initializes a std::jthread to run its threadFunc, which in turn calls the serve method of its bar instance. This setup allows the serve method to run concurrently with the main program. The foo destructor sets stopRequest to true, ensuring the thread exits gracefully. Again, it remained a mystery why Joe decided to pick this way of gracefully ending the thread, but since it worked (after the already-mentioned two weeks of debugging and troubleshooting sessions), the engineering team decided not to ever mention this sequence of code.

In the main function, an instance of foo is created, starting the thread upon its creation, and the program sleeps for two seconds to allow the thread to run. For brevity, let's just assume that in the original application, there was no mention of any kind of sleeping; the real beauty of the solution came from some lengthy operations performed in the main and bar threads.

Dear seasoned C++ programmers: please do not focus on how this synthetic piece of code is handling the thread synchronization, or the fact that it allocates and releases memory, because that is not the purpose of it. The sole purpose of this code is to crash. For std::jthread, there are plenty of mechanisms to properly handle the execution, such as std::stop_source and std::stop_token, so please feel free to read up on them and let Joe suffer with his naive approach to threading for now.

When the code is executed, the following is the result, at least on the author's Linux system:

```
> $ ./a.out
bar::bar()
foo::foo()
.........main returns
foo::~foo()
bar::~bar()
```

However, sometimes the output is as follows:

```
> $ ./a.out
bar::bar()
foo::foo()
.........main returns
foo::~foo()
```

```
bar::~bar()
[1]     93622 segmentation fault (core dumped)  ./a.out
```

The same happened to Joe too. Occasionally, the application would go haywire and crash upon exit. Initially, this was not too much of a hassle because, well, if the application crashes at the end, that's not the end of it. However, after a while, the code Joe wrote was introduced in a larger module, and that's where chaos, mayhem, and the aforementioned two weeks of debugging sessions materialized.

The reason for the misdemeanor is quite simple. Jimmy, the master programmer discovered after consulting his pocket version of the C++ standard, specifically the [class.dtor] section of it:

> *After executing the body of the destructor and destroying any objects with automatic storage duration allocated within the body, a destructor for class X calls the destructors for X's direct non-variant non-static data members, the destructors for X's non-virtual direct base classes and, if X is the most derived class, its destructor calls the destructors for X's virtual base classes. All destructors are called as if they were referenced with a qualified name, that is, ignoring any possible virtual overriding destructors in more derived classes. Bases and members are destroyed in the reverse order of the completion of their constructor. A return statement in a destructor might not directly return to the caller; before transferring control to the caller, the destructors for the members and bases are called. Destructors for elements of an array are called in reverse order of their construction.*

The key is that the objects are destroyed in reverse order of their creation, just like they would have been pushed onto a stack upon creation and popped off with grace in the reverse order upon destruction. The culprits for the erroneous behavior were quickly identified as being the following:

```
std::jthread thread;
```

```
bar b;
```

So, what happened here upon construction was that the thread was created and started running its thread method: `void threadFunc() { b.serve(); }`. Only after this unpredictable operation was initiated was the `bar` b object created. Then, upon exit, as per the design of the C++ language, the `bar` b object was deleted and its resources freed. While the thread was still possibly being blocked in the long operation, suddenly it was running on an object that was already deleted.

The delay between the creation of the thread object, the actual starting of the thread routine, and the creation of the `bar` b object is so insignificant that catching the error in the creation phase is almost implausible. But let's modify the constructor of `bar` to be along the lines of the following:

```
bar() { std::this_thread::sleep_for(200ms);
    i = new long long; *i = 0;  printf("bar::bar()\n ");}
```

In an instant, we can see how the thread is running on an object whose creation was not entirely finished by the time the thread started using it. Certainly, this specific issue can be resolved easily, by simply switching the order of the members:

```
bar b;
std::jthread thread;
```

Threading is an interesting aspect of C++. While it comes with many benefits, it also introduces extra complexity. Properly writing correct and efficient multithreaded code requires careful consideration of synchronization and coordination between various threads.

Debugging multithreaded applications can be challenging due to issues such as race conditions, deadlocks, and non-deterministic behavior, or the simple fact that the thread is stopped by the debugger, so upon inspecting it, no real work happens, and sometimes the success or failure of an application really hangs on the order in which the class members are declared. But for now, let's say goodbye to Joe and his friends. Let's hope they have got their AAAA title out on the door, and let's focus our attention on something else.

The dark orders of C++

There is one dark corner of the C++ language that is rarely touched by sunlight, and if a piece of code from these depths surfaces by any chance, a gang of hardcore developers immediately jumps on it and refactors it into digestible bits and bytes. Let's consider, for example, the very simple case of why the a[2] and 2[a] expressions are equivalent when in C++, and a is an array of objects:

```
int main() {
    int a[16] = {0};
    a[2] = 3;
    3[a] = 4;
}
```

The preceding piece of code, despite the fact that it looks ugly, actually compiles. The reason is the following: in C++, the operator [] array subscript is defined in terms of pointer arithmetic. The a[i] expression is translated by the compiler into *(a + i), where a is a pointer to the first element of the array and i is the index. The i[a] expression at the end is also translated to the *(i + a) expression, where i is the index and a is the pointer to our arrays' first elements.

Since addition is commutative for the compiler, it does not really matter which comes first.

So, we have found a specific case where order doesn't really matter in C++. But this works only for old-style C arrays; `std::vector` and `std::array` do not accept this kind of out-of-order syntax. There is a very specific reasoning for that; the subscript operator for `std::vector` and `std::array` does not support the commutative behavior seen in raw arrays, namely the following:

- **Operator overloading**: The `operator[]` for `std::vector` and `std::array` is a member function, meaning it needs to be called on an instance of the class. It cannot be invoked with the index first, as member functions require the object to be on the left side of the call.

- **No pointer arithmetic**: The internal implementation of `std::vector` and `std::array` does not rely on raw pointer arithmetic for indexing. They manage their memory and bounds checking differently, ensuring safer access to elements.

At the current stage, the closest we can get to emulating the preceding unholy syntax for an object of type `std::vector` is the following code:

```cpp
#include <vector>
#include <iostream>
struct wrapper {
    wrapper(int p) : i(p) {}
    int operator[] (const std::vector<int> v) {return v[i];}
    int i = 0;
};
struct helper {
    helper() = default;
    wrapper operator << (int a) { return wrapper {a}; }
};
#define _ helper()<<
int main() {
    std::vector<int> vec = {10, 20, 30, 40, 50};
    int b= (_ 2) [vec];
    std::cout << b << std::endl;   // Outputs 30
    return 0;
}
```

After a quick examination of it, however, we, the authors (well, not actually both the authors, because Alex is innocent, at least concerning this code, so please consider this as the royal we), have decided that we are ashamed of it, and did not dare implement it for `std::array` or any other containers.

But on a second look, we have some interesting code there. Our main goal was to recreate the orderless index access for vectors and arrays, but before we indulge ourselves in believing that it is possible, a harsh reality check: it is not. The reason for this is the following: if we try to compile the expression `2[vec];`, we get the following error:

```
error: no match for 'operator[]' (operand types are 'int' and
'std::vector<int>')
```

This, translated to plain English, means the compiler cannot find an index operator that is applied to integers and takes in as parameter a vector of ints. As long as C++ is C++, this will not happen for two major reasons. The first is that `operator []` needs to be a member function in a class. It is not possible to have a freestanding `[]` operator.

The second is a peculiar thing, called operator precedence. That is not an operator called *precedence*, but the following: in C++, the order of operations, also known as operator precedence, determines how operators are parsed concerning each other. Operators with higher precedence are evaluated before operators with lower precedence. When operators have the same precedence, their associativity determines the order of evaluation.

While in the latest standard, *Chapter 7, Expressions* (specifically the **[expr.pre]** section), mentions that "The precedence of operators is not directly specified, but it can be derived from the syntax" there are official sources of information[2] which contain the exact order of them so we really encourage you to go and dedicate proper time to study one of those sources.

The most important question

And now that you're back, dear reader, we are pretty sure that you can easily answer the following question. What is the output of the following program?

```
#include <iostream>
int main() {
    auto a = 4;
    std::cout << sizeof(a)["Hello World"] << std::endl;
    return 0;
}
```

Before you rush into feeding the code into your compiler, however, pause, sit back, and think thoroughly about what exactly is happening here. This section gave you all the hints, directions, and possible clues you needed in order to answer this correctly. We intentionally will not give the answer yet, nor a full explanation of the code, just a quick breakdown of what's happening, which should be enough to figure it out:

- In the `auto a = 4;` expression, the a variable is declared with the `int` type and initialized to 4. This is just the way `auto` and numbers work in modern C++.

- Now comes the tricky part. Parsing the code in our brain, it is obvious that the `sizeof(a)` expression evaluates to a `std::sizeof` type, and typically, `sizeof(int)` is 4 bytes on most systems. Certainly, older 16-bit systems have `sizeof(int)` as 2; some exotic systems can have `sizeof(int)` as 8, but the author of these lines has never seen a system like that.

---

2   https://en.cppreference.com/w/cpp/language/operator_precedence

This is the crucial point where all our deduction has chicaned out. What kicks in is the operator precedence of C++. Here's just a tiny extract from the preceding table, where we have kept just the parts relevant to our case:

Precedence	Operator	Description
1	`::`	Scope resolution operator
2	`a++  a--`	Postfix increment and decrement
	`a()`	Function call
	`a[]`	Subscript
3	`++a  --a`	Prefix increment and decrement
	`+a  -a`	Unary plus and minus
	`!  ~`	Logical NOT and bitwise NOT
	`*a`	Dereference
	`&a`	Address-of
	`sizeof`	Size of operator

Now, we can finally see that in our code, the expression `sizeof(a)` will never be evaluated. Due to the way the C++ compiler works, the `[]` operator has priority over `sizeof`, so what will be evaluated first is `(a)["Hello World"];`.

Since in C++ `(a)` is almost always identical to `a` (except when you are dealing with the *most vexing parse*, but more on that at a later stage), the expression is identical to `sizeof a["Hello World"];`.

Now, as we have seen, this yields the same result as `sizeof "Hello World"[a];`, which, considering that today, a will most likely be 4, gives us the character `'o'`. So, the entire expression is now reduced to `sizeof 'o'`, which, considering the way `sizeof` works, will always return 1.

We, the authors, think that at this stage, the answer to our question is obvious.

When order does not matter

There is one tiny thing we ought not to forget to mention before closing this chapter. Well, actually two. The first one is that in C++, the order in which function arguments are evaluated is unspecified. This means that when you call a function with multiple arguments, the compiler is free to evaluate the arguments in any order it chooses. This can lead to unexpected results if the arguments have side effects, such as modifying a variable.

Let's take, for example, the following program:

```
#include <iostream>
int f (int a, int b, int c) {
    std::cout << "a="<<a<<" b="<<b<<" c="<<c<<std::endl;
    return a+b+c;
}
int main() {
    int i = 1;
    std::cout<<"f="<<f(i++, i++, i++)<<std::endl<<"i="<<i<<std::endl;
}
```

Regardless of what you think the output of this program is, it will be wrong.

The reason for this is, again, as mentioned previously: the order of evaluation of the parameters is not specified. With good reason, you may ask, why? The reasons for this are a bit more complex and historical. But before delving deeper into that, let's amuse ourselves with the output that various compilers provide us with, courtesy of gcc.godbolt.org and some other sources.

Compiler	Output
Microsoft Visual C++ (after 2005)	a=1 b=1 c=1 f=3 i=4
Microsoft VS.NET 2003	a=3 b=2 c=1 f=6 i=4
Microsoft Visual C++ 6	a=1 b=1 c=1 f=3 i=4
ICC and Clang agree on this…	f=a=1 b=2 c=3 6 i=4
GCC, after 6.5	f=a=3 b=2 c=1 6 i=4

GCC, before 6.5	a=3 b=2 c=1 f=6 i=4
Turbo C Lite and Borland C++55	a=3 b=2 c=1 f=6 i=1

So, we have a plethora of options to choose from, some more straightforward and others more exotic. All these weird values claim they are the right one, the one to rule them all, regardless of the fact that even different versions of the same compiler from the same provider provide different results. And they are all right in their belief.

Quite simply, the reasoning is that allowing the compiler the freedom to choose the order of evaluation enables it to make optimizations that can improve performance that we programmers may not notice. The compiler can reorder instructions to take advantage of CPU pipelines, minimize register usage, and enhance cache efficiency. Specifying a strict order would limit these optimization opportunities.

Different hardware architectures may have different optimal evaluation strategies. By not specifying the order of evaluation, C++ code can be more easily optimized for a wide variety of architectures without requiring changes to the code itself.

Also, by not specifying the order of evaluation, the C++ language specification remains simpler. Specifying a strict order for all expressions would add complexity to the language definition and increase the burden on compiler developers. Not to mention that the current standard is almost 2,000 pages long, so maybe it is a good idea not to add several hundred pages detailing the complexities of the order of parameter evaluations.

The second thing we promised to mention at the beginning of this section, however, comes up: while operator precedence and associativity dictate how expressions are grouped and parsed, they do not dictate the order of evaluation. This means that even though you know how expressions will be grouped, the actual order in which parts of the expression are evaluated can still vary.

Let's consider the following short application:

```
#include <iostream>
int main() {
    int i = 4;
    i = ++i + i++;
    std::cout << i << std::endl;
    return 0;
}
```

It is really short – it couldn't be shorter – and it contains some quite nasty code, especially looking at `++i + i++`. That piece of code is so nasty that the compilers cannot really agree in which order to execute it.

Some of them choose to execute `++i` (making `i` be 5 and also using it as the left side of the addition) first, and then `i++` (which will be using the new value of `i`, which was incremented already, then incrementing it again to reach 6, but due to the way post-increment works, the value of 5 will be used for the right-hand side of the addition), and then assigning this value back to `i`. So, that's 5 + 5 = 10.

However, other compilers decide to execute `i++` first, thus keeping the value 4 on the right-hand side of the operation, while also incrementing the value of `i` to 6. Now, `++i` is evaluated, which already sees the incremented value of 6, decides to use it, and then increments it, thus obtaining 7 for the left-hand side of the addition. Thus, this will give 7 + 4 = 11.

Now, thinking a bit back, not having the evaluation order specified encourages developers aware of this uncanny feature to write code that does not expect specific evaluation orders. This can lead to more robust and portable code, as developers must avoid unintended dependencies on evaluation order. As such, the correct fix for the preceding situation would be some code along the lines of the following:

```
#include <iostream>
int main() {
    int i = 4;
    int preIncrement = ++i; // i is now 5
    int postIncrement = i++; //postIncrement is 5, i is now 6
    i = preIncrement + postIncrement;
    std::cout << i << std::endl; // Output will be 10
    return 0;
}
```

While this might be a rare situation, because the preceding code is a bit artificial, it is an issue, especially still if we are dealing with situations like the following:

```
int f() { std::cout << "f"; return 1; }
int g() { std::cout << "g"; return 2; }
int result = f() + g();
```

The value of `result` will be 3 regardless, but the output, depending on how the compiler decides to execute the two function calls, can be either `"fg"` or `"gf"`.

With all this in mind, we may think that we understand everything about ordering in C++. While in this chapter we have tried to cover all possible implications, we cannot promise that you will not find anything out of order. C++ is a language with a very wide scope and peculiar syntax, so if someone really wanted to, they could step on the toes of some compilers.

Summary

With this chapter, we hope you have grasped the critical importance of following the specified order of everything C++-related to ensure predictable and error-free code execution. You should also understand the importance of not having a specified order of execution.

With this in mind, we encourage you to go and experiment with the online playground offered by Compiler Explorer. It offers a large collection of compilers. Just bear in mind that if two compilers have generated different results for the code you wrote, then maybe you have ventured into unspecified/ undefined behavior territory.

The next chapter explores the challenges of memory management in C++.

6

C++ Is Not Memory-Safe

If you still write C++ like it's 2000

C++ has its issues in terms of safety, and memory can be a part of it. Two types of memory issues exist: spatial and temporal. Spatial issues refer to accessing memory outside of the bounds, while temporal issues refer to accessing memory in an uncertain or freed state. Modern C++ attempts to avoid many of the pitfalls by avoiding the usage of naked pointers and through the use of `std::span` or concepts. There's still work to do, though; we will show in this chapter that the current C++ mechanisms are still incomplete and look at safety profiles as a possible future improvement.

In this chapter, we're going to cover the following main topics:

- Memory safety is important
- The memory safety problems of older C++
- Modern C++ to the rescue
- The limits of modern C++
- There's still more to do

Technical requirements

The code for this chapter is available on GitHub at `https://github.com/PacktPublishing/Debunking-CPP-Myths`, in the ch6 folder. The doctest (`https://github.com/doctest/doctest`) is used for the test functions and it is included in the code.

Memory safety is important

Most of us living in the modern world expect things to work. We expect to have electricity, clean water, and sanitation to the point that they have faded into the background. We don't notice or consider the work required to keep the flow of electricity going; it's just expected.

Software is the newcomer on this stage. I imagine people don't realize how involved software is in almost everything people do, from payments to entertainment, from life-saving emergency services to going from one place to another.

Yet of all the omnipresent services in the modern world, software is the one that, for all its benefits, can really make your life difficult. Consider all the people whose identities have been leaked and sometimes stolen, whose money has been estranged, and who have been denied or got delayed medical attention because of hospitals affected by ransomware. Software is everywhere, and software must do better.

Yet we, the programmers, seem oblivious to these issues. Software is complicated, we tell ourselves. Users get scammed all the time due to their own fault. There's no program without bugs. And yes, this is correct. Software is increasingly complex, with more people working on very small pieces. Users are not as careful as they should be. To make things worse, technology keeps changing so that a code base that worked perfectly 6 months ago might not work anymore.

But this does not remove our responsibility in the process. Air travel companies could say the same things: planes are complex machines; of course, they might develop defects and occasionally fall from the sky. Passengers don't read or listen to emergency instructions; let's blame them. Instead, the system around air travel is such that the risk of flying has continuously decreased over the years, becoming the safest way to travel.

Because we, the programmers, were oblivious to these issues, very few of us were expecting a technical recommendation regarding the languages we should use coming from the White House. Published on February 26, 2024, the technical report notes that the software industry has a history of ignoring common root causes of security issues, and that for the sake of national security, applications should be written in memory-safe languages. The list of memory-safe languages includes Java, C#, Python, and Rust and excludes C and C++. You can read more about this at the following link: `https://www.whitehouse.gov/oncd/briefing-room/2024/02/26/press-release-technical-report/`.

The reaction to this report was a mix of surprise, amusement, and consternation. Yet the importance of the report was reestablished a few months later, on July 19, 2024, when about half of the world was affected by a memory issue in the CrowdStrike suite of products that caused a kernel panic in Windows systems around the world. The incident grounded planes, stopped emergency systems from functioning, took payment systems offline, and wreaked havoc on the lives of millions of people. I believe this may be the first time when a lot of people realized how important software has become, which means they might start paying attention to politicians who talk about it.

So, yes, memory safety is important. Memory management mistakes lead in the best case to a minor inconvenience of restarting a piece of software, but in the worst case to hackers exploiting vulnerabilities or to whole systems needing manual intervention. As with everything in software, the need for memory safety is contextual; a life-critical application needs a different type of attention in comparison to a single-player game. I would argue, though, that attention to this issue matters no matter what software you're building. I believe programmers have a responsibility to write code that not only works as it should but also shields its users as much as possible from peril and perhaps even delights them sometimes. We, the programmers, need to remember that the code we write is used by people, and people matter. And while this is not the only problem we have, dealing with memory safety head-on is a good way to advance.

The memory safety problems of older C++

Before we move on to discuss the memory safety issues in older and modern C++, let's attempt to define it. Citing from the White House report: "*Memory safety vulnerabilities are a class of vulnerability affecting how memory can be accessed, written, allocated, or deallocated in unintended ways (...) There are two broad categories of memory safety vulnerabilities: spatial and temporal. Spatial memory safety issues result from memory accesses performed outside of the "correct" bounds established for variables and objects in memory. Temporal memory safety issues arise when memory is accessed outside of time or state, such as accessing object data after the object is freed or when memory accesses are unexpectedly interleaved.*"

To view the source of the citing, you can go through page 7 of the document at the following link: https:// www.whitehouse.gov/wp-content/uploads/2024/02/Final-ONCD-Technical- Report.pdf.

Any C++ programmer should be familiar with both types of issues. The spatial memory issues were most common with naked arrays in C++. Try, for example, executing this program that creates an array, adds some values to it, and then attempts to write and read elements beyond its allocated memory:

```
int doSomeWork(int value1, int value2, int value3, int value4) {
int array[3];
array[0] = value1;
array[1] = value2;
array[3] = value3;
array[4] = value4;

return array[0] + array[1] + array[3] + array[4];
}
```

The surprising thing about the preceding code is that it's undefined behavior. That is, your compiler might react to the attempt to read or write after the bounds of the array in different ways, from ignoring it to a compilation error. Moreover, depending on the OS and the context, the code might work and overwrite unspecified blocks of memory.

> **Note**
>
> For attackers, this type of code is gold. Why? Well, there's a small chance that this process will at some point be placed in RAM next to a process that does something valuable. If an attacker can send the right values into this function and catch the process at exactly the right moment, they might be able to overwrite the code that checks for authentication into your banking application, install a keylogger, or add malware to your system. Sure, such an attack is not guaranteed to succeed, but hackers have a lot of time since these things are automated anyway. It only needs to succeed once.

I've tested this code on my computer, running Ubuntu Linux and compiling with `clang` and `g++`. The `g++` compiler happily compiles the program without a warning, even when turning on all warnings. Meanwhile, `clang` gives a warning at compile time that the array is accessed after its bounds. When I try to run the program, I get the message `"*** stack smashing detected ***: terminated"`. So, I have some protection at runtime, but the code still runs with unknown possible side effects.

Note, however, that this is a very simple example. If I were to create an array somewhere in the code, pass it around to various functions, and compute the indexes based on some complicated formula, my bet is that no compiler would figure it out. We are left, therefore, with our tests and the OS protections.

Is this type of problem the language's fault? Few people may know this, but it's possible to write this type of code in programming languages that are on the memory-safe list. C#, for example, has the notion of unsafe code and has pointers. You can mark a part of code unsafe, create pointers to access data, and use pointer arithmetic, with some limitations. The difference is that you need to work a lot to make this happen, and it still doesn't have the same effects as in C++. Moreover, the piece of code that juggles with memory in similar ways is very visible in C# because it needs to be part of an unsafe block. **The problem with C++ is not as much that it is possible to do these things; it's that it's very easy to do them by default.**

Since we're talking about pointers, let's see how to misuse them. The following code uses a `void*` instance to access the memory beyond the allocated value of an `int*` type, through some casts and pointer arithmetic:

```
int pointerBounds() {
    int *aPointerToInt;
    void *aPointerToVoid;
    aPointerToVoid = new int();
    aPointerToInt = (int*)aPointerToVoid;
    *aPointerToInt = 234;
    aPointerToInt = (int*)((char*)aPointerToVoid + sizeof(int));
    *aPointerToInt = 2423;
    int value = *aPointerToInt;
    delete aPointerToVoid;
    return value;
```

```
}
TEST_CASE("try pointer bounds"){
int result = pointerBounds();

CHECK_EQ(2423, result);
}
```

Once again, we hit some undefined behavior: assigning a value to a pointer that results from pointer arithmetic is left to the compiler to decide. This time, both g++ and clang give me warnings, but only about deleting a void pointer. None of the two have any problems with the fact that I try to write and read beyond the allocated region. Even more interestingly, the tests run perfectly fine, the result of the function is the expected one, and everyone is happy! Not even the OS is complaining about this nonsense – hopefully, because I haven't exceeded the process's allocated memory.

Hopefully.

We have looked until now at examples of spatial memory safety issues, and things don't look good. What about temporal ones?

Anyone who's used pointers has had to deal with the need to remember to do two things after they are no longer needed: free the allocated memory and reset them to NULL. Both things are important because forgetting one of them leads to temporal memory safety issues: a dangling pointer that still has access to an area of memory that has been released, or a memory leak when the pointer has not been freed and maybe the pointer was reset so that the memory area is no longer accessible.

Take as an example the following function that initializes a pointer to int with a value, frees the memory, and then returns the value stored in the memory:

```
int danglingPointer() {
    int *aPointerToInt = new int(234);

    delete aPointerToInt;

    return *aPointerToInt;
}
TEST_CASE("Try dangling pointer"){
int result = danglingPointer();

CHECK_EQ(234, result);
}
```

Once again, the program compiles fine. There's no warning in g++ or clang. It also runs, but the test fails because the value stored in the memory at that address is not the expected one:

```
test.cpp:8: ERROR: CHECK_EQ( 234, result ) is NOT correct!
  values: CHECK_EQ( 234, 721392248 )
```

The value stored at that address changes at each subsequent call, giving me other results such as the following:

```
test.cpp:8: ERROR: CHECK_EQ( 234, result ) is NOT correct!
  values: CHECK_EQ( 234, 1757279720 )
test.cpp:8: ERROR: CHECK_EQ( 234, result ) is NOT correct!
  values: CHECK_EQ( 234, -1936531037 )
```

It's unexpectedly easy to use this value in a computation later in the code and return a weird value. It's also a way to find out what's in a memory area if you know a little bit about the computation performed and can pass repeated inputs.

Temporal memory safety issues are worse since it's harder to keep track of the lifetime of a pointer in the labyrinth of a large code base than to ensure that we aren't reading past its bounds. So, yes – unfortunately, memory issues can be a big problem in C++.

You'll have noticed, however, that all the previous examples have been in the old C++ style. We used naked arrays, naked pointers, and pointer arithmetic. These are all constructs that you should use very sparingly in modern C++, for these exact reasons. I can't say never use them, because there are specific situations when we need naked pointers and naked arrays, but nowadays, they tend to be limited to memory optimization or low-level programming. Even in these situations, you can usually introduce a clear boundary between the unsafe and the modern C++.

So, does modern C++ solve all these issues?

Modern C++ to the rescue

Let's revisit the preceding examples but replace the naked arrays and naked pointers with their STL equivalents, as recommended in modern C++.

First, the array bounds example. We simply replace the naked array with a `vector<int>` instance and we get the following function:

```cpp
int doSomeWork(int value1, int value2, int value3, int value4) {
vector<int> values;
values[0] = value1;
values[1] = value2;
values[3] = value3;
values[4] = value4;
return values[0] + values[1] + values[3] + values[4];
}
TEST_CASE("try vector bounds"){
int result = doSomeWork(1, 234, 543, 23423);

CHECK_EQ(1 + 234 + 543 + 23423, result);
}
```

Unfortunately, the result of running this example is not great. Neither g++ nor clang complains, and we get the following result when running the test:

```
TEST CASE:   try vector bounds
test.cpp:5: FATAL ERROR: test case CRASHED: SIGSEGV - Segmentation
violation signal
```

Is std::vector<> unsafe? Well, we still need to pay attention to the space allocated for it. We have a few options: initialize it properly, use the methods provided to append to the collection, or ask to reserve memory for a specific number of items. The first two are what I would typically use since they are less likely to lead to issues. But even the third option results in a passing test:

```
int doSomeWork(int value1, int value2, int value3, int value4) {
vector<int> values;
values.reserve(5);
values[0] = value1;
values[1] = value2;
values[3] = value3;
values[4] = value4;
return values[0] + values[1] + values[3] + values[4];
}
```

A pleasant surprise is the behavior of std::vector, at least on g++, after reserve. I tried to access values[2], not set in this example, and I got the value 0. This is much better than accessing the value previously stored in that memory block, and I imagine it's a feature of the default allocator used by std::vector. This difference is due to the undefined behavior of operator[], and it is avoidable by using the vector::at() method. Still, we had to do some work. So, we can still write code that leads to memory issues, even with the modern STL. Of course, if we quit monkeying around and use one of the easy methods, this problem disappears completely. If we use the initializer syntax, the vector is created based on the data passed in without us having to do any more counting:

```
int doSomeWork(int value1, int value2, int value3, int value4) {
vector<int> values{value1, value2, 0, value3, value4};
return values[0] + values[1] + values[3] + values[4];
}
```

Of course, this syntax makes us add all the elements to the vector rather than some of them, thus preventing an off-by-1 error. The alternative is adding the elements one by one:

```
int doSomeWork(int value1, int value2, int value3, int value4) {
vector<int> values;
values.push_back(value1);
values.push_back(value2);
values.push_back(0);
values.push_back(value3);
```

```
values.push_back(value4);
return values[0] + values[1] + values[3] + values[4];
}
```

As expected, this version works perfectly as well. The moral: use the boring constructs, and you'll get the expected behavior 99% of the time. This is a good mantra for coding in any programming language, but even more so in C++.

Let's look now again at the example that uses pointer arithmetic and void* to access memory outside of the bounds. This is how it looks:

```
int pointerBounds() {
int *aPointerToInt;
void *aPointerToVoid;
aPointerToVoid = new int();
aPointerToInt = (int*)aPointerToVoid;
*aPointerToInt = 234;
aPointerToInt = (int*)((char*)aPointerToVoid + sizeof(int));
*aPointerToInt = 2423;

int value = *aPointerToInt;
delete aPointerToVoid;

return value;
}
```

I've done my best to convert this code to use std::unique_ptr or std::shared_ptr, and I believe it's possible but it's extremely convoluted. The first problem is dealing with all the pointer conversions we are using. There's no easy way to convert std::unique_ptr<int> to std::unique_ptr<char>; the only way is to convert the value and get a new unique_ptr<> instance.

The second problem is that void* doesn't have a direct translation into std::shared_ptr<void>; you can use it but only by allocating the memory manually and passing a custom deleter function. So, while it's possible to write something resembling this code with the modern STL, it takes so much work that programmers will stick to the safe methods unless they have very specific needs.

We encounter the same situation with the dangling pointer example:

```
int danglingPointer() {
    int *aPointerToInt = new int(234);

    delete aPointerToInt;

    return *aPointerToInt;
}
```

There's no straightforward way to delete the smart pointer and then return the value. We could reallocate using a call to `unique_ptr::reset`, but that would use pointers again. The simplest translation into pure smart pointers looks as follows:

```
int danglingPointer() {
    unique_ptr<int> aPointerToInt = make_unique<int>(234);
    return *aPointerToInt;
}
```

Only this works exactly as it should: the value is returned correctly, and the memory is released. No dangling pointer by default!

We could make it a dangling pointer if we allocate it manually and pass in a deleter that does nothing to `std::unique_ptr<>`. There's no reason to do this in most situations, therefore I would expect most programmers to avoid this issue altogether. Add in the option to use `std::shared_ptr<>` in case you need multiple owners of the memory block, and your most common situations are sorted out.

We can conclude from all this that modern C++ is much safer, reducing a lot of the potential issues by default. But it still has its limits, which is what we will focus on next.

The limits of modern C++

Let's assume for a moment that we use only STL collections, we avoid pointers, and when we really need them, we use the smart pointers implemented in the standard library, and we write our types with memory safety in mind. Are we done?

Herb Sutter, one of the well-known members of the C++ standardization committee, has looked at this issue and at the more general issue of avoiding security issues in C++, in a blog post titled *C++ safety, in context* (`https://herbsutter.com/2024/03/11/safety-in-context/`) published on March 11, 2024. His conclusion is that it's too easy to write C++ code that by default has security and safety vulnerabilities. The article identifies four areas that need more attention: types, bounds, initialization, and lifetime. Then, he states that there are already some mechanisms in place in C++ 20: span, `string_view` concepts, and bound-aware ranges. What is missing from the language, as the article discusses next, is safety rules that are enabled by default but that programmers can turn off if needed.

Let's unpack all this information and give some examples.

First on the list, the new `std::span` introduced in C++20. It represents a contiguous sequence of objects, extracted from a naked array, `std::array`, a pointer with a size, `std::vector`, or `std::string`. Its big advantage is that it automatically deduces the size of the sequence, thus removing the common instance of off-by-1 errors. Thus, we now have a safe way to pass a subset of a collection into a function without the fear of messing up the sequence length. Also, it allows us to completely forbid pointer arithmetic and use `std::span` instead.

Second, string_view. A std::string_view instance allows us to have a read-only view on a string, thus eliminating another source of potential safety issues, with strings being modified where they shouldn't or with operations on strings that are prone to being unsafe.

Third, concepts. Concepts allow C++ programmers to define constraints upon generic functions and classes, thus enhancing the safety of the types. For example, one could request that the value passed in a generic function has a type that has both an addition and a subtraction method. Concepts are still under development, with improvements coming in C++ 26, but they already help solve a lot of potential safety issues.

Fourth, bound-aware ranges. The ranges library allows C++ programmers to write efficient functional programming-inspired operations that work on collections, thus eliminating another source of potential misuse. Ranges know their bounds and shield the developers from passing in every function the begin and end iterators.

These improvements, if used, have gone a long way from C++ 98. Still, things are missing. Remember the code that accessed an index in std::vector that did not reserve any memory and got a bad memory error at runtime? Let's take a look:

```
int doSomeWork(int value1, int value2, int value3, int value4) {
    vector<int> values;
    values[0] = value1;
    values[1] = value2;
    values[3] = value3;
    values[4] = value4;
    return values[0] + values[1] + values[3] + values[4];
}
```

The problem with this code is that we can happily access indexes beyond the allocated vector size while skipping the initialization for index 2. A possible solution to this issue would be the following:

- Enable a safemode compiler flag
- The compiler generates a range check upon every index access that verifies that 0 <= index < collection.size()
- We get no error at runtime because nothing happens when we try to call this code

Such a compile option could be enabled on existing code with no change and prevent unknown issues. Sure, some programmers will have an issue with this because of the potential for reducing performance. That's precisely why such an option should be either turned on by a compiler flag, or, even better, turned on by default with the option to turn it off by a compiler flag.

This shows that there's still more to do to make C++ memory safe.

There's still more to do

The standardization committee is currently working on a proposal called **safety profiles**, which allows a combined approach formed of compile enhancements, static analysis, and profiler tools to eliminate most of these safety issues. It is unclear when it will be done, and I for one don't envy their task. There are millions if not billions of lines of C++ code used today, and any proposal needs to have a minimal impact on the existing code, other than pointing out potential security issues. It must also affect performance as little as possible, given how important it is for many existing applications.

On the other hand, the urgency is clear. C++ has issues with memory safety, and it might end up on a blacklist for US government projects, and likely for other governments as well. Only time will tell when the issue is resolved and how it impacts the usage of the language.

Summary

We have seen in this chapter how it's too easy to write unsafe code by default in C++. Despite the improvements introduced by subsequent standards, by the STL collections and smart pointers, it's still likely that programmers will make mistakes with a potentially huge cost. Sure, there are ways to catch these mistakes: automated developer tests, exploratory tests, penetration testing, and so on. But the defaults of the language matter, and C++'s defaults are still unsafe.

After examining these issues, my only option is to conclude that C++ is still memory-unsafe by default and that writing memory-safe code requires continuous attention and the appropriate tools. The safety profiles that will hopefully arrive soon in the standard will most likely alleviate many of the issues, but there's still an unfathomable quantity of C++ code in the world that was written like it's still 2000. So, a mixed bag.

In the next chapter, we will examine the state of parallelism and concurrency in C++.

7

There's No Simple Way to Do Parallelism and Concurrency in C++

Unless we rethink OOP and FP

To do parallelism and concurrency in C++, we used to require either separate libraries (for example, Boost) or OS primitives. With the introduction of functional programming constructs, parallelism and concurrency have become easier, within certain constraints.

In this chapter, we're going to cover the following main topics:

- Defining parallelism and concurrency
- Common issues with parallelism and concurrency
- Functional programming to the rescue!
- The Actor Model
- What we can't do yet

Technical requirements

The code for this chapter is available on GitHub at https://github.com/PacktPublishing/Debunking-CPP-Myths, in the ch7 folder. The code has been compiled with Makefiles using g++ and C++ 20. The example regarding the Actor Model uses **C++ Actor Framework (CAF)** (https://www.actor-framework.org/) so you'll need to install it before working on it. On Ubuntu, it can be installed by running apt install libcaf-dev. The CAF version that's used in the examples is the stable Ubuntu version of the library: 0.17.

Defining parallelism and concurrency

My first computer was an HC-90, a ZX-80 clone built in Romania. I owned two versions: the first required a cassette player to load programs. Despite this inconvenience, it had a big advantage over its main competitor at the time, the CHIP computer, yet another ZX-80 clone built in Romania. You see, the CHIP computer required a cassette to load into its OS, while the HC-90 had enough EPROM memory to boot directly into a BASIC interpreter. The second version I owned was much better: it had a 5-inch floppy disk reader, which meant that you could load programs much faster.

In both versions, the BASIC interpreter was your interface with the computer, and since not many programs were available other than games, I spent some of my time in high school writing BASIC programs and playing games. Eventually, I realized that I wanted more than BASIC. I played a bit with graphics and sound, but the problem was that everything was very slow. This made me learn ZX 80 assembler, which was an adventure. It was very easy to make mistakes in assembler, which resulted in a reboot and the loss of all work. It wasn't a sustainable way to program, but it made me appreciate the programming luxuries of today much more. Imagine this: I can compile and run tests on my programs on my computer and save my changes to a source control system.

I knew back then that I wanted the graphics and sounds to feel faster. What I didn't realize was that I had a fundamental limitation: there was only one CPU (or one core, as we would say today), which meant that the graphics, sound, and logic code had to run sequentially. The CPU could receive a command to play a sound, then go to display some graphics, and then make some computations, and since there was a very short lag between the instruction and the actual sound playing or the image showing, it seemed as if these tasks were running in parallel. But they weren't: they were concurrent. You could observe this if you loaded the system to the maximum since the image and sound were no longer synchronized.

What would have happened if I had more processors or more cores to work with? Well, I could have defined various tasks that can be run on separate processors. A capable scheduler could take these tasks and run them in parallel to fill the capacity of the idle CPUs. If the tasks are well-defined, we can squeeze a lot of the power from the available cores and get the answer faster. This is **parallelism**.

A nuance to this definition, which will become useful in this chapter, comes from the Haskell community (see `https://wiki.haskell.org/Parallelism_vs._Concurrency`). They make a big distinction between a parallel functional program and a concurrent functional program, therefore presuming both programs use immutability. Parallel functional programs use cores to execute faster, but they're deterministic, and the meaning of the program is unchanged whether we execute it sequentially or in parallel. Contrast this with functional concurrent programs that run concurrent threads, each doing I/O operations, and that are non-deterministic since we don't know the order of operations.

Unfortunately, as is common in software development, these terms have a life of their own. You might encounter people who believe concurrency and parallelism are completely different things. In researching this matter, I came upon a conversation on StackOverflow stating the argument that concurrency is a superset of parallelism since concurrency refers to a set of methods that are used for managing multiple threads. And this may well be how some computer science books treat the topic.

The need for clarity constrains us to pick one definition. I'll pick the definition that closely matches my formative years of programming: **concurrency** is when multiple operations seem to run at the same time, while parallelism is when they do. This difference, while seemingly simple, leads to a difference in intent when designing the program. When we design a program expecting it to run in parallel, we define operations that can run in parallel and figure out their order. We try to squeeze time from the CPU by splitting a larger task into parts that can run independently, without them affecting each other much. The intent is different when we design a program expecting it to run concurrently: we optimize the response time by pushing the longer tasks into the dead times of the CPU.

Both these programming models are challenging, albeit in different ways. Let's remind ourselves of the common issues we face when using them.

Common issues with parallelism and concurrency

I'm convinced that the fundamental problem of software development is to mentally translate the static view of a system – the code – into its dynamic behavior, or what the program does when it runs. Programmers run code in their heads every time they're considering a change, often automatically but always at the expense of mental energy. This is one of the reasons why I believe practices such as **test-driven development** (TDD) and incremental design are useful; they allow us to move part of this mental energy spending from our brains to running the tests repeatedly.

This fundamental problem is already difficult for single threads, but for parallel or concurrent designs, it adds a new level of challenge. We not only need to imagine what the code will do but also how the code will interact with the other parts of the code that run at the same time. So, imagination and the brain energy required to make sense of parallel execution is the first challenge.

Then, there are the purely technical challenges.

When resources are shared, resource management becomes much harder, particularly when multiple threads can modify values. One thread might be using a value that was already changed by another thread, thus leading to wrong results. A memory address might be freed by one thread and then another thread attempts to read or write to it.

Sharing the same infrastructure isn't easy either. One thread might take all the resources due to a bug, thus blocking other threads for long periods. This is less of an issue when the program is formed of separate tasks using multiple cores, but it still leads to reduced performance since the separate tasks need to converge at some point. Threads could wait for one another indefinitely or until a timeout occurs.

Implementing programs that work with parallel or concurrent tasks from scratch is one of the most difficult things you might need to do as a programmer. I remember when I once debugged a synchronization issue between threads for a week, and I knew my technical lead and my project manager were starting to doubt my abilities. I didn't doubt myself, but I didn't like how long it took me to finally figure it out.

For this reason, libraries and patterns have appeared that help us implement concurrent and parallel programs. Most of them invite us to pass a function that represents a thread to a method that sorts out some of the complexities of thread synchronization. This is possible by separating the tasks that we might need into types of tasks. Additionally, architecture models such as MapReduce that are implemented by Hadoop and inspired by functional programming help us deal with large-scale parallelization.

As we can see, we can't discuss modern approaches to parallel programming without discussing the functional programming approach to it.

Functional programming to the rescue!

As we've seen, one of the problems with parallel and concurrent tasks is the shared access to resources. Functional programming, in its pure form, solves this out of the box through immutability. Since everything is immutable by default, and since any change to a value is made by pointing to a changed value instead of modifying the initial one, threads are never at risk of modifying data used by other threads. We discussed how to achieve this when we discussed the different paradigms available in C++.

But there's more: functional programming offers us parallelizable algorithms out of the box. The C++ standardization committee recognized this when introducing functional algorithms along with an execution policy that allows you to run operations on collections in parallel.

Let's look at a simple example: we want to compute the sum of squares of the values in a collection. The functional version of this type of algorithm is a typical map-reduce one: first, we pass in the initial collection and map it to a collection that contains the squares of the values, after which we reduce it by adding all the elements. In STL, these operations are implemented in `std::transform` and `std::reduce`, respectively. A version that combines them is available in `std::transform_reduce`, but we'll ignore it for now to make the example more relevant.

Here's what the function looks like:

```cpp
long long sumOfSquares(const vector<int> numbers){
    vector<long long> squaredNumbers(numbers.size());
    auto squareNumber = [](const long it ){ return it * it; };

    transform(numbers.begin(), numbers.end(), squaredNumbers.begin(),
squareNumber);

    return reduce(squaredNumbers.begin(), squaredNumbers.end(), 0);
}

TEST_CASE("sum of squares in parallel") {
        vector<int> numbers{234, 423, 345, 212, 112, 2412};

        CHECK_EQ(6227942, sumOfSquares(numbers));
}
```

The only thing we need to do to run these operations in parallel is to add a parameter to both functional algorithms that specifies the execution policy. The execution policy we'll use is `std::execution::par`, an instance of `std::execution_parallel` provided by the standard library that specifies that the algorithms need to run in parallel:

```
long long sumOfSquares(const vector<int> numbers){
    vector<long long> squaredNumbers(numbers.size());
    auto squareNumber = [](const long it ){ return it * it; };

    transform(std::execution::par, numbers.begin(), numbers.end(),
squaredNumbers.begin(), squareNumber);

    return reduce(std::execution::par, squaredNumbers.begin(),
squaredNumbers.end(), 0);
}
```

From this example, we can notice a few things.

First, it's very easy to switch between the different execution policies when you use functional programming. This enables us to fix issues related to parallelization more easily and to optimize code. Running the algorithms in parallel isn't necessarily better than sequential execution in all cases. It's likely that for small numbers or short collections, the resources that are used to start threads and manage them are larger than the time saved.

Second, we can use the execution policy as a parameter or as a general configuration. This would allow us to test that algorithms work sequentially in isolation from thread synchronization. It also allows us to decide what policy to use at runtime, depending on a few factors related to the input data.

Third, each of these execution policies imposes limitations on your code. For example, the parallel policy we've used here requires that the iterators aren't invalidated in the process, thus disallowing write access and the usage of `std::back_inserter`. Other execution policies are available in STL besides `std::execution::parallel_policy`, `std::execution::sequenced_policy:`, `std::execution::parallel_unsequenced_policy`, and `std::execution::unsequenced_policy`, with the remark that the standardization committee might add built-in policies for `std::parallel::cuda` and `std::parallel::opencl`. Each of these policies has its limitations and constraints, so the most portable code is what's used for maximum immutability and functional algorithms.

Fourth, the algorithms run in sequence, but each of them is parallelized. If we need to squeeze more from our computing resources, we either use the combined `std::transform_reduce` algorithm or write our own algorithm combining the two. Once again, it's important to realize that running code in parallel is a trade-off: some of the computing resources will be spent on starting and synchronizing threads, which for some configurations might not add a big benefit.

Finally, the fifth point is that the map-reduce pattern is very powerful. Any unary function can be used for `map` and any binary function can be used for `reduce`, and we can bind the parameters of functions that require more values until we get unary or binary functions. Maps and reduces can be chained in many ways. If you start looking at your programs as data in/data out, you'll notice that all our programs can be written as data in/functional transformations/data out, with many of the functional transformations being `map`/`reduce` operations. This realization leads to a very powerful programming model since we can turn parallelization on or off for all or parts of the algorithms. Occasionally, we may want to write our own algorithms that optimize parallelization for important parts of the code, but we get most of it for free.

The only catch is that we need to use immutable data and functional algorithms.

The design style we've discussed so far is data-centric since it focuses on the data structures and their transformations. As always when it comes to software design and architecture, we have the alternative to focus on behavior. Surely enough, a design style that splits the program into behaviors and allows for parallel programming has emerged in the form of the Actor Model.

The Actor Model

The world around us moves in parallel very naturally. Each tree, plant, or person does their own thing, and occasionally they interact, and things change for the parties involved. So, we already have a mental model of how parallel programs could work: separate entities that encapsulate their behavior and communicate somehow, on an infrastructure that ensures proper synchronization.

This idea led to the creation of the Actor Model in 1973 by Carl Hewitt. This model splits a program into actors that can do three things:

- Send messages to other actors
- Create new actors
- Define the behavior for the next message the actor receives

Each actor has an address that's conceptually similar to an email address, and actors can only communicate with the actors whose addresses they have. This address can be received in a message or obtained by creating a new actor.

The actor model separates the communication mechanism from the functionality of each actor. This has resulted in implementations that allow us to write highly parallelizable code without having to deal with thread primitives.

The oldest and most stable implementation for C++ is CAF (`https://www.actor-framework.org/`). A newer alternative is **Hiactor** from Alibaba (`https://github.com/alibaba/hiactor`). However, the best-known implementation comes from the Java world: the **Akka toolkit** (`https://akka.io/`).

Let's look at a simple example of implementing a chat between two actors using CAF. The following code defines the behavior of an actor as a Lambda, instantiates two chatting actors, and sends messages between them. Each actor writes their message to the console:

```
behavior chatter(event_based_actor* self, const string& name) {
return {
[=] (const string& msg) {
cout << name << " received: " << msg << endl;
}
};
}

void caf_main(actor_system& system) {
        auto alice = system.spawn(chatter, "Alice");
        auto bob = system.spawn(chatter, "Bob");

        scoped_actor self{system};
        self->send(alice, "Hello Alice!");
        self->send(bob, "Hello Bob!");

        self->send(alice, "How are you?");
        self->send(bob, "I'm good, thanks!");

        sleep_for(seconds(1));
}

CAF_MAIN()
```

Running this code leads to different outputs. The best one is the one we expect:

```
Bob received: Hello Bob!
Alice received: Hello Alice!
Alice received: How are you?
Bob received: I'm good, thanks!
```

However, running the code repeatedly leads to various results, as shown here:

```
Bob received: Hello Bob!
Bob received: I'm good, thanks!
Alice received: Hello Alice!
Alice received: How are you?
```

We can also receive even worse outputs:

```
Alice received: Hello Alice!
BobAlice received: How are you? received: Hello Bob!

Bob received: I'm good, thanks!
```

These results make it obvious that actors run in parallel. It also shows that parallel programming can only mask its complexity so much underneath the magic of these frameworks.

However, the actor model offers us a way to think about parallel programming in terms of objects that respond to requests and allows us to pick the type of actors we need and the type of communication that's most fit for our system. The preceding example shows an event-based actor that receives asynchronous messages, but the framework supports blocking messages and various types of actors, depending on their life cycle.

An advantage of the actor model is that we can distribute the actors on separate computers, thus allowing us to scale a model relatively easily. Of course, this means that we hit the challenges of distributed systems head-on from the very first line of code that uses this model.

With that, we've seen what's possible today within the standard library and by using the venerable actor model. But what still isn't possible?

What we can't do yet

As you can see, using parallel and concurrent code isn't as easy as *"Write the code you want and let the tools and compiler make sense of it."* Perhaps we'll be able to do this in the future with the intervention of AI, although based on my current experience using coding assistants, I have to say this seems very far away.

Instead, you must structure your code for the programming model you choose. And if you start by writing the code base as a single-threaded application and without using functional constructs, changing it will prove difficult. I see parallels between objects and actors and, in theory, it might be possible to turn each object into an actor and each method into an event, but this seems idealistic. The reality is that there are still a lot of things that can go wrong when we switch from a synchronous to an event-based system, and a lot of them are very difficult to debug and require a deep understanding not only of the actor model but also of the framework you're using for the actors.

Your best bet is to redesign applications within the paradigm you choose: either the data-centric functional one or the behavior-centric actor model.

With a data-centric paradigm, you look at the data in and at the set of transformations required to get to the desired output. Each of these transformations is immutable, therefore taking data as input and returning another data structure as output. As we've seen, each of these transformations is parallelizable. Occasionally, we'll need our own algorithms or to optimize some of the existing ones, after which we can write our own implementations that follow the same pattern. We can fine-tune the system using the execution policy and end up with a system that's highly customizable and relatively easy to optimize.

With a behavior-centric paradigm, you look at your objects as actors that receive messages. This is closer to the original view of Alan Kay on object-oriented programming. As documented in the email exchange at `https://www.purl.org/stefan_ram/pub/doc_kay_oop_en`, a vision focused not on classes but on messaging, and most closely implemented in Smalltalk. You build your application from the ground up using actors and their messaging mechanics and test that the output is what you expect. You need to know about the types of actors and the types of messaging available in detail so that you can pick the ones that fit your problem. As shown in this example, actors don't necessarily guarantee the order of execution, which may or may not be a concern for your system. This leads to a highly scalable system, but one that's more difficult to understand and debug.

This means we can't automatically translate applications that are written to be synchronous and single-threaded into parallel or concurrent systems. Most of the time, a redesign is required.

Summary

Is there a simple way to do parallelism and concurrency in C++? It's easier than it used to be, in that we rarely need to create our own threads and deal with their synchronization unless we're building infrastructure code. We don't necessarily need external libraries or tools since STL supports parallel execution for many algorithms.

However, we can't avoid the essential complexity of parallel and concurrent programming. Programs that take advantage of it need to be structured differently, have additional constraints, and require a different mindset and a different design paradigm. This isn't a C++ problem – it's a problem for any attempt at parallelism.

Therefore, the conclusion is that it can be simpler than it used to be if we make the right choices, but it's still very complicated.

In the next chapter, we'll ask the question of whether the fastest form of C++ is inline assembly.

8

The Fastest C++
Code is Inline Assembly

Lower than this you should not get

In the fast-paced world of C++ developers, where efficiency is paramount, optimizing code to squeeze out every last drop of performance has always been a fascinating challenge. This journey often takes developers down to the very roots of computing, where C++ meets assembly language, and every CPU cycle counts.

Circa three decades ago, during the wild 90s, programmers frequently had to manually craft every byte of executable code, often diving into the murky waters of assembly language (and even lower) to achieve the desired performance. These early pioneers of optimization developed techniques that, while rudimentary by today's standards, laid the groundwork for understanding the power and limitations of both C++ and assembly.

This exploration delves into the specifics of optimizing a seemingly simple task, lighting up a pixel on the screen, by comparing handcrafted and optimized assembly routines from three decades ago with the modern-day output of advanced compilers such as Clang, GCC, and MSVC. As we navigate through the evolution of compilers, we'll see how the balance between human intuition and machine-generated optimization has shifted, offering new insights into the ever-evolving relationship between the code we write and the machine that ultimately runs our programs. As a side note, in this chapter, we'll focus on Intel's x86 family of processors and delve into specific features, while leaving coverage of the ARM architecture for another book, potentially by a different author.

In this chapter, you will learn the following:

- How to use assembly code to speed up your routines
- How not to use assembly code and trust your compiler's optimizer to come up with the fastest solution

Light me a pixel

Circa 30 years ago, at the nearer end of the wild 90s, the author of these lines spent quite a significant time optimizing code that was supposed to run as fast as possible, consuming the least amount of resources while showing incredible spinning graphics on a screen (there was also scrolling involved, too, and other not relevant calculations).

These applications were called demos (intros, etc.) and showcased some spectacular graphical effects, backed by a strong mathematical background, and had an in-house developed graphical engine; in those days, there was no DirectX to take all those nasty low-level details off your plate, so all had to be done by hand. Methods for pixel color calculation, color palette setting, vertical retrace of the CRT screen, and flipping of back and front buffers were all coded by hand, using C++ of the 90s and some assembly language routines for the time-critical bits.

One of these methods was putting a pixel on the screen, which, in its simplest incarnation of the method, looked like this:

```
void putpixel(int x, int y, unsigned char color) {
    unsigned char far* vid_mem = (unsigned char far*)0xA0000000L;
    vid_mem[(y * 320) + x] = color;
}
```

I'll spare you the very low-level details such as how segment/offset memory worked 30 years ago. Instead, imagine that the following apply:

- You are using DOS (in 1994, in the wild-far-eastern part of Europe, almost everyone who had a PC used DOS – kudos to the 0.1 percent of early Linux adopters)

- You are also using a special graphic mode, 0x13 (almost all the games used this mode because it allowed 256 colors to be drawn on the screen using the mysterious 320 by 200 resolution, whose origins only IBM engineers from 40 years ago know)

In this case, if you put a byte at the 0xA000 segment and a specific offset, the graphic card will light up a pixel at the specific coordinates, which can be obtained from the preceding formula.

Now, after several iterations of the code, the aforementioned programmer observed that the routine was not that optimal, and it could have benefited from some optimizations.

Please bear with me; the code that was generated by the affordable compiler (the one you just copied from the disk that we mentioned in *Chapter 2* of the book) is in the following screenshot:

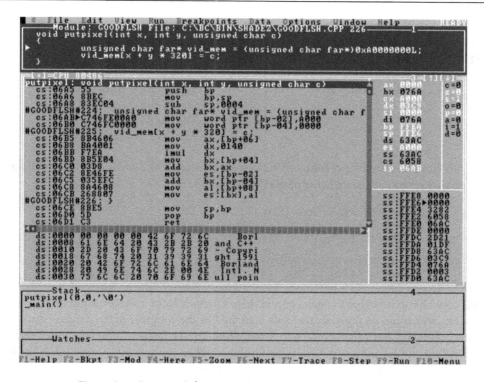

Figure 8.1 – Everyone's favorite Turbo Debugger from 30 years ago

Now, this looks pretty wild, considering the age of it, but again, we need just a bit of patience, and all the mystery surrounding why it's here will be revealed. You see, we were discussing how the code generated by the compiler is far from being optimal.

Let's take a moment to consider this piece of code. After giving it some thought, especially from the perspective of someone familiar with assembly language, which is becoming increasingly rare these days, it might be clear to them that the compiler didn't struggle as much as we might expect.

The following is the assembly code that the compiler generated for the `putpixel` routine:

```
putpixel    proc    near
  push bp                  ; Save the base pointer on the stack
  mov bp, sp          ; Set the BP to the current stack pointer
  sub sp, 4             ; Reserve 4 bytes for local variables
  mov word ptr [bp-2], 40960       ; Store 0xA000 at [bp-2]
  mov word ptr [bp-4], 0              ; Store 0 at [bp-4]
  mov ax, word ptr [bp+6]    ; Load the y-coordinate into AX
  mov dx, 320           ; Load the screen width into DX
  imul dx        ; Multiply AX (y-coord) by DX (screen width)
  mov bx, word ptr [bp+4]    ; Load the x-coordinate into BX
```

```
add bx, ax        ; Add y*screen width (AX) to BX (x-coord)
mov es, word ptr [bp-2]             ; Load 0xA000 into ES
add bx, word ptr [bp-4]         ; Final pixel address in BX
mov al, byte ptr [bp+8]     ; Load the color value into AL
mov byte ptr es:[bx], al               ; Light the pixel!
mov sp, bp                       ; Restore the stack pointer
pop bp                           ; Restore the base pointer
ret                              ; Return from the procedure
```

For those not familiar with the notation, `[]` represents the data at the address given in the square parentheses, so the parameters are being passed in like this:

- The x coordinate of the pixel (from `[bp+4]`)
- The y coordinate of the pixel (from `[bp+6]`)
- The color value to set (from `[bp+8]`)

Indeed, the code as is contains a lot of unnecessary memory access to move data around, when those operations could have been kept in registers, and there is quite a lot of unnecessary access to various memory areas, which can be skipped. The code compiled by the compiler of the day generated code that was easy to debug, but which could have been written much neater. Compilers today generate the same kind of code, having a very similar performance, when compiling in Debug mode but once you switch them to optimized Release mode, they will do magic.

Modern CPUs are highly complex beasts; when running in protected mode, they employ various techniques, such as out-of-order execution, instruction pipelining, and other techniques that make really low-level performance analysis nowadays quite difficult to nail down properly... but old machines were much simpler! Or just use DOS on a modern computer and you will get the same feeling.

Not considering that protected mode was introduced in the early 80286 processors, DOS simply could not handle it (and still can't), so it stuck to what it knew best: running programs in real mode. While running in real mode, the processor just executed one instruction after the other, and there even was an instruction table explaining how many cycles each instruction would take[1].

After spending a significant amount of time consulting those tables, we came to the conclusion that one `imul` can take longer than two shifts and an add on a processor of those days (the same conclusion was drawn by several other thousands of programmers all around the world after consulting those tables, but we felt that we must be some kind of local heroes for discovering this feature).

Considering that 320 is a very nice number, as it is the sum of 256 and 64, after several rounds of optimizations, we came up with the following slightly more optimized version for the routine:

```
void putpixel(int x, int y, unsigned char c) {
  asm {
```

---

1   https://zs3.me/intel.php

```
mov ax, 0xA000        // Load 0xA000 (VGA mode 13h) into AX
mov es, ax            // Set ES to the video segment (0xA000)
mov dx, y             // Load the y-coordinate into DX
mov di, x             // Load the x-coordinate into DI
mov bx, y             // Copy the y-coordinate into BX
shl dx, 8     // Multiply DX by 256 (left shift by 8 bits)
shl bx, 6     // Multiply BX by 64 (left shift by 6 bits)
add dx, bx // Add those, effectively multiplying y by 320
add di, dx    // Add the calculated y to DI (pixel offset)
mov al, c             // Load the color value into AL
stosb                         // Light the pixel
} }
```

It is not the most optimal routine that one can come up with for this purpose, but for our specific requirements, it was more than enough.

A significantly reduced amount of direct memory access (which was considered slow even in the old days), the lengthy multiplication by 320 using `imul` changed to multiplication by 256 (this is the shift to the left by 8 operations: `shl dx, 8`), and 64 (the same by 6), then a sum, which still adds up to fewer cycles than the power-consuming multiplication.

And thus, the foundation was laid for the myth that if you really want fast code, you have to write it yourself at the lowest possible level.

As an interesting mental exercise, let's jump forward in time 30 years, skipping several generations of compilers. If we feed the C++ routine as it is to a modern compiler (for our purpose, we have used Clang – the latest at the time of writing was version 18.1 – but using GCC will get also a very similar result, just using a different set of registers), we get the following output:

```
putpixel(int, int, unsigned char):
  movzx eax, byte ptr [esp + 12]
  mov ecx, dword ptr [esp + 4]
  mov edx, dword ptr [esp + 8]
  lea edx, [edx + 4*edx]
  shl edx, 6
  mov byte ptr [edx + ecx + 40960], al
```

This is way shorter than the one we concocted for our purpose and considered optimal targeting the processors from 3 decades ago, but processors have evolved a lot in the last 30 years, and a lot more advanced features have come in, with new commands (some more words about new commands a bit late in this chapter, so stay tuned) and we find it extremely satisfying how compilers' optimization routines have resolved the multiplication with that nice number, 320.

C++ compilers have evolved significantly over the past few decades, from their humble beginnings as Turbo C++ or Watcom C++, becoming incredibly sophisticated and capable of performing a wide range of optimizations that were previously unimaginable due to mostly hardware constraints because, well... 640 KB should be enough for everyone.

Modern compilers are no longer just simple translators from human-readable code to machine code; they have become complex systems that analyze and transform code in ways that can drastically improve performance and memory usage, taking into consideration some aspects that are all meant to help developers bring out the best of their source.

GCC, Clang, and MSVC all employ advanced optimization techniques such as inlining functions, loop unrolling, constant folding, dead code elimination, and aggressive optimizations that span across entire modules or programs, since, at their stage, they have an overview of the entire application, allowing these high-level optimizations.

On a side note, these compilers also leverage modern hardware features, such as vectorization and parallelism, to generate highly efficient machine code that can target a specific processor. We will soon see how these optimizations fall into place when we present the example in the next section, where we take a mundane task and let our compilers churn through it.

But till we reach that stage, just one more use case from 30 years ago. The subtitle of this chapter is *Lower than this you should not get*. Certainly, we meant coding at a lower level, not something else, and right now, we will proudly contradict ourselves. Again. Here is the contradiction: *in certain situations, you really should get to a level lower than assembly.*

If you are familiar with graphic programming, then I suppose you are familiar with the concept of double-buffering and back-buffering. The back buffer is an off-screen buffer (memory area, with the same size as the screen) where all the rendering (drawing of graphics) happens first. When the rendering is done, the back buffer is copied onto the screen in order to show the graphics, the back buffer is cleared, and the rendering restarts. At some time in history, Tom Duff, a Canadian programmer, invented a wonderful piece of ingenious code that was meant to accomplish exactly this task; the name of it is Duff's device and it has been discussed several times in several forums, and we are not going to discuss it now. Instead, we will show you the "highly optimized" code that we used to copy data from the back buffer to the screen:

```
void flip(unsigned int source, unsigned int dest) {
  asm {
      push ds    // Save the current value of the DS register
      mov ax, dest    // Load the destination address into AX
      mov es, ax      // Copy the value from AX into the ES
      mov ax, source    // Load the source address into AX
      mov ds, ax        // Copy the value in AX into the DS
      xor si, si  // Zero out the SI (source index) register
      xor di, di    // Zero out the DI (destination index)
      mov cx, 64000      // Load 64000 into the CX register
```

```
                    // (this is the number of bytes to copy)
    rep movsb          // Run  the`movsb` instruction 64000
        // times (movsb copies bytes from DS:SI to ES:DI)
    pop ds          // Restore the original value of the DS
  } }
```

The preceding trick consists of the `rep movsb` instruction, which will do the actual copying of bytes (`movsb`), repeated (`rep`) 64,000 times, as indicated by the CX register (we all know that 64,000 = 320 x 200; that's why they are magic numbers).

This code works perfectly given the circumstances. However, there is an opportunity for a tiny bit of optimization; you see, we are using a decent processor – at least, an 80386. Unlike its predecessor, the 80286, which was a pure 16-bit processor, the 80386 is a huge step forward, since it is the first 32-bit x86 processor coming from Intel. So, what we can do is the following: instead of copying 64,000 bytes using `rep movsd`, we can harvest the opportunities given by our high-end processor and put to use the new 32-bit framework, keywords, and registers. What we do is move 16,000 double words (we all know that a byte is measured as 8 bits, two bytes are called a word, measuring 16 bits, and two words are called a double word, totaling 32 bits) because that is exactly what the new processor has support for: operation on 32-bit values. The newly introduced `movsd` command does exactly this: copies 4 bytes in one step, so that could be a speed-up of 4 times compared to our older code.

Our anecdotical C++ compiler, introduced at the beginning of this book, is Turbo C++ Lite. Unfortunately for us, Turbo C++ cannot compile code for anything other than processors below 80286, so we are stuck with 16-bit registers and some really inefficient register handling.

And here is where the lowest level of hack anyone can see in C++ code comes in – we simply add the bytes of the `rep movsd` command as hexadecimal values in the code:

```
xor di,di
mov cx,16000
db 0xF3,0x66,0xA5 //rep movsd
pop ds
```

Nothing is simpler and more eye-watering than seeing this in production code, right? Now, regardless that our compiler cannot compile code for 80386 because it's stuck in the Stone Age (pretty much like half of the chapter you are reading right now), we can still produce code that runs optimally on your processor. Please don't do this.

A note on the past

Now, you might ask why we even bother mentioning assembly language in 2024, when the major trends exhaust themselves concerning the widespread adoption of AI-driven development tools, the growth of low-code/no-code platforms, and the continued rise of the Nth iteration of various JavaScript modules that have exactly the same output as the previous one, except that the syntax is different.

Regardless that these are the loudest happenings in the IT world nowadays, assembly language is still not obsolete. It might not get as much focus as everyone's favorite Rust language (Alex will debate Rust in a later chapter if all goes according to plan), but there are still major business branches where the assembly is a must, and still essential in several hardware environments that require precise control, performance optimization, or direct hardware access, such as the following:

- **Embedded systems**: Microcontrollers and IoT devices often use assembly for efficient, low-level programming. There isn't too much power on these small devices; every bit counts.

- **Operating system (OS) development**: Bootloaders and critical parts of OS kernels require assembly for hardware initialization and management. To achieve this feat, either you work for a large corporation or start your own project. Linux is pretty much accounted for.

- **High-performance computing (HPC)**: Assembly is used for optimizing performance-critical code, particularly in scientific computing or custom hardware (e.g., FPGAs). To pursue this, you must find someone wanting to pay you to pursue this.

- **Security and reverse engineering**: Analyzing and exploiting binaries often involves understanding and writing assembly. This is the most lucrative of all, and the most realistic way of getting into assembly programming, unfortunately.

- **Firmware development**: BIOS/UEFI and low-level device drivers are commonly written in assembly for direct hardware interaction. Here, again, you must be on the payroll of a large corporation, although there are a few open source projects too (coreboot, libreboot, or just google free bios to get a decent list).

- **Legacy systems**: Maintaining older systems or working with retro computing often requires assembly. This is the ideal chance to blend both fun and suffering into one experience.

- **Specialized hardware**: DSPs and custom CPU architectures may need assembly for specialized, efficient processing.

Please don't dismiss assembly language just yet. It remains relevant and will continue to be as long as computers exist. For those who are interested in the topic, it has its place. Otherwise, you can stick to standard C++.

The sum of all numbers

Dearest esteemed reader. It is a truth universally acknowledged that all developers at some stage in their lives must go through a technical interview. There are various levels of interrogations: some just on the level of "Please tell me something about yourself" (these are the hardest), while some go deeper and might even ask you to write some code on a blackboard or even a computer.

One of the programs that very frequently comes up in interview questions is to write some code that will calculate the sum of a series of numbers sharing a certain peculiarity, for example, the sum of all even numbers, the sum of all numbers divisible by, let's say, five, or the sum of odd numbers in a specific interval.

For simplicity's sake, let's stick to something simple: the sum of all odd numbers up to 100. The following quick program delivers exactly this:

```cpp
#include <cstdio>
int main() {
    int sum = 0;
    for (int i = 1; i <= 100; ++i) {
        if (i % 2 != 0) {  // Check if the number is odd
            sum += i;       // Add the odd number to the sum
        }
    }
    printf("The sum is: %d\n",sum);
    return 0;
}
```

Not an overly complicated program: just iterate through the numbers; check whether they are odd; if yes, add their value to the final sum; and, in the end, print out the sum (for everyone interested, the sum of odd numbers from 1 to 100 is exactly 2,500).

But our clear thinking was clouded by the well-known fact (at least, for C++ programmers) that the fastest C++ code is inline assembly, so we decided to sacrifice the portability and understandability of our program on the altar of speed and rewrite the main part of it using assembly language. Because, well, that is the fastest. Here is our attempt at this, using AT&T assembly syntax, just to demonstrate the widely available assembly dialects we can embed in a non-standard compliant C++ program:

```cpp
#include <cstdio>
int main() {
    int sum = 0;
    int i = 1; // Start with the first odd number
    __asm__ (
        "movl $1, %[i]\n"    // Initialize i to 1
        "movl $0, %[sum]\n" // Initialize sum to 0
        "loop_start:\n"
        "cmpl $100, %[i]\n"    // Compare i with 100
        "jg loop_end\n"        // If i > 100, exit the
        "addl %[i], %[sum]\n" // sum += i
        "addl $2, %[i]\n"     // i += 2
        "jmp loop_start\n"     // Repeat the loop
        "loop_end:\n"
        : [sum] "+r" (sum), [i] "+r" (i)
    );
    printf("The sum is: %d\n", sum);
    return 0;
}
```

Just a quick presentation of what the assembly code does, because I hope the other lines of code are self-explanatory.

Here is the assembly code breakdown:

1. `"movl $1, %[i] \n"`: This instruction sets i to 1. Although i was already initialized to 1 in the C++ code, this explicitly sets it again in assembly for clarity.

2. `"movl $0, %[sum] \n"`: This sets the sum to 0, ensuring that the sum starts from 0 in the assembly code. We have to admit that these two initializations are not required, but we wanted them to be a gentle introduction to the assembly code so as not to scare you away.

3. `loop_start`: This is just a label, and needs no further clarification.

4. `"cmpl $100, %[i] \n"`: Compares i with 100. The comparison is used to check whether i has reached or exceeded 100.

5. `"jg loop_end\n"`: If i is greater than 100, the program jumps to loop_end, exiting the loop.

6. `"addl %[i], %[sum] \n"`: Adds the current value of i to sum. This accumulates the sum of all odd numbers up to 99.

7. `"addl $2, %[i] \n"`: Increments i by 2 to move to the next odd number (e.g., $1 \rightarrow 3 \rightarrow 5$, etc.).

8. `"jmp loop_start\n"`: Jumps back to the start of the loop to repeat the process.

9. `loop_end`: This is the label where the program jumps when i exceeds 100, effectively ending the loop.

The weirdly looking `"+r"` (sum) and `"+r"` (i) parts are constraints that tell the compiler to treat sum and i as read-write variables, meaning their values can be both read from and written to during the assembly operations.

As a first drawback, the readability and understandability of the code have suffered exponentially. We intentionally use the AT&T syntax for assembly because it is much more cumbersome and harder to comprehend, and we want you to suffer with it and remember never to use assembly in your code unless you know what you're doing, and then you're excused.

Secondly, this code is not portable anymore because there is no such thing as __asm__ under Visual C++; they used __asm back in the day (or more recently, at the beginning of this chapter, Turbo C demonstrated the introduction of the asm keyword). And since we are here, the C++ standard does not include a common assembly block identifier because assembly language syntax is compiler- and platform-specific, and inline assembly is an extension rather than a core part of the language. You have been warned. I really hope that the preceding statement managed to entirely discourage you from ever considering writing assembly code in the body of your C++ function, regardless of the presence of the non-standard keyword to enable you to do this.

But now that we are here, courtesy of gcc.godbolt.org, we have asked the major compilers to churn through the original little C++ program (with no assembly incursion at all) at various optimization levels because we feel the urge to demonstrate to you that, indeed, entirely skipping the assembly language at this stage is the wisest decision you can take.

The first one to demonstrate how efficient the compiler is in generating optimal C++ code is Microsoft Visual C++. Microsoft's own tiny, squishy C++ compiler has several options to generate and optimize the generated code[2], but we have a saying here: the shorter the code, the faster it runs. So, we have explicitly told the compiler to generate the shortest code (/O1), which is the following:

```
`string' DB 'The sum is: %d', 0aH, 00H ; `string'
_main PROC
  xor ecx, ecx  ; Clear the ECX register (set ECX to 0)
  xor edx, edx  ; Clear the EDX register (set EDX to 0)
  inc ecx       ; Increment ECX, setting it to 1
$LL4@main:
  test cl, 1    ; Test the least significant bit of CL
                ; (ECX) to check if ECX is odd or even
  lea eax, DWORD PTR [ecx+edx] ; Load the effective
                ; address of ECX + EDX into EAX
  cmove eax, edx; If the zero flag is set
                ; (ECX was even), move EDX into EAX
  inc ecx       ; Increment ECX by 1
  mov edx, eax  ; Move the value in EAX to EDX
                ; (update EDX for the next iteration)
  cmp ecx, 100  ; Compare ECX with 100
  jle SHORT $LL4@main ; Jump to the start of the loop
                ; (loop until ECX > 100)
  push edx      ; Push the final value of EDX (the sum)
                ; after the loop onto the stack
  push OFFSET `string' ; Push the offset of the string
  call _printf  ; Call the printf function
  pop ecx       ; Clean up the stack (remove string)
  pop ecx       ; Clean up the stack (remove EDX)
  ret 0         ; Return from the _main function
_main ENDP
```

Interestingly, the assembly output from MSVC is very much in line with the one we concocted by hand; it has a loop, a bit differently dealing with the various registers based on whether we are currently dealing with an odd or even number, but besides this, it's similar to the one we wrote.

---

2   https://learn.microsoft.com/en-us/cpp/build/reference/o-options-optimize-code?view=msvc-170

Using the other combinations for optimization flags (/Ox, /O2, and /Ot) for MSVC did not produce a very different code, just a slightly different assignment of the registers, but nothing that would make us say VOW!

After switching to GCC (14.1) in order for it to churn through our simple code, we noticed that for the optimization levels of -O1 and -O2, the code generated was very similar to the one generated by MSVC: it had a variable, churned through the numbers, and made some test for oddness and sum. That's it, not black magic... unlike the code that was generated for -O3.

Using this flag, we were surprised to see how the **single instruction, multiple data (SIMD)** instructions were being pulled in by the compiler, in order to increase the speed, and the unexpected feature this compiler pulled in was that it calculated the sum of elements in an evolving 4-element array, starting with the values {1, 2, 3, 4} and incrementing each element by 4 over 25 iterations using SIMD instructions. The accumulated sum was stored in a SIMD register, and after the loop, it was reduced to a single integer, supplying the correct result.

The assembly code produced for this was simply too long (more than three pages), and we decided not to publish it here because it would have been useless, but as a fact of curiosity, we mentioned it.

The next compiler that we checked for how it deals with our simple C++ program is Clang. At this stage (meaning after the long SIMD instruction dump from GCC with -O3), we did not expect anything spectacular, but we had a surprise.

Even at -O1, Clang greeted us with the following, may I say quite short code:

```
main:
    push rax
    lea rdi, [rip + .L.str]
    mov esi, 2500
    xor eax, eax
    call printf@PLT
    xor eax, eax
    pop rcx
    ret
.L.str:
    .asciz "The sum is: %d\n"
```

What a surprise! It seems that Clang did all the calculations behind the scenes, and just simply put the result in the compiled binary. More optimized than this it cannot be. We were really thrilled that compilers have matured and grown into these clever beasts, so this tantalized us to check whether other compilers can be clever like this, too.

GCC exposes the same behavior at -O3, but surprisingly, only if we want to summarize odd numbers up to 71. At 72, something breaks inside and churns out again the long list of SIMD assembly sources.

We could not convince MSVC under any circumstance, combinations of numbers and parameters to go the Clang way, and precalculate the number required to print out the sum of odd numbers, so we just concluded that it cannot. Maybe it will be implemented in the next version, what do you say Microsoft Visual C++ developers?

A glimpse into the future

There is a phrase circulating amongst C++ developers that goes along the lines of *today's compiler optimizations are the best we've ever managed to cobble together and a not-so-gentle reminder of just how much better they could be.*

Taking into consideration that this book was written in 2024 (hopefully, it will be published in 2025, and if all goes according to plan, in 2027, it will be obsolete, and we will get a commission to come up with a more up-to-date version of it), we have a pretty clear overview of what is happening in the world today.

However, if you are reading this book while someone tries to grow potatoes on a different planet and the walls of your building are covered by graffitied monkeys, then you might have had some insights on how far the compilers have come in the last 10 years. Actually, it might even happen that Microsoft's own (yes, we know, tiny, squishy) C++ compiler managed to grow up to the stage where it can calculate the sum of a few numbers before compilation and GCC is not throwing a tantrum at 72. Even for a short, simple program like the one we have.

Welcome to the future.

One instruction to rule them all

Dear reader. In our previous section of this chapter, unfortunately, we exhausted the only pompous introduction we could borrow from various cultural sources concerning technical interviews, career and life choices, and whether should we take the red pill or the blue one, so let's focus our attention on more technical questions that our candidates might face at a technical interview (the word technical appears four times in this short introductory paragraph).

One of these questions, served to the author of these lines a few years ago, was to write a short code snippet that will count the number of 1 bits (the on bits) in a 32-bit integer. Let's draft up a quick application to do this:

```
int countOneBits(uint32_t n) {
    int count = 0;
    while (n) {
        count += n & 1;
        n >>= 1;
    }
    return count;
}
```

Here's what happens. Firstly, we initialize a counter, starting with 0. The next step is to loop through the bits. While n is non-zero, we add the least significant bit of n to the counter (n&1 gives us this value). Following this, we shift n right by one bit (discarding the least significant bit).

Once all bits are processed (when n becomes 0), return the total count of 1 bits. Not a very complicated process, just raw work.

It seems that this procedure of counting bits in numbers must be of a very peculiar interest in computing circles, such as for the purpose of error detection and correction, data compression, cryptography, algorithmic efficiency, digital signal processing, hardware design, and performance metrics, so no wonder it managed to creep itself into the STL (C++ STL, which is the standard template library) too in the form of std::popcount from C++ 20.

The interesting part of the story is that not only in the STL do we find this handy operation, but it was deemed so useful that it even exists at the level of the processors, under the infamous POPCNT mnemonic. Infamous it is, due to the fact that in 2024, it was effectively used in hindering the installation of Windows 11 on older machines that were not officially supported [3].

But what that means for our candidate, who has to write code to impress the interviewers, is that they can simply replace the complicated code from before with the following very handy snippet:

```
int countOneBits(uint32_t n) {
    return std::popcount(n);
}
```

Not forgetting to include the <bit> header, after feeding the preceding program into gcc.godbolt.org's compilers, we get a strange mishmash of results. The code compiled by GCC, regardless of the optimization level, always generates a variation of the following:

```
countOneBits(unsigned int):
  sub rsp, 8
  mov edi, edi
  call __popcountdi2
  add rsp, 8
  ret
```

So, the code at some level disappears from our eyes into a strange call deep inside the libraries offered by GCC, called __popcountdi2 [4]. In order to convince GCC to fully utilize the power of the processor that we are running the code on, we need to utilize some of the not-so-well-known command-line options, such as -march (or -mpopcnt for this specific purpose).

---

3   https://www.theregister.com/2024/04/23/windows_11_cpu_requirements/

4   https://gcc.gnu.org/onlinedocs/gccint/Integer-library-routines.html

According to the official documentation,[5] this command will select the appropriate processor instruction set in order to use the available extensions of the specific processor. Since, at this stage, we know that the POPCNT instruction was introduced in the early Core i5 and i7 processors, in the Nehalem family, we should simply specify the following to GCC: `-march=nehalem`. And now, not surprisingly, the compiler generates the following:

```
countOneBits(unsigned int):
  popcnt eax, edi
  ret
```

Interestingly, if we provide the compiler with just the `-mpopcnt` flag, then it generates an extra `xor eax, eax` (meaning it nulls the EAX register) so maybe we have witnessed some processor-specific extra optimizations by choosing the Nehalem architecture:

```
countOneBits(unsigned int):
  xor eax, eax
  popcnt eax, edi
  ret
```

We cannot squeeze more than this out of GCC; there is simply no lower level for this functionality, so we focus our attention on the next compiler on our list.

Without explicitly asking to optimize the code, Clang also generates a generic call to a `std::popcount` function, found somewhere in its libraries; however, explicitly asking to optimize the generated code, Clang at various levels of optimization yields the following:

```
countOneBits(unsigned int):
  mov eax, edi
  shr eax
  and eax, 1431655765
  sub edi, eax
  mov eax, edi
  and eax, 858993459
  shr edi, 2
  and edi, 858993459
  add edi, eax
  mov eax, edi
  shr eax, 4
  add eax, edi
  and eax, 252645135
  imul eax, eax, 16843009
  shr eax, 24
  ret
```

Surprising as it seems, there is a perfectly logical explanation for this code, found at the bit-twiddling site[6] of Sean Eron Anderson at Stanford. Not considering this extra detour, Clang behaves identically to GCC when it comes to handling architecture and specifying the subset of CPU extensions to use while generating code.

The last of the big three, Microsoft's own (we know, tiny, squishy) C++ compiler handles the situation very similarly to Clang. When asking to optimize the code while we specify an architecture that does not support the POPCNT instruction, it generates code like the one generated by Clang with low-level bit hacks, while if the architecture has support for the POPCNT instruction, it will adjust to the correct type and will call POPCNT for the proper parameters (/std:c++latest /arch:SSE4.2 /O1).

Good work, tiny, squishy compiler.

Summary

Myths related to C++ programming are shaped by the language's evolving history through time, the differences and various levels of mastery between the users of the language, and psychological needs within the developer community. Early C++ compilers, which often generated less optimal code compared to modern compilers, contributed to myths about the language's inefficiency and the necessity of manual optimization, such as rewriting entire routines using platform-specific assembly languages.

As compilers and language features have advanced, these myths persist, sometimes overshadowing modern best practices. This, combined with a culture of elitism and a sense of mastery among C++ programmers, reinforces outdated perceptions, even as C++ continues to be seen as a powerful and versatile language for serious, performance-critical applications.

In the upcoming chapter, we will host a beauty pageant of programming languages, quickly eliminating all but our favorite, and the process will culminate in the crowning of the undisputed queen, C++. Admittedly, our admiration for this language is so profound that one might suspect the contest was rigged from the very start.

---

6   https://graphics.stanford.edu/~seander/bithacks.html#Count-BitsSetParallel

9

C++ Is Beautiful

According to the mirror on the wall

Dear reader. In this chapter, we won't be focusing on teaching you specific concepts, techniques, or practical skills. Instead, our goal is to guide you through a different kind of experience, one that allows you to step back from the details and immerse yourself in the aesthetic aspects of coding.

This chapter is designed to inspire you to see code in a new light, to recognize the patterns, symmetry, and even the poetry that can emerge when we write code with thoughtfulness and care.

Beauty is a unique and personal experience because it arises from the intricate interplay of individual perception, emotional resonance, cultural influences, and personal identity. Each person interprets beauty through their own sensory and cognitive filters, shaped by their life experiences, memories, and cultural background. Emotional connections, mood, and personal taste further influence what one finds beautiful, making it a deeply subjective experience that reflects one's unique perspective on the world.

Some may find beauty in the fiery hues of a sunset over a Mediterranean island, while others might appreciate the crisp, cold allure of Scandinavian fjords. It is all personal.

So, while there may not be concrete lessons or objectives in this chapter, it offers a unique opportunity to connect with the craft of coding on a more emotional and intellectual level. Through this journey, we hope you'll come to see code not just as a means to an end but as something inherently beautiful in its own right.

In this chapter, you will experience that there is:

- Nothing new to learn here...

- ... except the appreciation of beauty...

- ... while crafting code with techniques in mind that may disqualify you from ever sitting in front of a keyboard while writing professional code in an enterprise environment

In search of beauty

Each programming language is a unique work of art, beautifully distinct in its design, philosophy, and the possibilities it offers; just as diverse are the programmers who use them, each bringing their own preferences, creativity, and personality to the craft.

Some developers are drawn to the elegant simplicity and structure of Python, relishing the clarity and expressiveness that its neatly organized whitespace brings to their code. Others, however, find their joy in languages such as Forth, where they can freely push and pop the stack with precision having full control and conciseness of such low-level manipulation, while seemingly enjoying the challenge of constructing powerful systems with minimalistic syntax. Now really, is there anyone using Forth anymore?

And then there are the bold adventurers who embrace the enigmatic world of Lisp, using its infamous long list of insipid and stubborn parenthesis. To these programmers, the apparent monotony of the syntax is a gateway to a rich and expressive metaprogramming landscape, where they can manipulate code as data in ways that feel almost alchemical, not to mention that they have direct access to Emacs.

Last but not least, there are those of us, the tribe of C++ programmers, who think the magical beauty of a program can fully be expressed by the following line:

```
auto main()->int{return<:]<class _>(_)->_<%return 7;}(1);%>
```

What more C++ beauty do we need on this planet? A line of code that looks like a series of winking smileys, and in the end, it returns the lucky number seven to the caller. There is not a huge amount of technicality lying in the preceding code, just a plain lambda returning a number, and to confuse you, dear reader, we have used the trailing returning type for the `main`, because why not?

Also, to add an even higher level of obscurity to our snippet, we have used, just for the sheer beauty of them, the infamous C++ digraphs. Unfortunately for them, the notorious trigraphs were deprecated in C++17 so we could not use them to spice up our code snippet. Actually, we could have used them, but we just wouldn't dare.

All that mayhem and confusion done in one line only. The real question that comes is can we make this even more ~~cumbersome~~ beautiful for you, dear reader, to read? And certainly, the answer to this certain question is a certain yes. And can we build it? Yes, we can! Almost... But firstly, we just have to get rid of the numbers, because hey...

Who likes numbers?

... or more specifically, who needs numbers? Numbers can be highly confusing to people due to their abstract nature, and the fact that we don't really need them in our everyday mundane life, which does not require higher-level thinking and the ability to grasp symbolic representations, makes them almost meaningless.

Maybe this is why some tribes in the Amazon jungle didn't even invent all of them (yes, I'm pointing at you, Munduruku tribe[1]). You have notions for none, one, two, up to five ... and then many. If it is enough for you, I can live with it.

Let's apply the ancient wisdom of the Amerindian people to our programming quest: to come up with the most beautiful C++ code snippet the world can see today. So, let's get rid of those pesky numbers, keeping just 0 and 1 (for the sake of the almighty bits so that they don't feel excluded), and let's go tribal with the following code snippet:

```
#define __(...)sizeof(int[]){0,\
                             ##__VA_ARGS__}/sizeof(int)-1
auto main()->int{return<:]<class _>(_)->_<%return
__(_(), _(), _(), _(), _(), _(), _()) ;}(__()) ;%>
```

Oh, the sheer beauty of it. It brings tears of joy to our eyes, doesn't it? Arguably, some picky programmers might have made some vitriolic comments about readability, maintainability, standard compliance, and so on... especially if they are using Microsoft's (tiny, squishy) C++ compiler, which flatly refuses to compile the preceding code. But we rejoice with trembling that we made one of the compilers break, while all the other major players happily digest it and compile.

But the code unfortunately contains a lot of duplicates, which we don't really like. Nor do we need duplicates, so we should also get rid of at least one of them, shouldn't we? Or all of them, why not?

Because that is the real beauty of the C++ language. The capability to always redefine yourself, to provide a better version of the code at all costs, not considering the sacrifice made. Death to readability. Death to maintainability! Long live the free code of chaos, mayhem, and confusion!

So, brave warriors, our quest has been laid, prepare arms (I mean keyboards), and let's save those bytes, just like the following code snippet shows us:

```
#define $$ sizeof
#define $ return
#define $_ int
#define __(...)$$($_[]){0,##__VA_ARGS__}/$$($_)-1
auto main()->$_<%$<::><class _>(_)->_<%$
__(_(), _(), _(), _(), _(), _(), _()) ;%>(__()) ;%>
```

Just look again at the sheer beauty of it. Again, the power of C++ shines through the dark clouds, like a thousand supernovae, and makes possible everything our heart desires, such as replacing a key element of the language, for example, the return keyword with a $ sign. Not that it is part of the standard character set the language specified as the valid character set, but we will have a discussion about this, and some bears, a little bit later.

---

1   https://www.amazon.com/Alexs-Adventures-Number-land-Alex-Bellos/dp/1408809591

But look at the bright side of the glass. At least we did not write the following code:

```
#define return(...) main
#define main(...) int
main(7)(return(7))(){
    return 7;
}
```

We have to admit, we contemplated writing it and adding it to the book, but after a glimpse at the future, we just thought that everything has its limits. Even the resilience of the most seasoned developers when it comes to nonsense (but regardless, fun) code.

This is highly possibly the most evil piece of code we will present in this book because the level of evilness is comparable to the level of pain felt when you try to write a properly parenthesized Lisp program. Because what happens if you remove a parenthesis because there are too many, or, God forbid, add another one because you think it'd be a great idea? Believe me, dear reader, just don't dare.

So, please pretend that the preceding code is not in the book, and even if it is, you haven't seen it. And even if you have seen it, you wouldn't dare change the number of parenthesis in it.

Enough of the piece of evilness; now it is time to return to our previous code, which is in the competition for the most beautiful piece of C++ code this book can present.

If only we could make it just a bit shorter, more concise, and more expressive, such as removing those ugly `define` and replacing them with something that expresses more beauty, more ... like the following:

```
#ifndef MINK
#define MINK
#include __FILE__
DD $$ sizeof
DD $ return
DD $_ int
DD _$ _()
DD __(_...)$$($_[]){0,##_}/$$($_)-1
auto main()->$_<%$<::><class _>(_)->
$_<%$ __(_$,_(),_$,_(),_$,_(),_$) ;%>(__());%>
#endif
#ifdef MINK
#define CAT(x, y) CAT_I(x, y)
#define CAT_I(x, y) x ## y
#define HH CAT(%, :)
#define DD HH define
#endif
```

Oh, it really hurts my eyes. Sorry about it, and apologies beforehand, but we cannot make this any more beautiful without incurring a very serious headache for the authors.

While reading this, we suddenly realize that just because there is already an obfuscated C code competition, we don't really need to overdo its C++ counterpart. C++ by definition can be obfuscated enough without us actively trying to obfuscate it, but now, after presenting the preceding chimera, we actively owe an apology and an explanation to you, dear reader (on the other end, chimeras can be beautiful too; you just need to have the right eye for it).

The first substantial observation we are concluding is that this code cannot be compiled by itself. If we try it, GCC will give errors, as follows:

```
error: stray '%:' in program
   15 | #define HH CAT(%, :)
```

ICC will complain, as follows:

```
error: "#" not expected here
  DD $$ sizeof
```

MSVC does not like that, as you can see:

```
error C2121: '#': invalid character: possibly the result of a macro
expansion
```

Clang isn't successful either:

```
error: expected unqualified-id
    4 | DD $$ sizeof
      |    ^
```

So, basically, the compilers have commonly agreed that they cannot agree on a common error message or a reason for failure, but at least none of them can compile that piece of code. There are a few very on-the-point error messages, such as # is possibly the result of a macro expansion (but the author of these lines would like to see a macro that expands to # because #define D # is just not working regardless of D) or another message concerning that stray %: in the program.

All this macro expansion and so on just leads us in the direction of macros. If you, dear reader, are not familiar with C or C++ macros, please go grab a book on them, such as *The C++ Programming Language*, by Bjarne Stroustrop, because this book (the one you are reading right now) deals only with macros of mythical fame, while that one (i.e., *the* C++ book written by the father and creator of the language) teaches you to not to use them unless you really, really have to. And even then, sparsely.

But back to our code. All decent compilers have the means to provide the result of the preprocessed C++ file, so let's examine it for our program. By invoking g++ with the −E flag (or Clang with the same flag, or MSVC with the /P flag if you use the command line for it; otherwise, they will be accessible from the build directory of the project you are working on in Visual Studio), we get the following listing:

```
%: define $$ sizeof
%: define $ return
%: define $_ int
%: define _$ _()
%: define __(_...)$$($_[]){0,##_}/$$($_)-1
auto main()->$_<%$<::><class _>(_)->
$_<%$ __(_$,_(),_$,_(),_$,_(),_$) ;%>(__());%>
```

We just show what is necessary for now and skip the compiler-specific line info, which is also added to the preprocessed output. So, as we can see, the preprocessed output looks like a very valid C++ file (albeit not very readable)... to our surprise, however, we can see several define directives actively present in the file. They are prepended by the %: symbol, which, after digraph substitution, will be transformed into the hashtag symbol (#) and yield a valid program.

In order to further understand what is happening here, we must understand how the compiler deals with macros.

The C compiler (and of course C++ too) expands macros through a methodical process managed by the preprocessor, beginning with tokenizing the source code and identifying macros for substitution. For object-like macros, a straightforward text replacement occurs, whereas function-like macros involve substituting the arguments provided in the macro invocation. Function-like macros (the ones that have a pair of parentheses) undergo an argument prescan, where macro arguments are fully expanded before being substituted into the macro body. This prescan ensures that nested macro calls within arguments are expanded correctly and that the final macro body is rescanned to catch any further macros for expansion.

However, the prescan does not apply when arguments are stringized or concatenated, nor does it affect macros that are already marked as ineligible for re-expansion. This behavior mandates that in order to have proper expansion, we force the compiler to do a second pass on the concatenation macros, as shown here:

```
#define CAT(x, y) CAT_I(x, y)
#define CAT_I(x, y) x ## y
```

The preceding snippet ensures that all the required arguments are properly expanded.

Special macros such as __LINE__ and __TIME__ are treated uniquely to prevent further unintended expansions. After all expansions are complete, the preprocessor ensures that no eligible macros are left unexpanded before passing the final code to the compiler. This comprehensive process ensures that macros are expanded efficiently and correctly, even in complex scenarios involving nested macros and stringification operations.

Now that we have tried to explain how the macro substitution works on a level that is not that obvious for the first time, it is time to get back and finally compile our program. As you can remember, the preprocessed source still contained some statements that had define directives in them.

Now, armed with this knowledge, we will reveal an arcane piece of knowledge to you, dear reader. In the end, this is a book about the mysticism of C++. This arcane piece of knowledge is something called **double preprocessing**. Before continuing, however, a small detour on how the compiler deals with your code.

During the initial stages of compiling a C++ source file, the compiler first undergoes preprocessing and compilation. In the preprocessing phase, the compiler expands macros (just like we have presented previously), processes conditional compilation directives (#ifdef, #ifndef, etc.), includes header files, and removes comments, resulting in a complete translation unit with all external files and macros fully resolved. Following this, in the compilation phase, the preprocessed code is broken down into tokens during a phase called lexical analysis, which are then checked against the language's syntax rules to construct a **parse tree** or **abstract syntax tree** (**AST**).

This is followed by the phase called semantic analysis, where the compiler verifies the correct usage of types, variables, and functions, and potentially performs early optimizations. Finally, the compiler translates the AST into an **intermediate representation** (**IR**), setting the stage for further optimization and eventual machine code generation, but this is way out of the topics covered in this book. However, we would like to direct those of you who are interested in this topic to the famous "Dragon book", also known as *Compilers: Principles, Techniques, and Tools*, by Alfred Aho, Jeffrey Ullman, Ravi Sethi, and Monica Lam. That is the go-to book for every programmer interested in developing a compiler, or just simply interested in learning about the techniques.

But back to our double preprocessing technique. By using this technique, we will pass in the previous preprocessed source file into a compiler, using a technique known in Linux as piping and on Windows as hacking.

The following is the Windows command that accomplishes this:

```
cl /P test.cpp & cl /Tp test.i
```

The first part is producing the preprocessed file, which, in Visual C++ land, usually has the .i extension and the second part will take the preprocessed output, place it in test.i, and compile it as a C++ file (the /Tp switch is responsible for this). The result of this is the expected test.exe, which, after execution, performs exactly as desired.

Under Linux, the sequence of commands is also very similar:

```
clang++ -E test.cpp | g++ -w -x c++ -std=c++20 -
```

The first part, before the pipe, produces the preprocessed code using `clang++`, which, using Linux pipe magic, is sent into `g++`, because why not 😏. For this simple scenario, it wouldn't have mattered if we had used the other way around, because these two compilers go hand in hand and they share the basic command-line options, such as `-x c++` to specify that the code it would compile is some sort of C++ code, or the version of the C++ standard this code complies to. The most important argument to the second compiler call is the last `-` sign, which tells the compiler to read the code from the stdin, instead of a file.

And that's it. Using this arcane technique, we can compile code that we thought would be impossible, but... please don't use it. This code is marginal insanity; it is presented just because this book is about unconventional, mythical techniques, targeting the advanced C++ programmer community, so don't let this piece ruin your programming style, or scare you away from the keyboard. We wouldn't want to lose our readers halfway through the book. Instead of focusing on this, in the upcoming chapter, let's occupy our minds with sheer nothingness.

The definition of zero

Zero is unique among numbers. The concept was present in ancient Egypt, and traces of it were found in ancient Babylon as a placeholder in their number system, but it wasn't treated as a true number at that point.

The ancient Greeks have had some resentment towards it because, regardless that they knew its importance, initially, due to some philosophical constraints, they didn't use it as a proper number, because not, to be or not to be, but how can nothing be, that was the question in the ancient Agora.

The breakthrough came in India around the 5th century CE when mathematician Brahmagupta defined zero as a number and established rules for its arithmetic use. This concept spread to the Islamic world, notably through the works of Al-Khwarizmi, and then to Europe, where Fibonacci played a key role in its adoption in the 12th century. Thank you, Wikipedia.

Zero has several important properties: it is the additive identity, meaning adding zero to any number leaves the number unchanged. Multiplying any number by zero results in zero, and division by zero is undefined. Zero is an even number and serves as a neutral element on the number line, being neither positive nor negative. In exponents, raising zero to any positive power gives zero, while any non-zero number raised to the power of zero equals one.

These properties make zero fundamental in mathematics, and with this, we can all agree that zero is one of the most important (if not the most important) numbers that ever existed; its place is up right next to π, or e, or i, which we all know is the square root of all evil, or -1.

Now we have presented concrete proof that there is no other number like zero, we also give the following statement: C++ is a unique language. In its latest iteration, as of 2024, at the current time, in C++, there are six different ways to initialize a value to zero, honoring the fact that zero is the most important number. Ever. Just see the following:

```
int z;
int main()
{
    int z1 = 0;
    int z2(0);
    int z3{0};
    int z4 = {0};
    int z5{};
    int z6();
}
```

Let's break it down, line by line, as there are not that many lines:

- `int z;` – Here, a global variable, z, of the `int` type is declared. Since it's a global variable, it is automatically initialized to 0 by the compiler (if a global `int` variable isn't explicitly initialized, it defaults to zero). This is something we can trust.

- `int z1 = 0;` – Copy initialization. The z1 variable is declared as an `int` type and initialized to 0 using copy initialization. This involves assigning the value of 0 to z1 after it is created.

- `int z2(0);` – Direct initialization. The z2 variable is declared and initialized to 0 using direct initialization, which involves passing the value of 0 directly to the constructor of the `int` type. Not that it has any, but you get the idea.

- `int z3{0};` – Brace initialization (uniform initialization). The z3 variable is declared and initialized to 0 using brace initialization. It helps prevent issues such as narrowing conversions and provides a consistent syntax for initializing different types. This is a peculiar initialization, and we will get back to this syntax a bit later in the next chapter.

- `int z4 = {0};` – Copy list initialization. The z4 variable is declared and initialized to 0 using copy list initialization, a combination of copy initialization and brace initialization. It's similar to z3 but explicitly uses the assignment syntax, and when we talk about simple things such as numbers, there is really no difference.

- `int z5{};` – Value initialization. The z5 variable is initialized using empty braces, `{}`, known as value initialization. For fundamental types such as `int`, this results in z5 being initialized to 0. This method is often used to ensure that a variable is zero-initialized without explicitly assigning a value.

Isn't it beautiful, the amount of consideration that was put into making a variable correspond to the number zero? So, one might just ask: why are the local variables of C++ not initialized to zero (or their default value), just in case?

The answer to this question is partly historical and partly pragmatic. Since C++ is based on C, and C was designed to be as close to the metal (silicone) as possible, the compiler did not waste precious processor cycles to initialize a value to their default value, if at some stage later it was used to set to a different value needed by the programmer. Elementary, dear reader, as one of the most famous detectives would say.

Last but not least, without me providing any more details, I really hope you have recognized the most vexing parse in `int z6();`.

The "most vexing parse" is a term used to describe a specific issue in C++ involving the declaration of objects that can be misinterpreted by the compiler due to ambiguities in the syntax. It usually arises when you declare a variable using parentheses, which can sometimes be interpreted as a function declaration rather than a variable definition, just like in our specific example.

A parenthesis concerning parentheses

Now that we are here, we have to mention that there were quite a lot of mentions of parenthesis in this chapter. So, we are presenting possibly the most important pair of parentheses you can encounter during the course of this book.

Please look at the following two functions:

```
static int y;
decltype(auto) number(int x) {
    return y;
}
decltype(auto) reference(int x) {
    return (y);
}
```

Those two functions look almost identical, except for the tiny pair of parentheses around the `return` value. But the presence of those two parentheses makes the biggest difference. The weird-looking `decltype(auto)` introduced in C++14 is a type specifier that combines the functionality of `decltype` with automatic type deduction, allowing you to declare a variable with a type that is determined by the expression it is initialized with, while also retaining certain properties of that expression. Unlike `auto`, which deduces types based on value categories, `decltype(auto)` retains the value category (e.g., reference or non-reference) of the expression it is based on.

More mundanely, the function number returns an `int`, while the function reference returns `int&`.

In order to verify the correctness of what we previously wrote, the following code snippets can be of great help:

```
using namespace std;
if (is_reference<decltype(number(42))>::value) {
    cout << "Reference to ";
    cout << typeid(typename
remove_reference<decltype(number(42))>::type).name() << endl;
} else {
    cout << "Not a reference: " << typeid(decltype(number(42))).name()
<< endl;
}
```

The preceding code snippet examines the return type provided by the number function. As the name hastily suggests, it will return, well... a number. When compiled with MSVC and executed, the following is the output of the code:

```
Not a reference: int
```

The other compilers also have the same behavior, except they do not print out the full type of the variable, because gcc and clang for the int type just return a single i and that wouldn't have been so spectacular.

Now, let's examine the following sequence of code:

```
if (is_reference<decltype(reference(42))>::value) {
    cout << "Reference to: ";
    cout << typeid(typename
remove_reference<decltype(reference(42))>::type).name() << endl;
} else {
    cout << "Not a reference: " << typeid(decltype(number(42))).name()
<< endl;
}
```

This is almost identical to the one before this, except that it uses the reference method instead of number. Not surprisingly, the result of the execution is (again, appealing to MSVC) as follows:

```
Reference to: int
```

So, with the preceding code, we have just proved that a pair of extra parentheses combined with decltype(auto) can provide some spectacular outcomes. Be warned. Let's say we omit decltype, such as in the following code:

```
auto reference(int x) {
    return (y);
}
```

The compiler then ignores the parentheses and just returns a normal number. The C++ standard specifies this behavior in the [dcl.type.decltype] section and the authors warmly recommend reading through it, in order to have a full understanding of what happens behind the scenes and a valid reasoning for it.

Now, because we are C++ programmers, always in pursuit of speed, high-quality, and clear code, you could ask why we had to duplicate the code to identify whether we have a reference or not. Wouldn't it have been perfectly valid to write something like the following?

```cpp
template <typename T>
void printType(T&& var) {
    if (std::is_reference<T>::value) {
        if (std::is_lvalue_reference<T>::value) {
            printf("lvalue ref ");
        } else {
            printf("rvalue ref ");
        }
        printf("%s\n", (typeid(typename
                std::remove_reference<T>::type).name())));
    } else {
        printf("%s\n", typeid(var).name());
    }
}
```

This is almost the same as above-above (above-above is like above, but refers to one above before the actual above), except that we have added an extra check to verify the type of the reference (and also removed std::cout in favor of printf because it generates much cleaner assembly code, and also put it in the body of a function). Indeed, let's say we put it into this context and call the following:

```cpp
printType(number(42));
printType(reference(42));
```

We get the correct and expected output:

```
int
lvalue ref int
```

As a side note, we get the same result with other, not-that-tiny-and-squishy compilers, too.

This function template uses a forwarding reference (T&& var) to handle both lvalue and rvalue references, making it capable of deducing and preserving the reference type of the passed variable. By using the type traits library, we check whether T is a reference type using is_reference<T>::value, and further distinguish between lvalue and rvalue references using is_lvalue_reference<T>::value.

If it's a reference, we print whether it's an `lvalue` or `rvalue` reference along with the type of the variable without the reference using `remove_reference<T>::type`.

If it's not a reference, we directly print the type of the variable. This approach works because of the perfect forwarding mechanics in C++, allowing T to be deduced as the exact type of the passed variable, preserving its reference nature.

Please note that it was mandatory to use the forwarding reference, `T&& var`; if we had used just `T var`, it would not work the same way for reference types. This is because, in this form, T would have been deduced as a non-reference type, so `var` inside the function would have been always a copy of the original argument, not a reference.

As an extra goodie for you, dear reader, here are some extracts of the assembly output of one of the compilers (GCC, in our case). You can see how it generates two distinct functions, and most importantly, what goes inside those functions:

void printType <int>(int&&):	void printType <int&>(int&):

push rbp
mov rbp, rsp
sub rsp, 16
mov QWORD PTR [rbp-8], rdi
mov edi, OFFSET
      FLAT:typeinfo
call std::type_
info::name()
mov rdi, rax
call puts
nop
leave
ret
	push rbp
	mov rbp, rsp
	sub rsp, 16
	mov QWORD PTR [rbp-8], rdi
	mov edi, OFFSET FLAT:.LC0
	mov eax, 0
	call printf
	mov edi, OFFSET
	      FLAT:typeinfo
	call std::type_info::name()
	mov rdi, rax
	call puts
	nop
	leave
	ret
	.LC0:
	  .string "lvalue ref "

Table 9.1: Comparing the assembly listings of various printType instantiations

We can see two instantiations of the `printType` function for each of the types returned by the two functions, and how in each of them the various calls to the type traits were successfully implemented at the source code level, thus leading to the removal of unnecessary branches. We can also observe the removal of the unnecessary strings (nowhere is `"rvalue ref "` found in the generated code because the compiler identified that the branch containing it is nowhere to be found in the final code).

Isn't C++ beautiful?

C++uties

It is time that the author of these lines has to admit something. He's tired of ugly code trying to win the C++ beauty contest. Regardless of how hard we try to convince ourselves that the code we presented a few sections before is beautiful and is worth remembering, well, it is not. It is ugly and horrible, and please forget, dear reader, that you ever had to read something like that. Apologies.

From this point on, we solemnly promise that we are up to no more mischief and will treat you only with beautiful code. No more ugly macros, no more shady substitutions, no more arcane techniques. Just pure, joyful, lovable C++.

As a result of this reinvention of ourselves (as the writer of beautiful C++ code), we present you the next program, which possibly is the cutest one you can get your hands on:

```cpp
using 🍜 = std::string;

#define 🔙 return

auto& 🗾 = std::cout;

struct 🐻 {
    virtual ~🐻() = default;
    virtual 🍜 🍲() { 🔙 "🐾"; }
};

struct 🐨 :public 🐻 {
    🍜 🍲() override { 🔙 "🐱"; }
};

int main() {
    std::unique_ptr<🐻> 🐾 { new 🐨 };
    🗾 << 🐾->🍲();
}
```

Please bear with us, for the sake of brevity, we have omitted the includes for `std::string`, `std::cout`, and `std::unique_ptr`. Who said C++ can't be cute?

But sadly, the preceding code is not widely recognized as being standard C++ (seemingly, there is no clear consensus among compiler developers on which Unicode identifiers to consider valid in the source code, regardless of [tab:lex.name.allowed] in the latest C++ standard), but not all hope is lost, as GCC accepts it. Maybe there was a bear hugger in the ranks of their developers.

As a side note, the code presented does not do too much, just feeds some bears with their proper meal, considering their nutrition needs, dietary requirements, and affiliations with various dietary patterns and current culinary trends present in Bearland. Didn't we deliver a cute program, a possible contender to the winner of the most beautiful C++ code?

There are a good number of books we encourage our dear esteemed readers to read, if they want their programs to follow common sense guidelines, be readable, stable, easily maintainable and up to the latest standards. Sadly none of those books detail how to write fun programs, because writing fun programs, or writing programs for fun involves a different mindset, and is rarely done for profit.

Programming can be an art form, producing code that surprises and delights, having code can include Easter eggs, humorous output, applying playful user interaction, or unusual visualizations. Playfulness could be as simple as using emojis as identifiers (as in our bear example) or making quirky applications with oddball logic. Fun programming often rejects the rigidity of formal practices in favor of creative solutions that may be inefficient or overly complex just for the sake of enjoyment, such as crafting an obfuscated piece of code, just because we find it to be fun.

Fun in programming can also come from solving intriguing puzzles or exploring unconventional programming paradigms (functional, esoteric languages such as Brainfuck or LOLCODE), or building projects purely out of curiosity.

While formal books on "beautiful" or "clean" code emphasize correctness, safety, and readability, fun programming opens the door to spontaneity, art, and entertainment, so no wonder that our last happening for this chapter is taking part in the last one. It is short, it is cute, and it looks like something out of a fairy tale. With bears. Because who doesn't like bears?

Summary

Not all that is shining is gold, and not every piece of code that seems exciting and bears complex features is necessarily of high quality. The allure of shiny, intricate code can sometimes overshadow the fundamental qualities that define good programming practices. Good, stable code is frequently characterized by its straightforwardness and predictability rather than its flair. This type of code may seem unremarkable or mundane compared to more fun constructs, but it is precisely this simplicity that ensures robustness and ease of understanding. When you have to, please try to write boring, simple code, as it will be much easier to read in half a year from now, but every time you can afford to, please squeeze in a bear or two in your fun side project. Unless you plan to read it, too.

In our next chapter, Alex will go on a crusade to advocate the proper use of modern C++ libraries, in order to debunk the myth that C++ libraries are also stuck in the Stone Age.

10

There Are No Libraries For Modern Programming in C++

Or maybe there are too many and they are not easily available?

C++ is the oldest language used in modern software development. Despite many attempts to replace it, it stayed up in both preference and usefulness. However, this legacy comes with its own challenges. The development style has evolved over time to include constructs that are easier to understand by developers, that solve problems with less code, or that sometimes just look nicer.

A big part of the ecosystem of any technology is the list of libraries available to it, including and complementing the standard library. Since C++ has been around for a long time, it has libraries. However, how do they compare with the experience of developers using other technologies? Do they match the needs and expectations of a modern developer, who is perhaps looking at the alternative solutions available in the marketplace of ideas?

These are a few of the questions we will examine next.

In this chapter, we're going to cover the following main topics:

- A modern developer experience
- Common needs
- Compatibility
- Supply chain security

How can we tell?

When pondering a question such as the title of this chapter, we are faced with the big challenge of selection. The choice of libraries for any project is completely contextual, and it fully depends on what the project is trying to solve. Of course, there are some features that are needed no matter what the project does, such as logging or unit testing, but what should we pick beyond these?

After all, it seems deeply unfair to compare web development in C++ with web development in Java, as it is to compare systems programming in C++ with systems programming in Java. Neither is C++ used for web development extensively, nor is Java for systems programming. In fact, C++ has had its own niche for a long time, and while it has been slowly eroded by Java, C#, Rust, and Python, it still holds the fort for use cases such as game development, firmware, high-frequency trading, engineering applications, automotive, systems programming, and probably others. The other languages have little traction in these domains, for very good reasons related to C++'s flexibility, performance, and control.

Another problem is the sheer number of libraries that exist for the aforementioned languages, particularly C++. An advantage of the venerable C++ is that programmers have had time to develop behemoth libraries such as Boost, which has no equal in the worlds of Java or C# (excluding the standard libraries), and absolutely no contender in the world of Python. We could argue that JavaScript has something similar to React and its surrounding ecosystem. However, in terms of the volume of available libraries, C++ looks dominant.

These observations leave us with one characteristic that we need to account for: how modern is the set of libraries? What would we want from a modern programming language and its ecosystem? Where does C++ stand from this perspective? Let's examine these questions.

A modern developer's experience

Let's step, for a moment, outside the C++ world and turn into a fly on the wall that looks at the experience of a developer using another technology. We will be with them as they are starting a new project, and later when they add new people to the team. The likely first step is that they will launch an IDE and create a new project or a project structure. The IDE is likely to be from Microsoft, such as Visual Studio .NET or Visual Studio Code, or from JetBrains, such as IntelliJ IDEA for Java, PyCharm for Python, or Rider for C#/.NET. A small set of strange programmers, such as myself, will use the command line and neovim. Even stranger programmers will use Emacs. I kid, of course; we all know that real programmers use changes in atmospheric electricity to manipulate the bits directly, as shown by a famous xkcd comic called *Real Programmers* (https://xkcd.com/378/). However, let's go back to our story.

Upon creating a new project, the IDE will suggest a few integrations and libraries to install. Once created, the project is ready to run, although it won't do a lot of useful things. During the creation, a source control repository will be selected, likely an existing one based on git. The project can then be committed locally and pushed to the shared repository.

After these steps, any member of the team will have a few things to do: fire up the IDE, clone the repository locally, and let the IDE do its thing to get the necessary dependencies, as specified in the project configuration.

It's likely that, at this point, the project will already include a logging and unit testing library. Let's pause for a moment to examine the libraries used.

Python has logging in its standard library, while Java has the open source Log4J and .NET uses either the Microsoft-built Microsoft.Extensions.Logging or the open source Log4Net. For unit testing, Python offers a standard implementation for both unit testing and mocking, but programmers tend to prefer open-source extensions such as pytest (https://docs.pytest.org/en/stable/). Java requires a unit testing library, usually JUnit or TestNG, and a mocking library, usually Mockito or JMock. Finally, .NET provides a standard framework for testing but knowledgeable tech leads will most likely select NUnit or xUnit instead, along with Moq.

Where does C++ stand here? Well, there's no shortage of logging libraries in C++, which shouldn't be a surprise since logging systems have matured at the same time as C++. We can say that logging libraries are quasi-standardized, having very similar behavior and features with small variations in the API. It's almost too difficult to choose a logging library for C++ unless you are using a technology that already comes with logging. I imagine that many projects use Boost and the logging that comes with it. A quick glance at GitHub shows that the spdlog library (https://github.com/gabime/spdlog) has 24k stars, although it only supports C++ 11.

What about unit testing? This is an interesting topic. Unit testing libraries exist for C++ in many forms. There's GTest and GMock, the two libraries started by Google, with the usual feature set. Similarly, CppTest follows the standard xUnit structure for unit tests. Then there's doctest (https://github.com/doctest/doctest), a single header library with no dependencies, which is why I prefer it for examples and the code accompanying this book. Finally, it's worth mentioning Cpputest (http://cpputest.github.io) because it allows embedded development, due to its small footprint and its features for identifying memory management problems. For mocking, FakeIt (https://github.com/eranpeer/FakeIt) is another single header framework that is very easy to integrate.

All these libraries would likely be set up through a package manager that stores the list of dependencies in a text file that's either plain text, a markup format, or a script. This file gets pushed to the central repository and can be used to recreate the dependencies, including the dependencies required by the installed libraries.

If, during the development, the team needs an additional library, they can simply add it to the dependencies. This process is a bit more restricted for enterprise environments due to security concerns: perhaps a pre-approved list of packages is available and provided from an internal source, perhaps each package requires approval, or perhaps only specific people can add a dependency.

Either way, when a new developer comes in, they will clone the central repository and run the installation commands, usually by just loading the project in the IDE and letting it do its thing, and everything should work fine. That's the end of our fly story.

Let's dive into more details about what happens behind the scenes if you use a package manager. Since I often use the command line in combination with neovim to program in Ubuntu Linux, I know a little bit more about the process in each of these technologies. For Python, a virtual environment is recommended so that the OS is not polluted with all the libraries required. A tool called `pipenv` combines the `pip` package manager and the `venv` virtual environment, both provided by the standard library, to allow for easy setup. The command line steps would be as follows:

```
pipenv init
pipenv install [library name]
```

In a new environment, you can simply run the following to install all the dependencies:

```
pipenv install
```

Java and .NET have similar workflows, minus the virtual environment. They both use open source package managers; for Java, Maven or Gradle are used, and for .NET, it's NuGet.

For all these three technologies, a central place for all the libraries exists: Pypi (`https://pypi.org/`) for Python, Maven Central (`https://mvnrepository.com/repos/central`) for Maven and the NuGet site (`https://www.nuget.org/`) for NuGet. As mentioned earlier, it's likely that large companies will pay more attention to the libraries used, and require more thorough security checks before using third-party code in their systems. These companies tend to provide their own repositories, for example, using Artifactory in Java (`https://jfrog.com/artifactory/`).

It is therefore very easy to search for libraries, update them, and install them in a new environment, with de facto standard tools available to any developer using that technology.

C++ has gone a long way since I was a junior C++ programmer in the 2000s. Back then, adding a new library required either downloading the binaries for the required targets or, more likely, compiling it yourself, which posed its own set of challenges. Nowadays, C++ is closing the gap through Conan and vcpkg, and it's likely that many programmers have a similar experience in C++ to the one I've described above for Java, Python, and .NET. Programmers in large companies are most likely to recognize it, since the organization provides a Conan or vspkg repository with approved libraries that can be found and installed easily. Adding a new library to the whitelist can be a bit of a pain and can take a long time, but that's understandable.

It's not as easy without that piece of infrastructure. The libraries are not available in a single location, and the tools don't seem to work as well. At least this was my experience: Conan gave me a bunch of errors when I tried to use it on a simple project and I had no idea how to fix them. While I dislike

Maven because it inexplicably downloads a lot of packages even for the simplest of setups, it works consistently and reliably, which is what we need from package managers. So, I'm afraid I will have to say this: while there are attempts to bring C++ package management on par with other technologies, it doesn't feel mature yet.

With this being said, I'm sure many developers working in large companies won't feel any of these issues. So, we'll assume that the package manager works fine. What will we do next? Depending on the project and the technology, we will need more libraries to help us. Let's look next at a few categories.

Common needs

Here are some needs that many developers have, in no particular order:

- Database connection, reading, and writing
- CSV file processing
- Compression, for example, `gzip`
- Date/time enhancements
- Various computations, for example: matrices, imaginary numbers, math equation solving, and so on
- UI, for desktop and mobile applications
- HTTP client
- HTTP server
- Asynchronous programming
- Image processing
- PDF processing
- Background jobs
- Cryptography
- Networking
- Serialization
- Email sending
- JSON processing
- Configuration file read and write: `ini`, `yaml`, and so on

It's safe to say that there are C++ libraries for all of these. Let's pick just a few random ones:

- `zlib` for `zip` and `gzip` compression
- Rapidcsv (`https://github.com/d99kris/rapidcsv`) for CSV processing
- For database access, an ORM such as TinyORM (`https://www.tinyorm.org/`) or SQLPP1 (`https://github.com/rbock/sqlpp11`) for type-safe DSL queries and results
- Poco libraries (`https://pocoproject.org/`) contain a lot of utilities for networking, sending emails, database access, JSON, OpenSSL, and so on
- UI libraries include Qt, GTK, wxWidgets, or Dear ImGui
- HTTP clients are implemented in Boost, Curl++, or cpp-netlib
- To implement a web application, Crow (`https://crowcpp.org/master/`) is inspired by Python's Flask, while Oat++ (`https://oatpp.io/`) and Drogon (`https://drogon.org/`) offer fast solutions for web APIs and microservices

We could go on, but I think we've made our point: C++ *has libraries*. It has *a lot of libraries*. Some of them have inspired the implementations of other technologies, while others took inspiration from the best solutions used by the alternatives. The advantages of the C++ implementations are obvious in terms of speed and low memory footprint. Some of these libraries pack many features into a few hundred kBs. It's also impressive how many header-only implementations exist, allowing for portability and simplicity.

C++ also has frameworks. We already mentioned a few and we can add others: GTK, QT, Boost, POCO, WxWidgets, and Unreal Engine, for example. Lists of libraries and frameworks are maintained on the internet, the best one I've found being **awesome-cpp** (`https://github.com/fffaraz/awesome-cpp`).

Even niche programming styles and practices have their libraries:

- Immutable collections? Use Immer (`https://github.com/arximboldi/immer`).
- Reactive Programming? Use RxCpp (`https://github.com/ReactiveX/RxCpp`).
- Microservices? Sure, CppMicroServices (`https://github.com/CppMicroServices/CppMicroServices`) can help (no, microservices are not niche, but they're rarely implemented in C++).
- Web Assembly? Yes, there's Emscripten (`https://github.com/emscripten-core/emscripten`) is a good choice.
- Serverless? There's `aws-lambda-cpp` (`https://github.com/awslabs/aws-lambda-cpp`).

I think it's obvious by now that we'd be hard-pressed to find any domain in which C++ lacks a library or framework. However, can we use them?

Compatibility

Let's assume that you find a very promising library and decide to add it to your project. Does it work? How *well* will it work?

Here's where the fragmentation of C++ shows its ugly side. The chance of any of the following undesirable things to happen is non-zero:

- The library uses a newer C++ version than your code and you can't compile it
- The library uses an older C++ version than your code
- You get a lot of warnings for different reasons
- The library compiles well with your version of C++, but its interface uses older constructs
- The library doesn't work on all platforms your project targets
- The library is incompatible with your compiler
- The library is incompatible with your compilation process
- The library is compatible with all platforms your project targets, but it has different behavior or performance issues or bugs on specific platforms

I hope you never encounter any of the preceding problems. Also, it's worth saying that you'd be much less likely to have them in the technologies we use as a comparison: Python, Java, and .NET have none of these issues. Well, almost none; it's possible, for example, to create Python programs that use C++ modules and face the same issues. Or you could create a Java program that uses OS primitives and has different issues on different OSs. In general, though, there's a continuous effort for consistency in these worlds.

To be fair, mature C++ frameworks and libraries such as Boost or `zlib` made the same effort and provided consistent behavior. It's just easier to create consistent libraries in languages that use virtual machines.

Let's say that your library works fine: no warnings, no weird issues, and it plays well with your code and toolkit. There's one last question: can we trust it?

Supply chain security

It should be obvious to anyone paying attention that software has always had a security problem. This problem is getting worse since software usage continues to increase and cover more and more areas of our daily lives.

There are two parts to improving security: the cybersecurity experts, who can find vulnerabilities and build protection tools, and the software developers, who need to find security issues before release and manage the accompanying risks. We know there's no perfectly secure software, but we also know that things can get much better.

A specific area of this increased protection is managing the potential vulnerabilities that come with the libraries we use. There are two situations: either vulnerabilities were introduced unknowingly, or they were injected on purpose by a malicious actor.

In all fairness, this can happen to any technology, and many of the high-profile C++ libraries are reviewed for security by large companies that use them. Moreover, if you're working in a large company, you have teams dealing with all these concerns. However, not all development is done in large companies, and not all libraries are treated the same, as we'll see with the **xz backdoor case**. Let's discuss the second case for a moment. A malicious actor can inject vulnerabilities in several ways:

- They can do this through a contribution to the code of an open source project.

- They can also fork an open source project and add vulnerabilities among useful features.

- They can also sometimes get away with becoming the maintainer of an open source project and then injecting vulnerabilities among useful features. See the story of the xz backdoor, which I commented on at length, at `https://mozaicworks.com/blog/xz-backdoor-and-other-news`.

- They can also replace the binary with a vulnerable version, for example, by offering it on another website than the original or managing to hijack the publishing process.

- They may also attempt hijacking the download, for example, through a DNS attack. Imagine a potential attacker managing to modify your local host's file to point the URL of your repository to another IP address on the internet.

All of the items in the preceding list are serious problems. In large companies, the security departments and IT/Ops tend to worry about them, but in smaller companies, it's likely that you'll need to pay extra attention. The solution we know is to validate all binaries with their digital signature or hash. While the package managers for programming languages and Linux do this automatically, manually downloading a binary from GitHub requires manual validation of the signature, hopefully provided along with the library file.

The first situation is even more complicated. How do you know whether a library has vulnerabilities? For open source code, the general belief is that many eyes look at the code and find all issues. However, that's very dependent on the number of contributors and their expertise.

The xz backdoor case mentioned is chilling, especially since the issue was found by a developer, Andres Freund, who got suspicious by the fact that `sshd` was using too much CPU during a micro-benchmark (`https://mastodon.social/@AndresFreundTec/112180406142695845`). This made the issue of overworked maintainers for open source libraries visible, only for it to return to obscurity soon after.

Let's assume that most open source libraries are not attacked by a malicious actor who gains maintainer status. It's still possible for vulnerabilities to escape, and more so in C++ since it has its own challenges in terms of security. A small team will need to stay informed of the reported vulnerabilities for the libraries they use, or license security tools that automatically do it for them.

Assuming that everything works fine, it's still best to store the list of libraries used in an application, so that the ops people know to periodically check for vulnerabilities in all the libraries used. The recommended practice in this area is to create what's called the **Software Bill of Materials (SBOM)** for your product. An SBOM contains the list of all the libraries and their dependencies. Specific tools are available to create the SBOM and to scan for vulnerabilities based on them; however, most of them work with docker containers. For example, consider Grype (`https://github.com/anchore/grype` and its companion tool Syft `https://github.com/anchore/syft`).

This leads us to the conclusion of this chapter.

Summary

We have seen in this chapter that C++ has a lot of libraries and frameworks that cover everything we might need. Compared to other technologies, the process of obtaining them is not as simple. They are not as easily discoverable since they are not in a central place, and they might bring additional issues such as incompatibility with the compiler or older code styles. We learned this in this chapter.

Similarly, like other technologies, the C++ libraries are prone to having vulnerabilities and are exposed to supply chain attacks. To protect against them, teams need to stay up to date with the stream of vulnerabilities discovered and authenticate the binaries upon download. Additional audits and scans are always useful, as we learned in this chapter. Thus, larger organizations have a security advantage since they have dedicated teams looking at these issues, at the cost of flexibility.

So, are there libraries for modern programming in C++? Yes, definitely. They are just harder to find and less compatible than in other widely used technologies.

In the next chapter, we'll look at whether C++ is backward compatible... with itself and beyond.

11

C++ Is Backward Compatible ...Even with C

And of course, with C, and B ... and even A ... and @ maybe?

In the beginning, there was the word, and the word was used in BCPL. Pronounced like Basic Combined Programming Language, not Baltimore County Public Library. It was the first of its kind that ruled the land of compilers with an iron syntax for several iterations. However, the trials of time were not kind to it. New features, doctrines, and syntax passed through and soon a new heir to the throne rose from the bits: B. Not too many considered B's typeless nature and advantage and soon B ceased to be, as a new contender to the throne of programming languages replaced B: C[1].

The rest is history. C became the de-facto language of low-level system programming, and its syntax crept into all popular programming languages of the last and this century (hello, curly braces). C is like glue, binding together various programming languages to perform sacred rites in Computerlandia.

And the programmers looked and saw that it was good.

Except for one Prometheus[2], a bringer of classes into C, soon to give people, *C with classes*, and *Cfront*, the first ever compiler that digested C++ code and spat out C code which sadly is long gone from our realm, but its legacy remains. The language, the dozens of C++ standard-compliant compilers (each, in their time was standard conformant... more or less), several hundreds of undefined behavior cases, and various iterations of the standard over the last three decades (the last working one being C++23, while the committee is laboring the latest and greatest C++26) are all here and constitute the programming language we all love: C++.

---

1   `https://www.bell-labs.com/usr/dmr/www/chist.html`

2   `Yes, Bjarne, we are talking about you`

This chapter will have you glued to your seat – like traffic at rush hour – with the following topics:

- Is C++ really backward-compatible with C?
- Is C++ really backward-compatible with C++?

Is C really forward-compatible with C++?

This chapter will be a bit of exploration, covering most of the banally boring bothersome beliefs concerning whether C++ is really backward compatible with C. As we were indoctrinated through the decades by our tutors, teachers, and trainers, C++ is mostly backward compatible with C. This means that much of C code can be compiled and run in C++ with little modification, as they share similar syntax and standard libraries.

```
<banalities reason="these were discussed somewhere else">
```

C and C++ may be closely related, like two siblings in a dysfunctional family, but still have many differences, leading to a love-hate relationship when it comes to compatibility. However, over time, the two languages have diverged significantly. According to the core rules, C is more permissive with looser typing rules, especially around pointers, and allows constructs like implicit pointer conversions, which C++ strictly forbids. For instance, in C, you can assign a `void*` to any other pointer type without a cast, while C++ will demand an explicit cast to maintain type safety.

Similarly, C++ (especially the newer iterations of the language) has stricter rules regarding enumerations, making them distinct types, whereas in C, enums are simply treated as `int`. This difference extends to many other areas: variable initialization, type qualifiers, and even memory allocation (`*alloc()`) work differently between the two. This is especially true of functions such as `malloc`, `calloc`, and so on. While in C they're just your run-of-the-mill functions, as mundane as your morning cup of coffee, if they occur in any kind of C++ code, suddenly it's like opening a portal to the seven circles of developer hell. This is particularly true during code reviews where acolyte C++ programmers are clutching their keyboards in terror, pointing out how you should not use C functions in C++ code when you have perfectly valid `new` and `delete`. They might also ask why you even need to allocate memory. It's 2024. We have smart pointers. Or at least, if you can restrain yourself, we beg you not to use C-style casting. That's because there are perfectly functioning cast operators introduced in the C++ standard more than a decade ago.

According to what was just discussed (but not exclusively), while young C++ emphasizes stricter type rules and more predictable, safe programming practices, granddaddy C remains the pragmatic and flexible, albeit riskier, option.

To the horror of C++ acolytes, the two languages are often used together, especially in C++ projects that need to use libraries written in C, but ensure code compatibility between the two languages. Oh, the nightmares of software development.

To aid the preceding scenario, developers often have to use extern "C" declarations, which prevent C++'s name mangling and allow smooth function linking across libraries written in various dialects. This is because, despite their similarities, the object files generated by C and C++ compilers are handled differently (yes, name mangling, we're talking about you).

To top the previous flat facts, in addition, there are a plethora of C99-specific keywords, such as _Alignas, _Alignof, _Atomic, _Bool, _Complex, _Generic, _Imaginary, _Noreturn, and _Static_assert, that are not part of standard C++, though some may have C++ equivalents or be available through compiler extensions. To make life more interesting, these were actually retired starting from C23, due to some efforts to bring C closer to C++.

And we didn't even mention designated initializers. Too late for them.

```
</banalities>
```

However, C was certainly not thought up with the idea that someday, there would be a future programming language called C++. That's why the following C code is perfectly valid while all law-abiding C++ compilers (and pure C++ developers too) will choke on it heavily:

```
int template(int this) {
    int class = 0, using = 1, delete;
    if (this == 0) return class;
    if (this == 1) return using;
    for (int friend = 2; friend <= this; friend++) {
        delete = class + using;
        class = using;
        using = delete;
    }
    return delete;
}
```

While looking like the nightmare out of the C pits, regardless of it, this piece of pure C code is perfectly valid, and what a surprise, it even calculates the Fibonacci numbers. But let's not be overly fiendish towards you, dear reader (although considering what other mythical code snippets you had to suffer through this book till you reached this chapter, I hardly doubt this piece of code may come as a shock to you ... no worries, this is the penultimate chapter, so the suffering is almost over ... till then, however: do you remember in *Chapter 9* where we defined main to be return and return to be main?), and let us present another interesting feature of C, that was not ported over to C++.

No, we are not talking about variable length arrays, regardless of the fact that just due to the peculiar syntax of `void funny_fun(int n, int array[][*])`, they also deserve a litany of their own (the syntax is an exemplification of how to pass in a 2D variable length array to a function in the declaration of its prototype). Variable length arrays have been discussed[3] in detail[4] throughout the last decade by authorities who are much more qualified to discuss this than our humble person. Regardless of those discussions, they (the VLAs) still did not make it into the C++ standard, so there must be a valid reason behind this decision (not just the potential stack-related issues, of assuming a theoretically unlimited stack, and the type mayhem the non-compile time type deduction might induce with VLAs, but also that in C++ there are much better mechanisms to handle this specific use case).

For this chapter of the book, we will discuss some C-specific features that the author finds highly useful, but that sadly still did not make it into the C++ standard in their original form.

The magic of the parameter list

Let's start with a simple function, the simplest of all, which is `int foo()`. It's not a very sophisticated function, but it does its job as expected, whatever that might be.

When compiled as C, a function with an empty parameter list means the function can take an unspecified number of arguments, which can lead to ambiguity and potential errors if arguments are passed to the function. That's because the compiler will not enforce parameter constraints.

To explicitly specify that a function takes no arguments in C, we must use `void` in the parameter list, as in `int foo(void)`, which clearly indicates that the function accepts no arguments and passing any would result in a compile-time error.

In contrast, C++ simplifies this by treating an empty parameter list as equivalent to specifying `void`, meaning that `int foo()` in C++ denotes a function that takes no arguments, just like `int foo(void)`, making the use of the `void` optional in C++.

This makes the syntax cleaner in C++, where functions with no parameters can simply be declared with empty parentheses. While C still requires `void` for clarity and correctness, C++ allows both forms, though the typical practice is to omit `void` and use the simpler `int foo()`. Neat, isn't it?

However, what if we want to add some parameters to our function? Let's modify it in the form of `int foo(int array[static 10])`.

The `int foo(int array[static 10])` declaration is a feature introduced in *C99* that provides additional information to the compiler about the parameters passed to a function, specifically when dealing with arrays.

---

3   `https://www.open-std.org/jtc1/sc22/wg21/docs/papers/2013/n3810.pdf`

4   `https://nullprogram.com/blog/2019/10/27/`

In this case, the `static` keyword within the array parameter indicates to the compiler that the `fun` function is expected to be called with an array that has at least 10 elements. The number 10 specifies the minimum size of the array that will be passed to the function, which can help the compiler make certain assumptions, such as enabling optimizations based on the guaranteed size of the array.

Additionally, when using static in the array parameter like this, the compiler assumes that the array pointer cannot be NULL. That's because a null pointer would imply that there are no valid elements, which violates the condition that the array must have at least 10 elements. This provides an extra layer of safety and clarity, as it eliminates the need for the function to check whether the array is NULL before proceeding, which can reduce runtime overhead.

~~Decent~~ Recent versions of **clang** (well, basically all above 3.1.0) even emit a warning if you call a function having this very specific declaration, with the infamous NULL pointer:

```
warning: null passed to a callee which requires a non-null argument
```

Sadly, this very handy feature did not make it into any of the C++ standards, nor can all today's C compilers digest it (we could not convince MSVC to successfully compile this piece of code, regardless of the requested C standard). Regardless, for programmers not targeting these platforms, this might indeed come in as a great help in times of need.

Another handy feature restricted to the circles of C programmers is the `restrict` keyword, introduced in C99, which is a type qualifier that provides hints to the compiler for optimizing memory access involving pointers. It tells the compiler that the pointer to which `restrict` is applied is the only means by which the referenced object (memory) will be accessed in the current scope. This allows the compiler to make aggressive optimizations because it can assume that no other pointer will alias or reference the same memory.

When you use the `restrict` qualifier on a pointer, you are promising the compiler that, for the lifetime of that pointer, the object it points to will not be accessed by any other pointer. This enables the compiler to generate more efficient code by avoiding unnecessary memory reloads or re-fetches, which might otherwise be required due to potential aliasing (multiple pointers pointing to the same memory).

Without `restrict`, the compiler must assume that any two pointers may reference the same memory, limiting its ability to optimize code.

For example, let's consider the following code:

```
void update1(int *a, int *b) {
    *a = *a + *b;
    *b = *b + *a;
}
```

In this case, the compiler must assume that `*a` and `*b` could alias each other, so it may reload `*a` or `*b` from memory just in case.

Here is its counterpart with `restrict`:

```
void update2(int *restrict a, int *restrict b) {
    *a = *a + *b;
    *b = *b + *a;
}
```

In this case, we have told the compiler that `*a` and `*b` do not alias, so it can optimize without worrying about memory aliasing.

The following listings (generated by **GCC** 14.2, using `-O3` optimization) are the assembly code generated for the two different functions, with some explanation:

```
update1:
  mov eax, DWORD PTR [rsi]; Load b from [rsi] into eax
  add eax, DWORD PTR [rdi]; Add a from [rdi] to eax
  mov DWORD PTR [rdi], eax; Store eax into [rdi] (a)
  add DWORD PTR [rsi], eax; Add eax to [rsi] (b)
  ret                      ; Return
```

Here's the other one:

```
update2:
  mov eax, DWORD PTR [rsi]; Load b from [rsi] into eax
  mov edx, DWORD PTR [rdi]; Load a from [rdi] into edx
  add edx, eax            ; eax + edx (result in edx) - a
  add eax, edx            ; edx + eax (result in eax) - b
  mov DWORD PTR [rdi], edx; Store edx into [rdi] - a
  mov DWORD PTR [rsi], eax; Store eax into [rsi] - b
  ret                     ; Return
```

Surprisingly, the one with `restrict` has a few more instructions, but once we go through the generated code, we can easily spot the effect of the `restrict` keyword. Supposedly, the parameters to the function are at the memory locations pointed at by `[rsi]` and `[rdi]`. The first one (without `restrict`) has to do all the addition work in memory, thus leading to slightly slower code, while the second one can delegate these costly operations to two ultra-fast register-based additions.

Also, a big difference between these two is that the second one (`update2`, with `restrict`) can assume that the value of the second parameter will not change after the first operation, so the carefully crafted register initializations and additions can play a vital part. The first one needs to consider that the `*a = *a + *b;` operation might change the value of b too (found at `[rsi]`). Hence, it needs to perform the operations in memory, always making the current value available to the upcoming operations.

While for a simple operation like these simple additions, the effects, and the outcoming result might not be as spectacular as for a larger example which would not have had enough space in this book, we still have enough evidence that the `restrict` keyword has factual effects on the generated code. Too bad this didn't make it into C++ either.

However, that's enough bashing of C++ and its lack of compatibility with C. They were never meant to compete, but rather, they complement each other. Let's move on to more interesting fields. Is C++ really compatible with itself?

Whitespace matters – until it doesn't

The following piece of code is not an extraordinarily complicated snippet:

```
#include <cstdio>
#define STR_I(x) #x
#define STR(x) STR_I(x)
#define JOIN(x,y) (x y)
#define Hello(x) HELLO
int main(void){
    printf("%s\n", STR(JOIN(Hello, World)));
    printf("%s\n", STR(JOIN(Hello,World )));
}
```

The not-so-complex code defines a series of macros to manipulate strings and concatenate tokens. `STR_I(x)` stringifies its argument, `STR(x)` ensures full macro expansion before stringification, `JOIN(x,y)` concatenates two arguments with a space, and `Hello(x)` is defined but, strangely, unused.

What comes up are two most important `printf` calls in the lifetime of this short program. In the first `printf` call, `JOIN(Hello, World)` expands to `(Hello World)`, which is then stringified to `"(Hello World)"`. That's nothing overly complicated.

However, the fun part comes now: in the second `printf` call, `JOIN(Hello,World)` (without the space between the comma and `World`) behaves differently depending on the GCC version.

In GCC 9.4 (and below), this results in `(HelloWorld)` without a space, while in GCC 9.5 (and above), the preprocessor adds a space between the tokens, making both `printf` calls produce `"(Hello World)"`.

This difference between GCC 9.4 and 9.5 stems from how each version handles token concatenation and whitespace between macro arguments, with GCC 9.4 not inserting spaces where none are explicitly given, and GCC 9.5 handling them more consistently by adding a space even when omitted in the macro invocation.

While the C and C++ standards do not explicitly say "whitespace is ignored between macro arguments and commas," it is implied by the way the preprocessor handles tokenization and macro expansion. Regardless, the rules state that arguments are separated by commas, and whitespace does not affect this separation. It seems that GCC (before 9.4) had a somewhat liberal interpretation of the lack of specification, which was re-interpreted in GCC 9.5 and after.

The whole misunderstanding is caused by the presence of the `Hello` macro, defined as a function-like macro, but used as a plain old replacement macro. It's highly possible that the main issue is (or rather, was) a bug in older GCC, which certainly we do not use anymore, because we all know, that newer compilers are more standard compliant, and certainly, we all write standard compliant code, don't we?

That's an interesting piece of historical forward compatibility.

The 11th guest

C++11 brought a range of new features while maintaining backward compatibility with C++98, ensuring that developers could adopt the modern capabilities incrementally without breaking existing code. One of the most transformative additions was **move semantics**, which introduced some new syntax that C++98 compilers could not digest. This was facilitated by rvalue references, a syntax again not supported by older compilers.

Similarly, the `auto` keyword simplified type declarations by automatically inferring types, yet developers could continue using it to explicitly specify that the variable has automatic storage, like they never did in C++98. This choice was made because let's admit it, no one ever used auto as it was intended for in the C language (from where it was inherited, but even there it was still useless, unless in the B language, where it originated, as correctly denoting the storage for a variable: the stack).

New syntax such as **range-based for loops** allowed for cleaner iteration over containers, but the classic `for` loops from C++98 remained fully functional, thankfully, because lots of people still use them. The introduction of `nullptr` replaced the old NULL macro with a type-safe alternative, though NULL was still supported for backward compatibility, regardless of the fact that it was not that different from 0.

In addition to these core language improvements, C++11 introduced modern functional programming features such as **lambda expressions**, which allowed anonymous functions to be written inline, facilitating cleaner and more concise code.

The new `constexpr` feature allowed certain functions to be evaluated at compile time, offering performance improvements, but developers could still rely on the C++98 approach of runtime function evaluation if needed with the use of overly complicated templated recursions because, well, `constexpr` is not supported by old compilers either.

However, none of those groundbreaking changes can be more confusing to older users of C++ than the change of parsing for the C++ templates double right-angle brackets. In C++98, when using nested template arguments, the parser required spaces between consecutive right-angle brackets (`> >`) to distinguish them from the shift operator (`>>`). This was necessary because, in C++98, the parser would interpret two consecutive > symbols as the bitwise right-shift operator rather than as the closing of two nested templates.

In C++11 and later, the compiler is smart enough to recognize that in this context, `>>` refers to closing two nested template brackets, not performing a right-shift operation. This makes the syntax cleaner and less error-prone, as developers no longer need to manually add spaces between right-angle brackets in nested template expressions. However, this also unfortunately means that the following program will display two different values depending on whether it was compiled with a compiler supporting C++11 standard, or with a compiler that only supports C++98:

```
#include <iostream>
const int value = 1;
template <class T>
struct D {
    operator bool() {return true;}
    static const int value = 2;
};
template<int t> struct C {
    typedef int value ;
};
int main() {
    const int x = 1;
    if(D<C< ::value>>::value>::value>::value) {
        std::cout << "C++98 compiler";
    } else {
        std::cout << "C++11 compiler";
    }
}
```

When we dig deeper into the intricacies of the program, it is perfectly clear why it has this strange behavior. If it is still not clear yet, let's break it down.

OK, let's not break down the entire program. That would be too long. Instead, we'll focus on just `D<C< ::value>>::value>::value>::value`, which is the key to all the feature identification.

Using C++98 syntax, this will be parsed as follows:

```
if(static_cast<bool>(D<int>::value)) { ... }
```

So, it all boils down to the value of `D<int>::value` due to the fact that `::value>>::value` will be parsed as `1 >> 1`, resulting in 0. This goes into `C<0>::value`, which is a plain `typedef` to `int`. From there, we reach `D<int>::value`.

Since we have defined it to be `2`, `if` certainly will be `true`, and we have executed the C++98 identification branch.

However, when parsing the code with a C++11-compliant compiler, the expression will be parsed as the following, slightly more complex expression:

```
if((static_cast<int>(D<C<1> >::value > ::value)) > ::value) { ... }
```

As may not be obvious from the long and complex set of right-angle brackets, in the end, this will be parsed like two comparisons. That's because the following `D<C<1>>::value` turns out to be 2 (because `C<1>` is also a type by itself, so we end up in a specialization of the D class with `C<1>`). Then, this is compared to `::value`, which will turn out to be true `(2>1)`. From this, in the end, after a series of interesting conversions, the end result will look like `1>1`. This turns out to be `false`; hence, we enter the C++11 branch.

With this in place, we have a nice and short, albeit overly complicated and useless, way to identify whether our code was compiled with a C++11 conforming compiler. However, checking for the value of `__cplusplus` is much easier than this and should be used in any production-ready code.

The auto surprise

If you, dear reader, do remember that in *Chapter 9*, we had an interesting section called *The definition of zero*, then all is good. That's because our next pitch will be about this highly influential number again. If you don't remember that chapter, then life is still good, because hopefully, you have purchased a full book with all the chapters inside, and you can turn the pages back to read it (again).

Let's consider the following program:

```
#include <iostream>
#include <typeinfo>
#include <string>
template<typename T> std::string typeof(T t) {
    std::string res = typeid(t).name();
    return res;
}
int main() {
    auto a1 = 0;
    auto a2(0);
    auto a3 {0};
    auto a4 = {0};
    std::cout << typeof(a1) << std::endl
            << typeof(a2) << std::endl
            << typeof(a3) << std::endl
            << typeof(a4) << std::endl;
}
```

The program is not an overly complicated one again. It just uses the fancy `auto` keyword and initializes variables to 0 using all kinds of mechanisms, mostly presented in the chapter mentioned earlier. If you do not know what the `auto` keyword does, then here is a short recap: the `auto` keyword in C++11 was hijacked from C, and its new role is to allow automatic type inference, enabling the compiler to deduce the type of a variable based on its initializer. This simplifies code by removing the need for explicit type declarations, and shortens the handling of complex or verbose types, such as iterators or templated types.

Anyway, back to our code. After careful consideration, we can conclude the following:

- `auto a1 = 0;`: For this simple case, `a1` is deduced to be `int` since 0 is an integer literal. This is a straightforward copy initialization.

- `auto a2(0);`: Again, a simple one, `a2` is also deduced to be `int` because 0 is directly initialized as an integer literal.

- `auto a3 {0};`: Then, `a3` is deduced to be `int`, as the `{0}` list initialization initializes it to an integer.

- `auto a4 = {0};`: This is a bit tricky, however. For this case, `a4` is deduced to be `std::initializer_list<int>` because `auto` with brace initialization deduces an `initializer_list`. This is a special rule for `auto` when used with brace-enclosed initializers.

The output of the program using MSVC is the following:

```
int
int
int
class std::initializer_list<int>
```

Using GCC (recent/decent versions), the output will be a bit less verbose, but you get the idea:

```
i
i
i
St16initializer_listIiE
```

However, there is a catch. If we compile this piece of code with GCC versions older than version 5.0 we get an ugly surprise. The output is as follows:

```
i
i
St16initializer_listIiE
St16initializer_listIiE
```

What an unexpected surprise of backward compatibility. The real help comes from clang (3.7), however. If we compile the program with it, we get the following rather helpful message:

```
<source>:19:13: warning: direct list initialization of a variable
with a deduced type will change meaning in a future version of Clang;
insert an '=' to avoid a change in behavior [-Wfuture-compat]
    auto a3 {0};
```

So, it seems that at some stage during its evolution, the meaning of {x} combined with auto but not =, in this very specific scenario, has changed (around the birth date of C++17). However, thankfully, early compilers had thought of this peculiar scenario, with this very specific and direct warning. Very backward compatible, isn't it?

So, with all this in mind, it should not come as a huge surprise that the following code does not even compile (considering that we are still in the confines of our previous short program):

```
std::cout << typeof( {0} );
```

Why should it? Which type would {0} be deduced to, considering all the chaos and mayhem with the preceding syntax? Would it be deduced to an int type? Or maybe to an initializer_list type? Would it be a null pointer (nullptr)? Or an object that can be built from a number, like the following:

```
struct D { D(int i) {} };
void fun(D d) { }
fun({0});
```

Or is this not so fun anymore?

Summary

In this chapter, we learned that C++ has evolved and diverged significantly from its humble C (as well as B and BCPL) origins. We learned that C++ has introduced modern features and stricter rules to enhance safety and efficiency, and to support modern programming paradigms. While it maintains much of C's syntax, the two languages have heavily branched off over time, leading to compatibility challenges, especially when mixing older C code with features requiring newer C++ standards. We discussed this extensively in this chapter.

Within modern C++ itself, the introduction of features such as move semantics, stricter template parsing, and changes in the behavior of keywords such as auto have added layers of complexity (not that there were not enough). We also learned this in this chapter.

Despite these challenges, we explored the fact that C++ continues to build on its rich legacy, offering powerful tools for developers while requiring careful attention to evolving standards and backward compatibility without incurring too much contradiction with its previous self. It remains a language where tradition and innovation meet, often in unexpected and fascinating ways.

But for how long? Will it survive the surfacing threat of the new kid on the block? Will Rust replace C++? That's up to you, dear reader, and it will be detailedly debated by Alex in our next chapter.

12
Rust Will Replace C++

If 4 things happen concomitantly

Rust rose as a contender for systems programming and C++ in the past years. There are good reasons for this: Rust is a modern language, providing a good toolset, simple syntax, and innovations that help reason about the code. The question of whether Rust will replace C++ is therefore on the minds of many programmers who would like to know where to invest their efforts for the future of their careers. We will look next at what makes Rust interesting and at what would need to happen for it to replace C++.

In this chapter, we're going to cover the following main topics:

- Why the competition?
- Core features of Rust
- Rust's advantages
- Where C++ is better
- What C++ still needs

Technical requirements

The code for this chapter is available in the GitHub repository (`https://github.com/PacktPublishing/Debunking-C-Myths`), in the `ch12` folder. To run the code, you will need Rust, using the instructions from their website:

`https://www.rust-lang.org/tools/install`

Why the competition?

As a junior C++ programmer working abroad in Paris around 2001, my biggest challenge was to make my code do what it needed to do. The project was a knowledge base for industrial printing presses, allowing operators to identify the source of printing errors. Back then, the main option for such desktop applications was C++ under Windows, developed with Visual C++, **Microsoft Foundation Class** (**MFC**), and Windows APIs, designed with the Document-View model, a weaker cousin of Model-View-Controller promoted by Microsoft. The project challenged me to the maximum: not only was I struggling with C++ memory management but I also had to deal with the quirks of MFC and Windows APIs. My support back then was the official documentation, the `https://codeproject.com` website, and one more experienced colleague who was rarely available. Basically, I had to deal with a complex technology, as a sole developer, without a lot of support. Welcome to software development in the 2000s! Don't get me wrong, I'm not complaining: because of its challenges, the experience was deeply helpful and educational.

My sole focus at that point was the technology I was using. I had heard of things such as PHP, and I had used Java before for applets and web applications, but C++, MFC, and Windows APIs were filling my bandwidth. It didn't help that the commute took around 90 minutes, enough time to read the whole *Lord of the Rings* book on public transport over the course of a year.

A second important project in my career was completely different: still C++, but a very structured and mentored approach to building a NoSQL database engine before such a thing was named. At that time, I learned how to write tests, and we wrote our own testing engine since there was none for C++. I learned a lot about software design by writing design documents and reviewing them with colleagues. I learned about code reviews. I learned C++ ins and outs through a deep dive into seminal books that included Scott Meyers' *Effective C++* and *More Effective C++*, and Andrei Alexandrescu's *Modern C++ Design*. So, I went even deeper into the same technology.

Then C# appeared, and I decided to switch technologies. After doing some Java, having a deep knowledge of C++, and going in a structured manner into C#, I realized two things: changing technologies is easier the more you do it, and each technology has its own advantages and disadvantages. Desktop applications were much easier to build in C# since we had to pay less attention to memory management and its potential issues. Programming was more fun, and more importantly, we were developing faster. We traded these two benefits for two downsides: less control and a less rigorous approach to programming.

Later in my career, I started wondering about the plethora of programming languages available in the marketplace. In my estimation, we would need about 5-7 programming languages for purely technical reasons: one for web, one for systems programming, one for scripting, and the rest for various niches like AI, workflows, solving equations, and so on. Let's say I'm wrong and we would need 20. However, the reality is that we can use hundreds of programming languages today, including mainstream, niche, and esoteric languages such as Brainfuck or Whitespace. We can see many of them in the TIOBE Programming Community index that monitors the popularity of programming languages. Why are there so many?

My best guess is that it's not a matter of technical needs, but one of culture. Sure, the technical aspects are important. Object-oriented and later functional programming features were introduced in all mainstream languages. Security, parallelism and concurrency, ease of programming, the community, and the ecosystem are all important aspects of a programming language. However, the decision to make a new programming language comes from people, and the decisions they make when designing the language come from their personal preferences. Trends in literature and philosophy follow the same pattern: current and counter-current or reactionary. In literature, Romanticism was a reaction to Classicism, and realism was a reaction to Romanticism. Something similar happens with programming languages: Java was a reaction to C++, and Ruby on Rails was a reaction to Java. While in literature, currents are partially determined by societal changes, in technology, the currents are determined both by the movements in the landscape and the preferences of younger generations of programmers, added at a very high pace. An example of the technological landscape change is the rise of the internet, which has favored the rise of Java as a reaction to C++ for web applications. Interestingly, the movement of computation from server to client nowadays seems to favor the apparition of Web Assembly applications that currently require low-level programming in C++ or Rust. As for the new generations of programmers, Ruby on Rails was very much a reaction to the perceived old-style Java language. Rails offered freedoms of expression that Java didn't, along with a feeling of satisfaction with the progress. This feeling had little technical basis, but technical aspects aren't everything for people, not even for software developers.

You should see now where this is going: Rust is a reaction to C++. It is a reaction both to current technical annoyances of C++ and to the ways C++ does things. Let's therefore look at what Rust brings to the table.

Core features of Rust

The first place we can use for understanding Rust's core features is the official website, `https://www.rust-lang.org/`. The site does a very good job of emphasizing the most important features of Rust:

- Fast and memory-efficient

- No runtime

- No garbage collector

- Integrates with other languages

- Memory safety and thread safety through a rich type system and ownership model

- Great documentation

- Friendly compiler with useful error messages

- Integrated package manager and build tool

- Auto formatter

- Smart multi-editor support with auto-completion and type inspections

From this description only, we can already see a few similarities with C++, along with improvements on the current state of C++. The similarities are in the level of control: native compilation, no garbage collector, speed, and memory efficiency are qualities that C++ touts as well. The differences point to things that we discussed at length in this book: standard package manager, standard tooling, and friendly compiler. This last quality is music to the ears of any C++ programmer who got huge error messages; I remember back in the 2000s, I got an error in Visual C++ that said something along the lines of "error messages are too long and we can't display them". While today's C++ is friendlier, figuring out what didn't work while using templates is still a pain.

However, let's look beyond what's written on the front page of the website. We'll look next at a few features that I selected because I found them very useful and interesting compared to C++.

Project templates and package management

As an avid user of the command line and neovim code editor, I love technologies that allow me to create projects directly from the command line. Rust comes with the `cargo` tool that allows creating projects, building, running, packaging, and publishing. To create a new project, just call `cargo new project-name`. You run it with `cargo run`, check that it doesn't have compile errors with `cargo check`, compile it with `cargo build`, package it with – you guessed it! – `cargo package`, and publish it with (drum rolls) ... `cargo publish`.

We can, of course, create libraries and executables with `cargo`. More than that, we can use the cargo generate tool found at `https://cargo-generate.github.io/cargo-generate/` to start from a project template.

I know this might not look like much to most of the C++ developers out there because you rarely create a new project. This has been one of my surprises when teaching unit testing or test-driven development to C++ programmers: we had to work together to set up a test project with a production project and the corresponding references, something I took for granted. Believe me when I say that this is very nice to have not only at the beginning of a project but also for small experiments, personal or practice code bases, and reducing compilation times. A simple thing C++ offers you if your project compiles too slowly is to create a new compilation unit formed out of the few files you are modifying and refer to the rest as a binary. I used this technique extensively before SSD hard drives sped up compilation considerably.

Enough on new projects. Let's write some code. Let's modify some variables... or maybe not.

Immutability

Rust features immutability by default. The way the documentation puts it is *"once a value is bound to a name, you can't change that value."* Let's look at a simple example where I assign a string value to a variable, display it, and then try to modify it:

```
fn main() {
    let the_message = "Hello, world!";
    println!("{the_message}");
    the_message = "A new hello!";
    println!("{the_message}");
}
```

Trying to compile this program results in a `cannot assign twice to immutable variable` `the_message` compilation error. Helpfully, the error message includes the `For more information about this error, try `rustc -explain E0384`` notice. The explanation for the error message contains an example for the error, and a very helpful notice on how to make variables mutable:

`"By default, variables in Rust are immutable. To fix this error, add the keyword must after the keyword let when declaring the variable"`

Following is a code example that, when adapted, makes the program compile:

```
    let mut the_message = "Hello, world!";
    println!("{the_message}");
    the_message = "A new hello!";
    println!("{the_message}");
```

As you can see, mutable variables must be specified as `mut`, so the default is immutability. As we've seen in previous chapters, this helps with a lot of problems such as parallelism and concurrency, automated testing, and code simplicity.

Simple syntax for compound types

Rust borrows from languages such as Python or Ruby the syntax for arrays and tuples. Here's what that looks like:

```
let months = ["January", "February", "March", "April", "May", "June",
"July", "August", "September", "October", "November", "December"];
println!("{:?}", months);

let (one, two) = (1, 1+1);
println!("{one} and {two}");
```

This might not look like much, but it helps simplify code.

It's worth mentioning here that C++ has introduced a similar syntax in C++ 11 and has improved it in consequent versions, through the list initializer, using curly braces:

```
std::vector<string> months = {"January", "February", "March", "April",
"May", "June", "July", "August", "September", "October", "November",
"December"};
```

I would love to see further improvements on this front, but the C++ syntax is already complex, so I don't expect it.

Optional return keyword

Functions in Rust allow the return of the last value in the function. The next example uses this construct to increment a number:

```
fn main() {
    let two = increment(1);
    println!("{two}");
}

fn increment(x:i32) -> i32{
    x+1
}
```

I usually avoid this in functions such as the preceding, but avoiding the `return` keyword simplifies closures, as we'll see next.

Closures

Let's increment all elements of a vector:

```
fn increment_all() -> Vec<i32>{
    let values : Vec<i32> = vec![1, 2, 3];
    return values.iter().map(|x| x+1).collect();
}
```

As usual for functional programming constructs, and similarly to the `ranges` library in C++, we need to get an iterator, call the map function – equivalent to the transform algorithm in C++ – with a closure, and call `collect` to obtain the results. The closure has a very simple syntax, made possible by the optional return statement.

Unit tests in Standard Library

Unit testing is a very important practice in software development, and it's surprising that only a few languages offer support for it in the standard library. Rust does it by default, and it's quite easy to use. Let's add a unit test to verify that our `increment_all` function works as expected:

```
#[cfg(test)]
mod tests {
    use super::*;

    #[test]
    fn it_works() {
        assert_eq!(vec![2, 3, 4], increment_all());
    }
}
```

As a plus, I like that it's very easy to write unit tests in the same compilation unit (called a **crate** in Rust) as the production code. This might not seem like much if you see unit tests as an obligation, but I often use unit tests to experiment and to design so I love this facility a lot.

Traits

A big difference between Rust (or Go) and the other mainstream languages is that Rust does not support inheritance, instead favoring composition. To allow for polymorphic behavior without inheritance, Rust offers traits.

Rust traits are similar to interfaces in object-oriented languages in that they define a set of methods that need to be implemented for every object that derives from them. However, Rust traits have a specific feature: you can add a trait to a type you don't own. This is similar to extension methods in C#, although not the same.

The Rust documentation provides an example of traits by using two structures, one representing a tweet and the other a news article, and adding the `Summary` trait to both is meant to create a summary of the corresponding message. As you can see in the example that follows, the trait implementation is separate from both the structure implementation and the trait definition, which makes it very flexible.

Let's start by looking at the two structures. First, the `NewsArticle` contains a few fields:

```
pub struct NewsArticle {
    pub headline: String,
    pub location: String,
    pub author: String,
    pub content: String,
}
```

Then, the `Tweet` structure contains its own fields:

```
pub struct Tweet {
    pub username: String,
    pub content: String,
    pub reply: bool,
    pub retweet: bool,
}
```

Separately, we define the `Summary` trait with a single method summarize returning a string:

```
pub trait Summary {
    fn summarize(&self) -> String;
}
```

Let's now implement the `Summary` trait for the `Tweet` structure. This is done by specifying that the implementation of this trait applies to the structure, as follows:

```
impl Summary for Tweet {
    fn summarize(&self) -> String {
        format!("{}: {}", self.username, self.content)
    }
}
```

The test works perfectly:

```
#[test]
fn summarize_tweet() {
    let tweet = Tweet {
        username: String::from("me"),
        content: String::from("a message"),
        reply: false,
        retweet: false,
    };

    assert_eq!("me: a message", tweet.summarize());
}
```

Finally, let's implement the trait for the news article:

```
impl Summary for NewsArticle {
    fn summarize(&self) -> String {
        format!("{}, by {} ({})", self.headline, self.author, self.
location)
    }
}
```

```
#[test]
    fn summarize_news_article() {
        let news_article = NewsArticle {
            headline: String::from("Big News"),
            location: String::from("Undisclosed"),
            author: String::from("Me"),
            content: String::from("Big News here, must follow"),
        };


        assert_eq!("Big News, by Me (Undisclosed)", news_article.
summarize());
    }
```

Traits in Rust have much more capabilities. We can implement a default behavior, specify that the type of a parameter needs to be of one or multiple trait types, implement traits generically on multiple types, and so on. In fact, Rust traits are a combination of OO interfaces, C# extension methods, and C++ concepts. However, this is outside the scope of this chapter. What's worth remembering is that Rust treats inheritance very differently from C++.

Ownership model

An interesting characteristic of Rust, and perhaps its most advertised feature, is the ownership model. This is Rust's reaction to memory safety issues in C++, only instead of going into garbage collectors like Java or C# do, the designers have solved the problem with a more explicit ownership of memory. We'll look at a quote from the Rust book (https://doc.rust-lang.org/book/ch04-01-what-is-ownership.html):

"Memory is managed through a system of ownership with a set of rules that the compiler checks. If any of the rules are violated, the program won't compile. None of the features of ownership will slow down your program while it's running."

There are three rules of ownership in Rust:

- Each value in Rust has an *owner*

- There can only be one owner at a time

- When the owner goes out of scope, the value will be dropped

Let's first look at an example that works the same as in C++. If we have a variable allocated on the stack, such as an integer, then copying the variable works in a very familiar way:

```
#[test]
fn copy_on_stack() {
    let stack_value = 1;
```

```
        let copied_stack_value = stack_value;

        assert_eq!(1, stack_value);
        assert_eq!(1, copied_stack_value);
}
```

Both variables have the same value, as expected. However, if we try the same code with a variable allocated on the heap, we get an error:

```
#[test]
fn copy_on_heap() {
    let heap_value = String::from("A string");
    let copied_heap_value = heap_value;
    assert_eq!(String::from("A string"), heap_value);
    assert_eq!(String::from("A string"), copied_heap_value);
}
```

When running this, we get the `error[E0382]: borrow of moved value: `heap_value`` error. What happens?

Well, when we assign the value of `heap_value` to `copied_heap_value`, the `heap_value` variable is invalidated. This behaves the same as the move semantics in C++, only without any additional work from the programmer. Behind the scenes, this works through the use of two traits: `Copy` and `Drop`. If a type implements the `Copy` trait then it works as in the first example, while if it implements the `Drop` trait then it works as in the second. No type can implement both traits.

To make the above example work, we need to clone the value instead of using the default move mechanism:

```
#[test]
fn clone_on_heap() {
    let heap_value = String::from("A string");
    let copied_heap_value = heap_value.clone();

    assert_eq!(String::from("A string"), heap_value);
    assert_eq!(String::from("A string"), copied_heap_value);
}
```

This example works fine, so the value is cloned. This indicates, however, a new allocation on the heap, not a reference to the same value.

The move semantics work the same for function calls. Let's initialize a value and pass it to a function that returns it unchanged to see what happens:

```
fn call_me(value: String) -> String {
    return value;
}


#[test]
fn move_semantics_method_call() {
    let heap_value = String::from("A string");

    let result = call_me(heap_value);

    assert_eq!(String::from("A string"), heap_value);
    assert_eq!(String::from("A string"), result);
}
```

When trying to compile this code, we get the same error as before: `error[E0382]: borrow of moved value: `heap_value``. The value is created on the heap, moved into the `call_me` function, and therefore dropped from the current scope. We can make this code work by specifying that the function called should only borrow the ownership instead of taking it over. This is done through the use of reference and dereference operators, which are the same as in C++:

```
fn i_borrow(value: &String) -> &String {
    return value;
}

#[test]
fn borrow_method_call() {
    let heap_value = String::from("A string");

    let result = i_borrow(&heap_value);

    assert_eq!(String::from("A string"), heap_value);
    assert_eq!(String::from("A string"), *result);
}
```

The important difference between C++ references and Rust references is that Rust references are immutable by default.

There is, of course, a lot more to learn about the ownership model in Rust, but I believe this is enough to give you a taste of how it works and how it's meant to prevent memory safety issues.

Rust's advantages

To summarize, Rust has a few advantages over C++. By being a newer language, it has the advantage of learning from its predecessors and using the best patterns available. I find the combination of immutability with the ownership model to be very good at code that works well by default. It might take a bit to learn since it's not the typical memory management style, but once you understand how to use it, it allows you to write code that works without much challenge.

The unit testing support in the standard library, the package manager, and the multi-editor support should be part of any modern programming language. The syntax is nicer when it comes to closures and compound types.

We might wonder at this point: does C++ stand a chance? Why and where?

Where C++ is better

C++ is a very capable, advanced programming language, under continuous improvement. The language is progressing quite fast. It's very difficult to equal the C++ ecosystem: its community, the staggering number of libraries and frameworks available, and the articles, blogs, and books that teach you how to use C++ in various ways for any possible problem you might have. For all its benefits, Rust is a young language compared to C++, which should give you pause when considering the choice of technology for systems programming. However, Rust has been adopted for subsystems of Linux and Android, so it proves itself a worthy competitor.

The C++ standardization committee has shown a continuous focus on simplifying syntax and reducing the mental burden of programmers for various code constructs. Part of the effort comes from the competition, with many of the features introduced in C++17 and later being an answer to the Rust design choices. While I don't expect C++'s syntax to evolve to be as simple as Rust, the other factors mentioned here must contribute to the choice just as much, if not more.

What C++ still needs

In this book, we have seen some of the challenges of C++. A standard package manager would be very helpful, even if the community follows in the footsteps of Java and C# and picks an open source de-facto standard. A standard unit testing library would be very beneficial, even if the existing code might take a long while to migrate if it ever does.

Unicode and utf-8 support still need improvement. Standard support for multithreading is at the beginning. Safety profiles would be extremely useful for minimizing memory safety issues.

It's clear from this list that C++ has a lot of things to improve. The good news is that the standardization committee is hard at work on some of these issues. The less good news is that it takes time to define these improvements, more time to adapt compilers, and even more time to adapt existing code. Hopefully, Gen AI will be capable enough to speed up these improvements while maintaining code integrity.

Summary

We saw, in this chapter, that Rust is a very interesting language, whose designers knew to take advantage of the knowledge gathered by their predecessors and to innovate in the right places. The result is a nice syntax, a more natural way to deal with memory without using a garbage collector, and an overall modern development experience. We explored this in this chapter.

However, C++ is hard to compete with. The sheer number of libraries, frameworks, blogs, articles, code examples, books, and experience available in the world on C++ is impossible to equal in a short time. Rust has found its niches in Web Assembly applications and various tools, but it's far from replacing C++.

Still, we have to remember that languages are not necessarily picked based on technical reasons and that cultural reasons matter as well. Newer generations of programmers might enjoy Rust much more than C++, and with the NSA and the White House leading the focus on memory-safe languages, Rust might gain ground for newer projects.

The conclusion? It's hard to predict the future, but we can imagine how Rust could take over. The way I see it, it would require four factors: Rust is preferred by more and more programmers, it is required by regulation, C++ fails to evolve on memory safety fast enough, and generative AI gets good enough at translating from C++ to Rust.

So, there's a chance, but I think it's safe to say that it's over 50% that C++ is here to stay at least for another decade.

Index

R

range-based for loops 180
Rapidcsv
  reference link 168
Rust
  advantages, over C++ 196
  URL 187
Rust, features 187
  closures 190
  immutability 189
  optional return keyword 190
  ownership model 193-195
  package management 188
  project templates 188
  simple syntax, for compound types 189, 190
  traits 191, 192
  unit tests, in Standard library 191
RxCpp
  reference link 168

S

safety profiles 119
Scrt1.o 59, 60
section headers 77
section mapping 57
sections 78
SIGBUS fault 91
single instruction, multiple data (SIMD) 142
sinth 68
smart pointers 38
Software Bill of Materials (SBOM) 171
spdlog library
  reference link 165
SQLPP1
  URL 168

stack canaries 83
Stack Overflow
  reference link 21
static initialization order fiasco 63
static library 70
sum of all odd numbers program
  compiling 139-142
supply chain security 169-171
Syft
  reference link 171
synth library 72

T

test-driven development (TDD) 9, 123
  misconceptions 10
test-driven method, for C++ 9, 10
  features 14
  language, exploring 12
  memory issues 12, 13
  setup 10-12
TinyORM
  URL 168
Turing complete 46
types
  ignoring 50-52

V

variable length array 27

W

whitespace 179
Windows PE format 76

packtpub.com

Subscribe to our online digital library for full access to over 7,000 books and videos, as well as industry leading tools to help you plan your personal development and advance your career. For more information, please visit our website.

Why subscribe?

- Spend less time learning and more time coding with practical eBooks and Videos from over 4,000 industry professionals

- Improve your learning with Skill Plans built especially for you

- Get a free eBook or video every month

- Fully searchable for easy access to vital information

- Copy and paste, print, and bookmark content

Did you know that Packt offers eBook versions of every book published, with PDF and ePub files available? You can upgrade to the eBook version at packtpub.com and as a print book customer, you are entitled to a discount on the eBook copy. Get in touch with us at customercare@packtpub.com for more details.

At www.packtpub.com, you can also read a collection of free technical articles, sign up for a range of free newsletters, and receive exclusive discounts and offers on Packt books and eBooks.

Other Books You May Enjoy

If you enjoyed this book, you may be interested in these other books by Packt:

Expert C++ - Second Edition

Marcelo Guerra Hahn, Araks Tigranyan, John Asatryan, Vardan Grigoryan, Shunguang Wu

ISBN: 978-1-80461-783-0

- Go beyond the basics to explore advanced C++ programming techniques
- Develop proficiency in advanced data structures and algorithm design with C++17 and C++20
- Implement best practices and design patterns to build scalable C++ applications
- Master C++ for machine learning, data science, and data analysis framework design
- Design world-ready applications, incorporating networking and security considerations
- Strengthen your understanding of C++ concurrency, multithreading, and optimizing performance with concurrent data structures

Data Structures and Algorithms with the C++ STL

John Farrier

ISBN: 978-1-83546-855-5

- Streamline data handling using the std::vector
- Master advanced usage of STL iterators
- Optimize memory in STL containers
- Implement custom STL allocators
- Apply sorting and searching with STL algorithms
- Craft STL-compatible custom types
- Manage concurrency and ensure thread safety in STL
- Harness the power of parallel algorithms in STL

Packt is searching for authors like you

If you're interested in becoming an author for Packt, please visit `authors.packtpub.com` and apply today. We have worked with thousands of developers and tech professionals, just like you, to help them share their insight with the global tech community. You can make a general application, apply for a specific hot topic that we are recruiting an author for, or submit your own idea.

Share Your Thoughts

Now you've finished *Debunking C++ Myths*, we'd love to hear your thoughts! Scan the QR code below to go straight to the Amazon review page for this book and share your feedback or leave a review on the site that you purchased it from.

https://packt.link/r/1835884792

Your review is important to us and the tech community and will help us make sure we're delivering excellent quality content.

Download a free PDF copy of this book

Thanks for purchasing this book!

Do you like to read on the go but are unable to carry your print books everywhere?

Is your eBook purchase not compatible with the device of your choice?

Don't worry, now with every Packt book you get a DRM-free PDF version of that book at no cost.

Read anywhere, any place, on any device. Search, copy, and paste code from your favorite technical books directly into your application.

The perks don't stop there, you can get exclusive access to discounts, newsletters, and great free content in your inbox daily

Follow these simple steps to get the benefits:

1. Scan the QR code or visit the link below

https://packt.link/free-ebook/9781835884782

2. Submit your proof of purchase
3. That's it! We'll send your free PDF and other benefits to your email directly

www.ingramcontent.com/pod-product-compliance
Lightning Source LLC
Chambersburg PA
CBHW080523060326
40690CB00022B/5014

* 9 7 8 1 8 3 5 8 8 4 7 8 2 *